The Culture of
Public Problems

The Culture of Public Problems

Drinking-Driving and the Symbolic Order

Joseph R. Gusfield

The University of Chicago Press
Chicago and London

The University of Chicago Press, Chicago 60637
The University of Chicago Press, Ltd., London

Library of Congress Cataloging in Publication Data

Gusfield, Joseph R   1923–
  The culture of public problems.

  Bibliography: p.
  Includes index.

  1. Drunk driving—California—San Diego Co.
  2. Traffic violations—California—San Diego Co.
  3. Sociological research—Case studies.   4. Social
problems—Case studies.   5. National characteristics,
American—Case studies.   I. Title.
HE5620.D7G87   353.0087'83   80-17007
ISBN   0-226-31094-9   (paper)

To David Riesman

Contents

Preface and Acknowledgments

The presentational procedure of the scholar is justly summed up in the legal phrase, *res ipsa loquitor*—"the thing speaks for itself." Whatever the motives or intentions of the author, he or she must be understood and judged within the confines of the text. Whether or not my book was written under the duress of tenure considerations is hardly relevant to its worth. Whether the writing and research were supported by the Department of Defense or a legacy from a doting grandmother is unimportant in examining my logic or the character of my evidence. Even my use of the personal pronoun here is an affectation. The work is no longer mine. Having written, the writer must step back as the manuscript becomes the creation of its readers and the words are no longer controlled by their original inventor. The preface is a device that permits me one final illusion that my manuscript is not yet alien unto me.

In May 1971, I was asked by the Urban Observatory of San Diego County to undertake a study for the Traffic Safety Department of the County Highway Division. The study, financed by a federal grant to the California State Highway Division, was an analysis of sentencing practices in drinking-driving cases in San Diego County courts and their relation to rearrests for the same offense. A number of personal and organizational considerations led me to accept the proposed study, although it represented the

kind of team project and applied research that I had generally avoided in
my professional life. I agreed to prepare a proposal, eventually accepted,
for a study that I thought would be dull, hackneyed, and intellectually
unrewarding. This book, I hope, is the best evidence that my view of
what would happen was vastly incorrect.

That initial study was completed in 1972 (Gusfield 1972) but the
present book bears only a slight relation or resemblance to it. Out of my
experience in studying the police, the courts, and the safety agencies, I
developed curiosity and interest in the accepted realities of the drinking-
driving phenomenon. These were shared by everyone with whom I came
in contact. I had studied the temperance movement in great detail in the
past (Gusfield 1963a) and had been attuned both then and recently to
sociological perspectives toward symbolic actions. The San Diego study
left me with a new problem: why is it that driving an automobile under
the influence of alcohol is at all a public problem? The present work is
part of an effort to answer that question.

A fellowship from the Guggenheim Foundation in 1973–74 enabled
me to begin observations of probationary procedures in San Diego
County courts, and of schools for offenders. I examined the corpus of
research on the basis of which assertions about drinking and driving were
justified, and began to read and to think through the issues of the present
study. In this period I also started writing parts of the manuscript. During
1974–77 I continued research, aided by several grants for research assistants and typing from the University of California, San Diego Graduate
Research Board. In 1977–78 a grant from the National Science Foundation Program in Law and Society enabled me to complete the research on
the study and to bring the writing to conclusive manuscript form. (The
NSF grant also enabled me to undertake additional research in the area of
drinking-driving.) The final manuscript was completed in summer 1979.

The present book represents only a portion of the entire study. In
writing the manuscript, and in completing additional ethnographic work,
I realized that the entire study had become too much for one volume.
Accordingly, I have restricted this book to cultural analysis, keeping
social structural analysis subordinate to the main plot. The focus here is
on the symbolic aspects of social problem formation. The more structural
pieces of the problem will be dealt with in a future volume.

All aspects of my studies in drinking-driving from the initial study to
date have informed and influenced this present book. Some of those I
acknowledge have helped more at one stage than another. They have all
aided the present work even when their efforts were largely accomplished
in relation to past or future publications. I am indebted to Carole A. B.

Warren, Jerold Cloyd, Steven Phillips, David Petraitis, and Herbert Isen-
berg, who served as research assistants on the original San Diego study.
Mary Thoune, Peter Hayward, and especially Judith McIlwee helped
immensely in the historical research. Joseph Kotarba and Paul Rasmussen conducted much of the ethnographic investigation in the
National Science Foundation study. To all of them I am grateful for
conversations, suggestions, ideas, and reports that in one way or
another have gone into the making of this book.

Colleagues and students are an indispensable part of a scholar's intellectual environment although it is often difficult to pinpoint each instance of aid and to express debts accurately. The Social Research Group
in the School of Health at the University of California, Berkeley, nurtured
my ideas in several colloquia, offered substantial services through their
superb library of alcohol studies, and contributed in many and myriad
ways through innumerable conversations and criticisms. I am especially
indebted to Don Cahalan, Harry Gene Levine, and Ron Roizen. My
obligations to Robin Room, presently director of the Social Research
Group, are far too great for listing. More than anyone, he has served me
as guide, goad, and guru in the swampy morass of alcohol studies. His
scholarship is awesome and his acute understanding unmatched.

I gained from conversations and correspondence with H. Laurence
Ross, Lawrence Freidman, Michael Overington, Stephen Wasby, Richard Brown, Richard Zylman, Bruno Latour, and Norman Scotch. My
departmental colleagues David Phillips, Jack Douglas, Fred Davis,
Aaron Cicourel, and Bruce Johnson were especially helpful in suggestions and references. Teaching a joint seminar on alcohol with Jacque-
line Wiseman was a most significant element in the thought going into
this work. Her deep knowledge of alcohol research provided a special
colleagueship. Chandra Mukherji and Bennett Berger provided a sustaining friendship and a critical reading of the manuscript that did much
to improve it. I am deeply grateful to them. Murray Edelman and John
Kitsuse gave the initial manuscript that sensitive and critical reading
without which any book would be deficient in thought and style. I am
greatly appreciative of all that each of these colleagues has contributed
to whatever merits this work can claim. There is a special obligation that
I bear to my graduate students whose willingness to argue with their
mentors is essential to both of us.

As always, a secretarial and library staff is the quiet help that makes
projects possible. Anita Schiller and Robert Westerman of the University
of California, San Diego, library provided great help in purchasing,
finding, and suggesting sources. My secretaries at various times during

this period were invaluable: Sue Miller, Amy Silverberg, and Ann Knight. Marlene Philley served as secretary to the NSF project and typed the initial manuscript which has appeared as a National Science Foundation report. Her help and her efficiency deserve my deepest thanks. Dorothea Nero and Judith Sherer typed the final manuscript. Mignon Furqueron assisted in bibliography.

I am particularly indebted to several sources for funds enabling this project to be completed. This is an opportunity to express my thanks to Les Earnest, then at the Urban Observatory of San Diego County, and to Powell Harrison, then with the Traffic Safety Division of the San Diego County Highway Department; to the Guggenheim Foundation and its staff; to the Graduate Research Board at the University of California, San Diego; and to the National Science Foundation, especially to H. Laurence Ross, then director of the Law and Society Program. I also wish to thank the Travelers Insurance Companies, for permission to reprint their advertisement, "Is Putting Drunk Drivers Behind Bars the Only Way to Teach Them a Lesson?" and the National Safety Council, for the graph from the 1977 edition of *Accident Facts*. The advertisement entitled "Alcoholism: The Lonely Disease" is reprinted by permission, CareUnit Program, Comprehensive Care Corporation, Newport Beach, CA.

As always, Irma Geller Gusfield provided that companionship, love, and support "without which none." I have dedicated this work to David Riesman in appreciation for years of friendship, help, and intellectual colleagueship. More than anyone, he taught me to look.

The use of the automobile is a microcosm on a large scale of the problems created by the conflict of restraint and release in American life. The issues embedded in the use of alcohol and the auto present the tensions and complements of a world at once at work and at play. Driving has accentuated the difficulties in keeping the borders between self-control and self-release closed. The contemporary motorcar is a piece of mechanical equipment inherently dangerous and yet relatively unsupervised in its use. Driving requires a high degree of motor coordination, rational judgment, and a level of skill that must be maintained by constant practice and attention, qualities of mind calling for a rational attitude and a serious intent. But this area of rational existence intersects day and night, work and play. Unlike the airplane, the railroad, or mass transit it is not in the care of highly trained, paid, and certified personnel. The automobile is available as an accesory to the gamut of our moods, our arenas of living, and our daytime and nighttime tasks and adventures.

This book is about how situations become public problems, but it is also about drinking and driving. The particular case informs us about the macrocosm, the more general case. In general, this is a book about culture—public meanings—and social structure—authority, control, and deviance. It is about consistencies and inconsistencies between public ceremony and routine behavior. In particular, it is also a book about motorists, police, judges, lawyers, scientists, journalists, doctors, and government officials, about how and why driving an automobile under the influence of alcohol is an act publicly condemned yet privately observed.

The introduction is a ritual of transition which permits the reader to become acquainted with the writer—his style, his outlook, his intent. It is a literary device that enables me to ease you into this study. If I have written well and you have read well, it will outline what is to come and foreshadow the thrust and significance of the work.

The phrase "research essay" conveys both what this book is and what it is not. It is a book of general ideas developed and expressed in the context of a particular subject matter and experience. The phenomenon constituting the public issue of alcohol and auto safety—the "drinking-driving problem"—is the occasion for creating a theoretical perspective with which to examine public problems. This is neither a conventional report on research nor an essay setting forth an abstract system of theoretical ideas or propositions, not grounded in specific subject matter. Perhaps it is both. In the word *research* I call attention to the grounding of my ideas in the experience of performing a detailed analysis and description of a specific body of data on a particular issue—drinking-driving. Some of the data are original with me; some are the result of reading, activity, and exposure to the field. By the word *essay* I point to the effort to create a theoretical perspective, grounded in the particular phenomenon of the empirical research, but reaching for a general and wider application. I am less bound by data here than in the research report; more constrained by them than in the essay of abstract theory. The door of my book is now opened. Let us move into the foyer.

The Construction of Social Problems: How Phenomena Become Real

There is an apocryphal tale about the American philosopher Morris Raphael Cohen. He was reputed to begin a course in ethics with the following problem for his students:

> Suppose an angel came down from Heaven and promised the people of the United States a marvelous invention. It would simplify their lives; enable the injured to receive quick treatment; decrease the time of transportation by a large magnitude; bring families and friends closer together and create a life of far greater ease and convenience than exists today. However, in grateful return for this boon to human

welfare, the angel demanded that every year 5,000 Americans be put to death on the steps of the Capitol. Having posed the question, the philosopher then asked the class what answer should be given to the angel. After the ethical dilemma had been discussed for some time, the professor pointed out that every year many more than 5,000 were killed in automobile accidents in the United States.

Of course, public issues seldom emerge in such clear-cut fashion. Only in seminars can a philosophical problem be posed in so hypothetical and deliberate a manner. The problems connected with most public issues emerge long after events and processes have been set in motion. No seminars on the ethical consequences of technological change were held in Henry Ford's shop to decide if the venture was a wise public action and worthy of continuation. Technological assessment comes later.

The Plurality of Possible Realities

At the outset I have had the problem of naming the problem. To talk about the "drinking-driving problem" is already to assume the character of the phenomenon (automobile safety) and to define it as having such and such a shape. Human problems do not spring up, full-blown and announced, into the consciousness of bystanders. Even to recognize a situation as painful requires a system for categorizing and defining events. All situations that are experienced by people as painful do not become matters of public activity and targets for public action. Neither are they given the same meaning at all times and by all peoples. "Objective" conditions are seldom so compelling and so clear in their form that they spontaneously generate a "true" consciousness. Those committed to one or another solution to a public problem see its genesis in the necessary consequences of events and processes; those in opposition often point to "agitators" who impose one or another definition of reality.

The existence of a "drinking-driving problem" is the result of a procedure by which the automobile and fatalities have been construed as a problem of societal concern, to be acted upon by public officials and agencies. Alcohol has already been perceived as important in the genesis of such fatalities and accorded an importance as a target in the resolution of the problem. That target character is not a given, is not in the nature of reality as a *Ding an sich* (a thing in itself), but represents a selective process from among a multiplicity of possible and potential realities which can be seen as affecting auto fatalities and injuries. Before the nineteenth century drinking and drunkenness were seldom used to account for accidents or crime (H. G. Levine 1978). The problematic character of the "drinking-driving problem" is the first concern of the sociologist interested in understanding the character of public problems. He must account for its status as a matter of public concern rather than accept it as given in the nature of things.

The sociologist has come to recognize that many human situations and problems have histories; they have not always been construed and recognized as they are today or will be in the future. What is now labeled and seen as "mental disorder" has a history in which the same behavior was accorded different statuses in different historical periods, and sometimes seen as valued, sometimes as condemned and irremediable. Its present place in the spectrum of medical "illnesses" is another way of talking about it. Recent criticisms of the concept of "mental illness" have built upon this theme of its historical diversity (Rosen 1968; Foucault 1965; Rothman 1971). The same has occurred with the phenomenon now labeled in American society as "poverty." At some periods in Western history, the poor were objects of reverence; at others they were the objects of condemnation. In the 1950s the issue of poverty was a minor one in American public consciousness. In the 1960s, with little changed in the levels and distribution of income, it became a significant part of public actions. Where poverty had once been a term for a margin below which incomes fell it has become instead primarily a matter of the distribution of income; a question of equality rather than penury (Matza 1966; Bell 1972).

It is then a major effort of this essay to illuminate the process by which the association between alcohol and driving has come to be a public problem. In this we follow the advice of Malcolm Spector and John Kitsuse (1973): "the process by which members of groups or societies define a putative condition as a problem—is the distinctive subject matter of the sociology of social problems."[1] Pressed to the wall to solve the problem of drinking-driving I can only shout "Why do you ask?"

The Public Character of Social Problems

Some years ago I passed a movie marquee with the title *Marriage Is a Private Affair*. And so it is in American life today. Much attention, time, and money are devoted to problems of marital relationships. Divorces are daily lamented, accepted, or exulted over in public communications, but the situations, perceived as painful or problematic or even immoral, do not result in public actions to assure their resolutions. Marital happiness, parent-child satisfactions, sexual frustration, unrequited love, disap-

pointment in friendships are among the most keenly felt of human experiences and their joys and sorrows the occasions for some of the
deepest and most profound aspirations. Yet no public agency exists to
provide for their quick or beneficent satisfaction. Only in musical com-
edies do political parties campaign on platforms that promise to bring
everyone love and sexual fulfillment.

It is useful to distinguish public problems from private ones. That is
why I prefer the term "public problems" to that of "social problems." All
social problems do not necessarily become public ones. They do not
become matters of conflict or controversy in the arenas of public action.
They do not eventuate in agencies to secure or in movements to work for
their resolution. Whether or not situations should be public problems is
itself often a major issue. The abortion question is today a source of great
and bitter political conflict in the United States. It poses the question as to
the place of public authority in accepting responsibility for providing
sanction to private abortions and entitling citizens to facilities for
achieving abortions. It is not straining the imagination to perceive a
somewhat similar destiny in store for sexual pleasure. In the past decade
sexual dissatisfaction has become the source of a new, growing
occupation—sexual therapist. I can imagine in the next quarter-century
the movement to define sexual disappointment as illness and a governmental program to provide sexual therapy as part of medical insurance.
What may be visible and salient in one period of time may not be so in
another. Issues and problems may wax and wane in public attention, may
disappear or appear. How is it that an issue or problem emerges as one
with a public status, as something about which "someone ought to do
something"?

In analyzing the public character of a problem it is vital to recognize
again the multiple possibilities of resolution. Who and what institution
gains or is given the responsibility for "doing something" about the
issue? As phenomena are open to various modes of conceptualizing them
as problems, so too their public character is open to various means of
conceiving their resolution. It is only in the past ten or fifteen years that
automobile safety has been seen as a matter of responsibility for the
federal government and the automobile industry through the development of public standards for safe automobiles.[2] Income security in old
age has ceased to be left largely to personal and familial obligations.
Social security legislation has established a public, governmental
responsibility.

The problem of responsibility has both a cultural and a structural dimension. At the cultural level it implies a way of seeing phenomena. Fixing responsibility for preventing accidents by laws against drinking-driving involves seeing drinking-driving as a choice by a willful person. Seeing it as a medical problem involves an attribution of compulsion and illness. At the structural level, however, fixing responsibility implies different institutions and different personnel who are charged with obligations and opportunities to attack the problem. Here, too, change from one set of causal definitions, of cognitive conceptualizations, to another carries implications for institutions. The relation of causal responsibility to political responsibility is then a central question in understanding how public problems take shape and change.

In the case of drinking-driving this has involved such institutions as the church, the courts and police, government, medicine, and the world of engineering. That there is transition or conflict between institutions claiming or rejecting claims to authority in controlling the phenomenon of drinking-driving leads us to a recognition of the categories in which the phenomenon is conceptualized, thought about, becomes a matter of consciousness. For example, to see alcohol problems through the metaphor of medicine, as diseases, has consequences for efforts to utilize law enforcement measures in their resolution. Such modes of conceiving of the reality of a phenomenon are closely related to the activities of resolution. They affect the claims to authority over the area and over the persons connected with the phenomenon.

The Structure of Public Problems

My obsession with the uses of knowledge as a basis for authority in public problems was aroused by an earlier phase of what has become this study. In 1971 local traffic safety officials in San Diego County asked me to undertake an analysis of the effectiveness of court sentencing practices on recidivism in arrests for driving under the influence of alcohol (Gusfield 1972). While completing that initial study, it seemed to me that all the parties with whom I came in contact—police, offenders, judges, attorneys, academic colleagues, Department of Motor Vehicle officials—were locked into a consciousness of drinking-driving which narrowly shut out possible alternative conceptualizations and solutions. There were other ways of "seeing" the phenomenon, other resources that might have been explored as solutions to the problem. The definition of the problem, which participants to the process took for granted, was to me problematic. This situation became something that required my explanation and understanding. An alternative consciousness was possible, and it seemed the task of this sociologist to develop it and to understand how the existing consciousness persisted.

The people whom I talked with in the course of that original study presented a fairly uniform view of the problem. Alcohol leads to impaired driving and increases the risk of accident, injury, and death. Since drinking coupled with driving "causes" auto accidents, solutions lie in strategies which diminish either drinking or driving after drinking. The available strategy is to persuade the drinker not to get behind the wheel of the car. Law enforcement and punishment perhaps supplemented by education are the most useful and acceptable means to diminish auto accidents due to drinking. Some people thought in longer range terms and wanted drinking-drivers screened for alcoholism and treated for their illness.

This homogeneous consciousness of alcohol and automobile use appears to the sociologist as a salient form of social control. It eliminates conflict or divergence by rendering alternative definitions and solutions unthinkable. This subtle, unseen implication of cultural ideas is perhaps the most powerful form of constraint. Unlike the conflict of power it goes unrecognized. What we cannot imagine, we cannot desire.

Earlier in my academic career I had studied the American temperance movement and Prohibition (Gusfield 1963a). That study had sensitized me to other modes of seeing issues of alcohol. It made me critical of the intensively individualistic character with which the auto safety problem and the drinking-driver problem were seen by those I studied and met in the San Diego courts research in 1971–72: it was taken for granted by those I studied that the problems of auto safety and alcohol use were chiefly problems of individuals, of motorists. Institutional explanations and loci of responsibility were eloquently absent from the consciousness of officials, observers, and offenders.

Two things struck me as especially significant by their absence: the lack of involvement of alcohol beverage distributors—bartenders, sellers, manufacturers—and the inability or unwillingness of people to see the problem of drinking-driving as a problem of transportation. The producers and distributors of liquor and beer were almost never represented in the conferences, meetings, classes, and committees which fill the organizational agenda of local alcohol agencies. But so, too, was there little representation from medicine, government, planning, or other possibly interested groups. In speaking to audiences throughout the country as a presumed "alcohol studies expert" I often pointed out that the city of San Diego had developed an area of hotels alongside a major interstate highway. The hotels all had public bars which provided part of their income and depended on more than their temporary residents for clientele. Autos were almost the only means of transportation to or from such bars in a part of the United States where the spatial spread made taxis expensive. Research on drinking-drivers was similarly silent on alternative means and possibilities of transportation. Little was known about where drinking-drivers were going or had come from. Although such questions were part of the standard arrest form in these cases, the item was not deemed important and answers were inconsistent and poorly asked.[3]

My attention was in this way led to the realization that there were alternative ways of being conscious of the drinking-driving problem. I came to conceptualize the issue in a number of different ways, even to conceive of it in terms of consequences, rather than causes (Gusfield 1976). It was possible to drop attention to drinking and to think only about the injury or fatality incurred, concentrating only on preventing that and not the crash. Later I discovered that indeed there were a whole literature and a set of programs and movements since the mid-1960s that had done exactly that (cf. chapter 2, below).

Causal imputation in itself, of course, is ambiguous and open to multiple attributions and imputations. The absence of alternative modes of transportation is logically as much a cause of drinking-driving as is the use of alcohol. To see public problems as the application of values to an objective set of conditions puts the car in front of the motorist. The conditions are themselves part and parcel of the process through which problems are attacked. There was a structure of thought and action, of institutions and groups within which the problem was contained and alternatives were excluded.

The idea of structure implies an orderliness to things. Ideas have structure insofar as they follow from generalized rules of thought. Behavior has structure when it, too, is orderly. Analyzing public problems as structured means finding the conceptual and institutional orderliness in which they emerge in the public arena. The public arena is not a field on which all can play on equal terms; some have greater access than others and greater power and ability to shape the definition of public issues. Nor do all ideas have public problems as their consequences.

The social construction of public problems implies a historical dimension. The same "objective" condition may be defined as a problem in one time period, not in another. But there is more to the analysis of public issues than the idea of historicity. As my experience with the initial study suggested, there is a pattern to how issues and problems arise, emerge, and evidence a structure. At any specific moment, all possible parties to the issue do not have equal abilities to influence the public; they do not possess the same degree or kind of authority to be legitimate sources of definition of the reality of the problem, or to assume legitimate power to regulate, control, and innovate solutions. To describe the structure of public problems is to describe the ordered way in which ideas and activities emerge in the public arena.

The concept of "structure" lends itself too much to a distorted sense of public events as having a fixed, permanent, unchanging character. I do not want to convey that interpretation. At any moment the "structure" itself may be fought over as groups attempt to effect the definitions of problems and authority to affect them. At any moment the structure is itself problematic in its implementation. Structure is process frozen in time as orderliness. It is a conceptual tool with which to try to make that process understandable. What is important to my thought here is that all is not situational; ideas and events are contained in an imprecise and changing container.[4]

Cognitive and Moral Judgments

As ideas and consciousness public problems have a structure which involves both a cognitive and a moral dimension. The cognitive side consists in beliefs about the facticity of the situation and events comprising the problem—our theories and empirical beliefs about poverty, mental disorder, alcoholism, and so forth. The moral side is that which enables the situation to be viewed as painful, ignoble, immoral. It is what makes alteration or eradication desirable or continuation valuable.

The moral side of a problem suggests a condemnable state of affairs from the perspective of someone's morality. Even medical conceptions of illness contain the moral admonition that sickness is not preferable to health, that the patient should want to be well. Someone who elects to continue an unhealthy occupation because of the value of its rewards may decide, however, that illness is preferable to health. Issues of equality, of justice, of economy all involve judgments of goodness, badness, and morality.

But events and situations are also cognitively assessed. A world of fact is posited. Crime may be seen as a result of broken homes, poverty, genetics, community disorganization, or any number and type of variables. Significantly there are beliefs about the alterability of phenomena. They are, but need not be. The aging process is seen as physiologically painful and unwelcome in contemporary societies, but it also is seen as inevitable and unalterable. Inequality between races is also seen by many as painful and unwelcome but believed to be alterable. In that is its status as a problem.

Without both a cognitive belief in alterability and a moral judgment of its character, a phenomenon is not at issue, not a problem. In recent years biologists have begun to take the aging process as potentially alterable and have begun to study it. It may become a problem and the reality of aging itself a center of public controversy. At present it is not. The reality of a problem is often expanded or contracted in scope as cognitive or moral judgment shifts. The composition of the criminal has been open to considerable argument over such phenomena as "war crime," "white collar crime," "victimless crime," and "juvenile delinquency" (Quinney 1971; Cressey 1953; Platt 1969; Schur 1965).

The Ownership of Public Problems

The concepts of "ownership" and "responsibility" are central to this work and are used in a very particular manner. Much of the study examines the fixation of responsibility for public problems, and the concepts must be discussed with care.

At the outset I will separate three aspects of the phenomenon of responsibility. The first will be given the term "ownership" and the other two discussed as different types of "responsibility." The concept of "ownership of public problems" is derived from the recognition that in the arenas of public opinion and debate all groups do not have equal power, influence, and authority to define the reality of the problem. The ability to create and influence the public definition of a problem is what I refer to as "ownership." The metaphor of property ownership is chosen to emphasize the attributes of control, exclusiveness, transferability, and potential loss also found in the ownership of property.

I have pointed out that the status of a phenomenon as a problem is itself often a matter of conflict as interested parties struggle to define or prevent the definition of a matter as something that public action should "do something about." At any time in a historical period there is a recognition that specific public issues are the legitimate province of specific persons, roles, and offices that can command public attention, trust, and influence. They have credibility while others who attempt to capture public attention do not. Owners can make claims and assertions. They are looked at and reported to by others anxious for definitions and solutions to the problem. They possess authority in the field. Even if opposed by other groups, they are among those who can gain the public ear. Thus the American Psychiatric Association has been the owner of the problem of homosexuality, and their support or opposition to the definition of homosexuality as a psychiatric problem has been significant.

What the Chamber of Commerce does about homosexuality is far less significant in its influence on others.[5]

Different groups and institutions have authority and influence for different problems and at different times. The orbit in which religion has control over health has greatly diminished while that of medicine has expanded in Western countries. At one stage in the history of the social organization of health, ecclesiastical authorities possessed great power and influence; today they do not.

The history of the control of alcohol problems illustrates the concept of ownership in an area central to this study. During the nineteenth and early twentieth centuries in the United States, the Protestant churches wielded a heavy club over alcohol problems, providing by themselves, or through allied organizations, much of the public, persuasional material on temperance and Prohibition. When they defined the legitimate cognitive and moral approaches toward alcohol use, many listened. The churches, the Woman's Christian Temperance Union, the Anti-Saloon League all acted to place and keep alcohol high on the public agenda.

The churches came to "own" the problem of drinking in American society. They set the pace and much of the framework of the debates, Other possible sources of competing ownership were absent. The medical profession was poorly organized and unable to gain a loud voice in suggesting alternative perceptions of the problems of drinking and drunkenness. The same was true of the universities. They were far from autonomous from religious influences. The sciences were less well organized and equipped to play a role in public affairs than at present. The effort of the Committee of Fifty, a group of private citizens, to be arbiters of fact in the area was short-lived. Government was less the initiator than the recipient of alcohol policies.

With Repeal, the authority of the churches to be judges of public tastes was "disowned." Whatever the desires and attempts of temperance and Prohibitionist organizations, theirs was no longer the authoritative voice. Their pronouncements no longer commanded attention but were the "kiss of death" for proponents of alcohol control policies. Ownership passed to the universities, the medical profession, and the problem drinkers themselves. In recent years government has entered the field as federal agencies have been charged with solving alcohol problems (Room 1979).

Disowning Public Problems

Some groups, institutions, and agencies are interested in defining, affecting, and solving public problems. Others may be especially interested in avoiding the obligation to be involved in the problem creating or problem solving process. They deliberately seek to resist claims that the phenomenon is their problem. For much of the active period of the temperance and Prohibition movements the liquor and beer industries made little effort to counter temperance assertions, took little notice of the issue, and derogated the importance of alcohol as a cause of suffering, crime, or other public woes. Today theirs is a similar, though unstated, aloofness from attempts to provide definitions or solutions to the problems associated with alcohol. The slogan of the alcohol beverage industry is "The fault is in the man, not the bottle." Little money is spent by the alcohol beverage industry in research on problems connected with its use. The industry makes no claims to ownership of the alcohol problem and, in word and deed, disown it.

In a somewhat similar fashion, the automobile safety problem has been characterized until recently by a less than benign neglect. The National Highway Traffic Safety Administration (NHTSA) came into existence in 1968. Prior to that, automobile safety on a federal level was the purview of the Public Health Service. At the state level it was usually an arm of the department of roads or of motor vehicles. The automobile industry, while it has sponsored some safety research, has not devoted much of its resources to questions of safety improvement. Prior to 1966, the total spent by American automobile companies on safety research was a small fraction of that expended on style research.[6] Similarly the insurance industry has, until the late 1960s (cf. chapter 2 below), played a minor role in developing or supporting research or education on auto safety. The National Safety Council, discussed at length in chapter 2, has been a source of public information and a source of agitation chiefly for improved drivers' education. The major research on automobile safety, until the late 1960s, was sponsored by the U.S. Army and the U.S. Public Health Service (U.S. Senate 1966).

The question of ownership and disownership is very much a matter of the power and authority groups and institutions can muster to enter the public arena, to be kept from it, or to prevent having to join. The power to influence the definition of the reality of phenomena is a facet of a politics of reality. Senator Abraham Ribicoff stated this in one form during the Senate hearings on the National Traffic Highway Act in 1966: "I think Detroit has fostered the idea that the whole problem was the 'nut behind the wheel' . . . and they brainwashed Americans into thinking that the automobile did not have a real role to play in the safety field (U.S. Senate 1966, p. 47).

Ribicoff's remarks imply a set of empirical assertions and a theory of how public consciousness is formed. Without judging those assertions and that theory at this point, the implications of the remarks are pertinent. Public problems have a shape which is understood in a larger context of a social structure in which some versions of "reality" have greater power and authority to define and describe that "reality" than do others. In this sense—of responsibility—the structure of public problems has a political dimension to it. The existence of overt conflict and debate makes the politics of an issue manifest. The lack of such conflict may hide the very features of the structure which make for its absence, which prevent the opposite forms of consciousness from being observed. They contribute to "what everyone knows," what is "common sense"—the taken-for-granted by which the objective world is made into experienced life. This absence of alternative modes of consciousness is also the subject of analysis of the structure of public problems. Acceptance of a factual reality often hides the conflicts and alternative potentialities possible. Ignoring the multiplicity of realities hides the political choice that has taken place.

Responsibility: Causal and Political

Ownership constitutes one piece of the structure of public problems. It indicates the power to define and describe the problem. It tells us who but not what: it does not specify the content of description and solution. Here we need to add two other concepts: causal responsibility and political responsibility.

The Dual Meaning of Responsibility

To say that "cancer was responsible for someone's death" is to use the term *responsibility* in a manner different from saying that "parents are responsible for preventing their children from making noise." The first usage looks to a causal explanation of events. The second looks to the person or office charged with controlling a situation or solving a problem. The first answers the question, How come? The second answers the question, What is to be done? The first—causal responsibility—is a matter of belief or cognition, an assertion about the sequence that factually accounts for the existence of the problem. The second—political responsibility—is a matter of policy. It asserts that somebody or some office is obligated to do something about the problem, to eradicate or alleviate the harmful situation.

The second usage is close to the legal use of "responsible" in much of Anglo-Saxon law:

> Usually in discussions of law and occasionally in morals, to say that someone is responsible for some harm means that in accordance with legal rules or moral principles it is at least permissible, if not mandatory, to blame or punish or exact compensation from him. In this use . . . the expression "responsible for" does not refer to a factual connection between the person held responsible and the harm but simply to his liability under the rules to be blamed, punished or made to pay. . . . There is no implication that the person held responsible actually did or caused the harm. [Hart and Honoré 1959, p. 61]

The political, or policy, concept of responsibility has a wider scope than the legal one but is similarly distinguished from causal explanation. In my usage the responsible office or person is the one charged with solving the problem and open to reward or punishment for failure to do so. To look to government agencies and actions to diminish inflation is to hold governmental officials politically accountable, subject to electoral and other responses for the continued or curtailed existence of the economic problem, although government may not be seen as its cause. The medical profession and medical science are not seen as causes of cancer, but they are seen as sources of potential solution. Priests, astrologers, civil engineers, and sociologists are not responsible for curing cancer or nephritis in American society although they may be in some others.

Ownership and the Fixation of Responsibility

A primary question of this study is the relation between these three aspects of structure—ownership, causation, and political obligation. While all three may coincide in the same office or person, that is by no means necessarily the case. Quite often those who own a problem are trying to place obligations on others to behave in a "proper" fashion and thus to take political responsibility for its solution. The environmental "lobbies," operating under a theory of causal responsibility which finds the source of "impure air" in the automobile, have used their ownership of the pollution problem to fix political responsibility on the automobile industry. Government shares that responsibility through undertaking to determine standards of gasoline fume emission.

In the example of clean air, causal and political responsibility are related. The design of the automobile is seen as cause, and the designers are looked to for liability and repair. The Prohibition movement owned the alcohol problem during the early part of the twentieth century. Whatever the causal theory of alcohol problems, the movement tried, succeeded, and later failed to fix responsibility for solution on the beer and liquor industries. Government and law intervened but not as solvers of the problem. The definition of alcohol problems, their cause, and their cure were given by the programs of the movement.[7]

The unique position of the state makes it a key figure in fixing responsibility. In some historical periods and for some issues it may be a processing machine, taking in inputs in the form of demands and processing them into policies that meet the demands, serving as a broker of inconsistent and equally powerful demands.[8] This was the case in the Prohibition period, but seems less and less so in many areas of contemporary life. Today the state appears more often as an active agent, the owner of the problems it seeks to solve. Governmental officials and agencies operate to define public issues, develop and organize demands upon themselves, and control and move public attitudes and expectations:

> To explain political behavior as a response to fairly stable individual wants, reasoning, attitudes, and empirically based perceptions is therefore simplistic and misleading. . . .
> Government affects behavior chiefly by shaping the cognitions of large numbers of people in ambiguous situations. It helps create their beliefs about what is proper; their perceptions of what is fact; and their expectations of what is to be done. [Edelman 1971, pp. 2, 7]

Knowledge and Responsibility

The structure of public problems is then an arena of conflict in which a set of groups and institutions, often including governmental agencies, compete and struggle over ownership and disownership, the acceptance of causal theories, and the fixation of responsibility. It is here that knowledge and politics come into contact. Knowledge is a part of the process, providing a way of seeing the problems, congenial or contradictory to one or another way in which political responsibility is fixed. It may emerge from religious institutions, from science, from folklore. Whatever its source, the appeal to a basis in "fact" has implications for the practical solutions sought to public problems.

In analyzing drinking-driving, I am examining the theoretical and scientific perspectives which have emerged from universities and technical institutes and which have operated in attributing causal responsibilities. These perspectives constitute the "state of the art" in explanations of automobile fatalities and provide the consciousness of the auto safety problem. The ownership of that problem in different and sometimes conflicting circles of alcohol occupations and engineering and legal agencies provides the arenas within which the drama takes place. The spectatorism and occasional participation of the liquor, beer, auto, and insurance industries provide absent actors whose empty chairs must also be explained. The interaction between these elements of ownership, causal theories, and political responsibilities is the central focus of this study. The crux of the political issue of drinking-driving lies in the choices of one or another theory of cause and one or another locus of political responsibility. The consciousness of the drinking-driving problem is my subject.

In the midst of profound issues of war, human equality, and violent crime, the case of drinking-driving may seem too prosaic and unimportant to merit the attention of the sophisticated reader let alone the time and energy of a mature sociologist. But that very prosaic and unimportant quality of drinking-driving is itself the incitement for curiosity, because of its theoretical importance. If drinking-driving seems not to excite political passions, it may tell us something about how dissensus occurs. That a matter seemingly connected with so many deaths and injuries arouses far less demand for cessation or resolution than did the Viet Nam War may tell us something about how public demands do arise. Thus do we "by indirections, find directions out."

The Cultural Perspective toward Public Actions

The perspective which informs this study represents a departure from the characteristic way in which sociologists have approached the study of public actions. It has more in common with the orientations that have been in use among cultural anthropologists and literary critics than those that have marked sociological studies until recently.

The view of public actions as cultural forms can be introduced by analyzing two terms used in this book: rhetoric and ritual. The terms are drawn from literature and anthropology. They describe behavior as language and drama. Their usage thus appears as an aspect of culture—of the systems of symbols by which meaning is constituted and conveyed (Sahlins 1976; Geertz 1973a). "A symbolic system of meanings is an element of order 'imposed' as it were on the realistic situation" (Parsons 1951, p. 11). As a generalized perspective on human behavior sociology has emphasized the cultural realm as "superstructure," as implicated, generated, and supported by human interests located within the diversities and hierarchies of social structure, of group life and position. "Our primary aim," wrote Robert Merton in his classic paper on nonconformity, "is to discover how some *social structures exert a definite pressure upon certain persons to engage in nonconformist rather than conformist conduct*" (Merton 1949, pp. 125–26).

This is not to maintain that I am uninterested in the social structural side of the coin of behavior. How culture and social structure affect one another is a significant piece of the puzzle of social life, and in a complete analysis both must be explored (A. Cohen 1976). I am, however, approaching the phenomenon of drinking-driving and the public actions connected with it while keeping their status as cultural forms uppermost in my bifocals. Only after I have viewed them as cultural products can I analyze the structural relationships.[9]

There are then two levels of social life: that which is constructed in the act of talking about it, defining it, and organizing our thought about it; and that which exists in social action itself. The former presents an ordered, consistent, understandable set of rules—a social structure. It is what sociologists and others construct in describing a "society." The latter is the raw data of existence, the initial acts which we, as human beings, cast into types in order to think about them. Edmund Leach, in his classic work on highland Burma, has made us aware of the sharp discontinuity between these:

> social structure in practical situations (as contrasted with the
> sociologist's abstract model) consists of a set of ideas about the distribution of power between persons and groups of persons. Individuals can and do hold contradictory and inconsistent ideas about this system. They are able to do so because of the form in which their ideas are expressed. The form is cultural form; the expression is ritual expression. [Leach 1954, p. 4]
> In practical field work situations the anthropologist must always treat the material of observation *as if* it were part of an overall equilibrium, otherwise description becomes almost impossible. All I am asking is that the fictional nature of this equilibrium should be frankly recognized. [Leach 1954, p. 285[

The two terms—rhetoric and ritual—will appear here in contexts of incongruity. Each will be used as a primary term of reference to describe an area in which the term is unfamiliar and even contradictory. They emphasize the nonutilitarian, uninstrumental quality of the products of science and law. It is precisely this noninstrumental quality, the cultural character of these products, that lends such areas of life their potent instrumental and cultural consequence. My attention is fixed more on how meaning is constituted, less on how behavior is influenced.

Part 1 treats the product of science—the "state of the art" in drinking-driving research—as a form of rhetoric. To describe science as rhetoric diminishes or ignores its status as a means to an end—a way of determining a factual reality. It emphasizes the research document and its presentation in communities of science and in the public arena as a form of argument. To complete the metaphor, I analyze documents and public presentations as performances—as materials which dramatize the drinking-driving phenomenon as both a cognitive and a moral matter.

Considering science as a form of art means in practice examining its style, its modes of persuasion, its fictional components—in short its literary substance. That science is not literature is accepted. I treat it as if it were literature in order to bring out those aspects which are better understood through literary analysis.

The significance of this cultural analysis for social structure lies in understanding how the construction of a factual reality rests on the authority of research and scientific study. That "reality" has a definitive, consistent facticity which enables the social control of drinking and driving to proceed. The artistic rhetoric of science has produced a cognitive and moral order which appears external and unyielding to human choice and design.

Part 2 continues the analysis of authority and drama, this time placing them in the arena of law. It is a story of contradictions—of the gap between formally stated intentions and aspirations of law and legislation and the day-to-day routines of courts and police. It is a story of moves to decrease automobile accidents and deaths that prove to be ineffectve and inconsequential. In law, drinking-driving is a delinquency which differs from ordinary traffic violations in its moral status and its prescribed punishments. In everyday action, it appears more like traffic violation than crime. The legal punishments exacted are far below those prescribed and advised. The law of drinking-driving has only a limited effect in deterring the phenomenon of driving while under the influence of alcohol, a limited effect in preventing the accidents which are the objects of attention.[10]

The key terms in part 2 are *myth* and *ritual*—the consideration of law as a stylized form of public drama whose impact is not only in its instrumental consequences as a utilitarian means to an end. As a cultural performance at levels of both formal and routine activity, law embodies and reinforces meanings. It creates a day-to-day authority and legitimates control through building the image of a social and natural order based on moral consensus. It presents a public version of the ethical and social character of drinking-driving which has its own existence as a public performance. The public drama creates a public culture whose relation to private culture is as problematic as the relation of the stageplay to the life of the audience. In part 2 the issue of law and deterrence becomes the occasion for analysis of public performance as an effort to establish a public authority among private people.

The Illusions of Authority

In the chapters to come I make some assertions about the modes of authority and develop a general theory of public acts as carriers of meaning. These can only be foreshadowed in this introductory chapter, but it is essential to sketch them out at this point so that the substantive material can be visualized in the framework which the author has intended.

In describing authority as illusory I am intentionally creating an ambiguity of meaning. In one sense authority is illusory in that its sources are illusory. The base of knowledge about drinking and driving is not so certain, consistent, and constant as is claimed when experts speak in a voice of authoritative wisdom. The analogy between alcohol problems and disease is a metaphor, and their affinity to other medical ailments is a matter of discretion and choice—not scientific truth. The claim of technicians to moral neutrality hides ethical and political values at work.

There is still another meaning to the illusion of authority, in which the fact of authority is illusory. The effectiveness of legal sanctions as methods for deterring drinking-driving and for preventing accidents is more limited than the legislative and judicial acts that fill libraries will lead one to think. The medical model of alcohol problems, so carefully nurtured over the past thirty years, has not given medicine a dominant voice in the healing of this sickness or convinced more than a slim sliver of the body politic of its validity.

There is a third side to the problem of authority, especially in relation to knowledge but also relevant to the issues of law and deterrence. This point of view is derived from sociological perspectives which place at the center of human action the image of the actor interacting with his social and natural surroundings—selecting, choosing, typifying, generalizing. The seminal theorists here are George Herbert Mead (1934) and Afred Schutz (1967). What this perspective does is to emphasize the activity of the human actor in creating and constructing the world in which he lives, in carving out of the "big, buzzing, blooming confusion" (William

James's phrase) a consistent and orderly universe in which to act. The concept of "ethnomethodology" contains in its etymology an entire theory of human behavior. It suggests that ordinary people—the ethnos, the folk—also follow a methodology, make the world logical, consistent, and operative in theoretical terms. Thus Garfinkel: "Every feature of sense, of fact, of method, for every particular case of inquiry without exception, is the managed accomplishment of organized settings of practical actions" (Garfinkel 1967, p. 32).

Translated from the abstract pages of theory into the particular acts of men and women this leads us to ask how it is that the illusions of certainty, consistency, effectiveness, or political and ethical detachment are constructed into realities. It is a one-sided version of human activity which sees only an external stimulus and a responding animal. That is not what is happening in the public arenas—the media of communication, the courts, the experts' professional endeavors, the scientists' studies—in which auto safety, alcohol, drinking, and driving are topics of analysis and targets of policy. Knowledge and law are not shiny marbles lying on the beach and awaiting only the sharp eyes of skilled men and women to be found. The "facts" of alcohol are picked out of a pile, scrubbed, polished, highlighted here and there, and offered as discoveries in the context of the particular and practical considerations of their finders.

The Artful Realm of the Public

The last of the illusions is that public authority is only a bridge to private behavior, a mechanism through which control is attempted. That illusion is the premise, as I will show, behind the disappointment with law as a deterrent device. It has been the incitement for much of sociology in its use of empirical study to establish the great divide between official versions of what is and what *really* is. A great deal of modern sociological work has been debunking writ large, showing that the clean face of organizations, movements, governments, forms of social organization hides from public view the dirty backside of hierarchy, narrow interests, and group antagonisms.

The hiatus between the public and private sides of reality is interesting or shocking or provocative only as the observer expects or demands a closer fit, assumes that public authority is a means to a private end—control of the behavior of persons. Suppose that instead, or in addition, public acts—laws, legislation, official speeches, mass media descriptions, brochures, and the other mechanisms of public action—can be considered sui generis, as events in and of themselves without reference to possible functions as means to ends? If we drop the premise that drinking-driving knowledge, as portrayed in the policies of governments and the opinions of experts, conveys much about drinking-driving, and operate on the premise that it tells us much about how public actors behave toward this phenomenon in public arenas, what then? If we assume that the legislation and appellate court decisions about drinking-driving are dramas for the consumption of an audience and not a technique for controlling alcohol abuse and automobile use, what would law and legislation look like?

Like any methodological device, this form of study, now called dramaturgical analysis, says more than it can frequently show.[11] But using it uncovers more than was there without it. I will retreat to less radical conclusions than implied above but will still find that the analysis of drinking-driving knowledge and policies as forms of literary art casts a strong footlight on some of the problems of policy implementation. It helps reveal the otherwise unrecognized political and moral conflicts that public presentations disguise and camouflage.

Although the dramaturgical perspective has not been well developed in social science or applied to social behavior by literary analysts, its use is not unique or new. Erving Goffman's development of it in analyzing interaction has been the major source of its introduction into social science (Goffman 1956, 1974). I build on the past work of several writers who have used it in analyzing politics, including Murray Edelman (Edelman 1964, 1971). In my own earlier work I distinguished between instrumental and symbolic political acts (Gusfield 1963a). Instrumental acts, such as social security legislation, effect behavior in a direct fashion. Symbolic acts "invite consideration rather than overt action" (Wheelwright 1954, p. 23). I interpreted the temperance movement and Prohibition less as politically significant through controlling alcohol use than as ceremonial actions which affected the social status of those who supported or rejected an abstinent style of life and a moral condemnation of alcohol. In this study I am more conscious of the mix of the instrumental and the symbolic and much more aware of the complexity of symbolic actions as modes by which public consciousness is itself constructed and defined.

Kenneth Burke, the literary critic who has been the seminal figure of dramaturgy, has taught us to be attentive to the language of metaphors by which phenomena are presented, and in this study I am concerned with knowledge, law, medicine, and technology as cultural patterns, as metaphors by which a reality is presented.[12] This method of analysis is itself dependent on a metaphor, that of the theater. To see public actions and public policies as theatrical is to emphasize the ritual, ceremonial, and dramatic qualities of actions. It is to see public actions, like plays, as artistic, as constructed within conventions particular to that genre of actions, just as dramas are staged within conventional understandings between audience and performers.[13]

To see public actions as performances does not negate group interests in the character of those performances, as I stressed in finding social status interests in the temperance issue. Nor does it absolve the sociologist from looking for self-serving and instrumental elements in otherwise symbolic and ceremonial behavior. Metaphors are important for what they ignore as points of difference as well as for what they include as marks of similarity.

I am also better informed about language and about the social construction of reality than was the case when I developed the view of symbolic politics more than a decade ago. The belief that language and logic are analyzable only as means of making statements about a factual world has undergone much criticism in recent years under the influence of J. L. Austin and other linguistic philosophers, as well as rhetoricians and linguists (Austin 1962, 1971; Perelman and Olbrechts-Tytecka 1969; Jakobson 1966). To see that language can be itself action is crucial to how I interpret the theater of public life—as modes of presentation of the speaker. To say that "there are nine million alcoholics in the United States" is more than a statement about numbers; it is an expression of the concern of the speaker with alcohol issues and his commitment to their seriousness.

Public consciousness is then drawn into the actions of policymakers, experts, and journalists. The rules of public performance "front stage" are not those of private behavior "backstage." In their behavior in the public arena they create the order and consistency with which "society" is endowed. Public authority is engaged in preserving the illusion of a predictable, consistent, and morally controlled universe, one in which the facts about drinking and driving are clear. Consensus exists about heroes and villains, and policy can be made because the moral and rational grounds of authority are discoverable and evident. Jack D. Douglas has phrased my viewpoint well:

> In such an uncertain and conflictful society, the belief in an absolutist set of moral rules is important not only because it is reassuring and because it helps one to control his nightmares of social chaos and violence, but also because it helps the individuals involved in political

action to solve the fundamental problems of constructing order . . . the belief that a rational and ordered society is both possible and already existing gives individuals the belief that their attempts to construct social order will be successful. [Jack D. Douglas 1971, p. 308]

In its utilitarian and rational emphasis, social science has sought to replace mysticism, irrationality, and blind conflict in public policy with reason, knowledge, and scientific method. This study is less than enthusiastic about the success of this Enlightenment attitude. Peter Gay's description of the confidence of and "ideological myopia" of the Enlightenment *philosophes* is appropriate: "They never wholly discarded that final, most stubborn illusion that bedevils realists—the illusion that they were free from illusions" (Gay 1966, p. 27).

Part One

Rhetoric and Science: Creating Cognitive Order

The Organization of Public Consciousness

Rhetoric and science! The title imposes an obvious contradiction. Science is the discovery and transmission of a true state of things. Rhetoric is the art of persuasion. Aristotle defined it as "the faculty of observing in any given case the available means of persuasion" (Aristotle 1941, p. 1329). Such persuasion is an art usually considered more characteristic of the politician, the advertiser, the artist than part of the skills of the scientist. It is associated with men or women who attempt to move people to action. "It is chiefly involved with bringing about a condition rather than discovering or testing a condition" (Bryant 1965, p. 18; also see Winterowd 1968, p. 14). It was the skill perfected by the Sophists, and now it exists in the nefarious arts of advertising, propaganda, and political campaigns. These, not scientists and technical experts, need rhetoric to produce deliberate effects on their audiences. The scientist reports what he finds and the technician applies such findings to solve problems. Is it not to replace rhetoric that science has come into the world?

Yet, as Alvin Gouldner has pointed out, scientific canons of rationality and evidence provide a system for claiming authority and establishing conclusions and techniques. They confer legitimacy on those who carry out scientific prescriptions. Modern discussion of ideology partakes of this distinction in its modes for compelling legitimacy:

Ideology thus entailed the emergence of a new mode of political discourse: discourse that sought action but did not merely seek it by invoking authority or tradition, or by emotive rhetoric alone. It was discourse predicated on the idea of grounding political action in secular and rational theory . . . policies shaped by rational discourse in the public sphere, and premised that support can be mobilized for them by the rhetoric of rationality. [Gouldner 1976, p. 30]

Both science and ideology are grounded in a culture of careful discourse, one of whose main rules calls for *self-groundedness,* requiring that . . . [the speaker's] conclusions do not require premises other than those he has articulated. [Gouldner 1976, p. 42]

Science, scientific pronouncements, technical programs, and technologies appear as supports to authority, and counterauthority, by giving to a program or policy the cast of being validated in nature, grounded in a neutral process by a method that assures both certainty and accuracy. The advertisement reproduced in figure 1 shows how the scientific study, or report, is used as support for an argument.

It is this aspect of science and technology that is my focus in part 1—the ways in which science provides compelling argument. To examine scientific and technical knowledge from the standpoint or perspective of rhetoric is to view it as a species of argument and ask about the techniques and methods by which affirmation is achieved. "The object of the theory of argumentation," write Perelman and Olbrechts-Tytecka, "is the study of the discursive techniques allowing us to induce or to increase the mind's adherence to the theses presented for its assent" (Perelman and Olbrechts-Tytecka 1969, p. 4). It is useful, I assert, to think of scientific presentations of drinking-driving research not as reported material which happens to compel assent but as a form of rhetoric which is calculated to induce belief. I shall examine how it is that a factual world is presented and believed in by relevant audiences in the public arena. Programs of control depend, in part, on the willing belief in a certain and consistent reality established by valid and unambiguous method. My attention is to the construction of that reality as a ground to authority.

The most subtle forms of social control are those we least recognize as such. Precisely because the categories of understanding and meaning provide so powerful a constraint to what we experience and how we think about that experience, they prevent awareness of alternative ways of conceiving events and processes. Because they lead us to "see" the accustomed forms as the only reality they minimize and obscure the possible conflicts and the volitionary decisions that have helped construct that "reality."

Is putting drunk drivers behind bars the only way to teach them a lesson?

There are many ways to punish drunk drivers. Jail them, fine them, suspend their licenses, or sometimes all three.

One of these, says the California Department of Motor Vehicles, appears to have a particularly strong educational effect.

The department recently studied a group of drivers with multiple drunk driving convictions who received various combinations of punishments. Drivers who lost their licenses in addition to fines or jail had better records when they got their licenses back. Over six years, they had 40% fewer reckless driving convictions, fewer crashes and fewer moving violations than drivers who kept their licenses.

The agency doesn't see suspension as a panacea. But for the moment, it seems the best lesson for drinkers should include license suspension.

A lot of people think there's nothing much to be done about the problem of drunk driving. But that's no reason to stop trying. We'd like to know what you think. Just write The Travelers Office of Consumer Information, One Tower Square, Hartford, Connecticut 06115. Or dial, toll-free, weekdays from 9 to 5 Eastern Time, 800-243-0191. In Connecticut, call collect, 277-6565.

THE TRAVELERS
Raising our voice, not just our rates.

The Travelers Insurance Company, The Travelers Indemnity Company, and Affiliated Companies, Hartford, Conn. 06115

Figure 1. "Is Putting Drunk Drivers Behind Bars the Only Way to Teach Them a Lesson?" Advertisement, *Newsweek*, April 17, 1977

Zygmunt Bauman, in an argument for a socialist program oriented to cultural revision, puts the issue of dominant and alternative consciousness in a clear light: "the dominant culture consists of transforming everything which is not inevitable into the improbable...an over-repressive society is one which effectively eliminates alternatives to itself and thereby relinquishes spectacular, dramatised displays of its power" (Bauman 1976, p. 123).

Auto injuries are no less amenable to such analyses than more dramatically exciting political programs. In 1968 the Department of Transportation issued a report to the U.S. Congress on alcohol and highway safety, as required by the National Highway Safety Act of 1966. That report began with a summary two paragraphs which have been, and continue to be, conventional wisdom on the subject of auto accidents and alcohol:

> The use of alcohol by drivers and pedestrians leads to some 25,000 deaths and a total of at least 800,000 crashes in the United States each year. Especially tragic is the fact that much of the loss in life, limb and property involves completely innocent parties.
> ...every competent investigation has demonstrated that the immoderate use of alcohol is a very major source of highway crashes, especially of those most violent. In fact, it contributes to about half of all highway crashes, and to appreciable percentages of the far more numerous nonfatal crashes. [U.S. Congress, Committee on Public Works, 1968, p. 1]

The "facts" described in these paragraphs have not risen to the consciousness of observers as natural and self-evident experience. Implicit in their emergence is an organization of thought and of activities which has impelled some persons to be publicly accepted as legitimate and authoritative observers, to look in some directions and not in others, to select certain avenues of concern and to neglect others. These structures of thought and of activities that lead to the "facts" of drinking and driving are the subject of this chapter. A theory of causal responsibility and an accompanying attribution of political responsibility form the consciousness of automobile accidents in the United States. Alternative modes of being conscious of automobile accidents are logically possible and have occurred.

More pointedly, the framework in which the drinking-driving problem is couched in the United States is a framework of assumptions about accidents and about automobile operation. In order to search for the "cause" of accidents they must be conceived as amenable to understanding and knowledge. They cannot be assumed to be random events and products of chance. It must also be assumed that they can be acted upon. Thus, accidents, in the 1968 report, are potentially capable of human and public control. They *can* be the object of social policy. The phenomenon of accidents is treated as an object that can be explained, made accountable, and rationally manipulated (Starr 1969). Writing on the problem of drink and driving in a *Science* editorial, Robert Morrison said: "The general problem of technology assessment is exceedingly complex.... The alcohol-automobile problem provides a simple model with which to begin...many of our law and order problems seem to have no known solution. This one does" (Morrison 1970).

Beyond such general frameworks are more specific ones which direct the observer, the scientist, the policymaker toward one or another of the manifold possibilities of conceiving the causes of accidents. In this chapter my concern is with the theory of the individual motorist as the source of automobile accidents. The theory of the "incompetent driver" has been the major framework within which drinking and driving have made sense as foci of accident research. That attention to individuals can be contrasted with alternative frameworks which focus on the "unsafe car" as the source of concern. It is apparent from my discussion in the introduction that the thesis of this book is that such foci are *not* results of external, objective realities in any direct, compelling fashion but are deeply influenced by the social and cultural organization by which attention is directed down some avenues and away from others.

Lastly, it is part of the framework of "facts" about drinking and driving that they have become public wisdom. They constitute the believable and accepted body of knowledge for a large number of people who have personal knowledge neither of all the instances of accident described nor of the scientific knowledge alluded to in the 1968 report summary. The "facts" of drinking and driving are not esoteric. They are known by scholars in the field, practitioners in alcohol programs and traffic safety organizations. They constitute the working assumptions of journalists and policymakers who write about, speak about, or create policy toward auto accidents. They are the "facts" which make up the knowledge of auto accidents which interested and informed citizens believe to be *the* reality.

In this chapter my examination of the structure of knowledge about auto accidents will develop two components of the process that formed it. One component is cultural organization. It is found in the linguistic and logical categories used to think about auto accidents. Such categories have important implications for the types of causal and political responsibility involved. The conceptualizations with which auto accidents are framed influence the policymaking apparatus—the points at which political responsibility is placed. And vice versa—conceptions of political responsibility influence the accepted and acceptable theories of causation.

The second component is that of social organization—the pattern of activities through which phenomena become accessible and systematized into data and theory. Here the role of ownership is significant. The analysis of cultural organization tells us what "automobile accidents" mean, how they are interpreted, and how they are made an object of thought. The analysis of social organization tells us what facts are collected, how and by whom, as well as how they are processed and transmitted. The former is a study of cognitive order; the latter, of organized actions.

Conceptual Framework: The Structure of Accident Consciousness

How can "accidents" be a matter of public action? The very concept of the accidental would seem to suggest unpredictable and random events. How can causal and political responsibility be adduced to explain or control what is unpredictable and unexplainable? To speak of cause or of control would imply that the event can be understood and that there is some capacity to control its appearance.

Science and Accident

Science seems to stand at the opposite pole from "accident." Ordinary language usage often prefaces an explanation by saying "It is no accident that...." When Sigmund Freud published *The Psychopathology of Everyday Life* he took an entire area of human behavior—mistakes, slips of the tongue, everyday errors—and perceived them as determined events. The epochmaking character of this new conceptualization of old experiences was that acts that had been presumed to be accidental and not an object of scientific explanation were now seen as explainable and determined (Freud 1938). The psychoanalytic weapons of theory and insight could be brought up to the front to subject the "accidental" to explanation. In their seminal work on accidents, *Accident Research,* William Haddon, Edward Suchman, and David Klein argue for a science of accident control and criticize people of education and science for believing that "accidents are 'acts of God' that 'just happen' ... that accidents are as uncontrollable as the weather; that, in short, accidents somehow mysteriously defy any systematic study beyond mere tabulation" (Haddon, Suchman, Klein 1964, p. 6).

In these usages commonsensical versions of accident are ways of placing events outside any scheme of analysis and accountability. Both Freud and Haddon, et al. attempt to place phenomena considered "accidental" into categories of analysis. They seek to provide causal explanations.

From another standpoint, the issue of "accident" is akin to problems of political responsibility because it provides answers of blameworthiness, of liability. In Anglo-Saxon tort law, accidents are distinguished from negligence. In their exhaustive treatise on the concept of cause in legal uses, Hart and Honoré define the distinction: "The expression 'accident' perhaps strictly applies to those causes where the agent does not anticipate the consequences and the consequences are not what would reasonably be expected in the circumstances. A negligent act is unintentional but not accidental, for such act would reasonably be expected, in the circumstances, to lead to harm" (Hart and Honoré 1959, p. 143). As an example, Hart and Honoré cite a highway "accident" case in which the defendant had, by his actions, obstructed walking on a sidewalk. To avoid the obstruction, the plaintiff walked into the street and was killed by a passing car. The court held that the question of causation was a rightful one for the jury to consider. The court was saying that the obstruction could be seen as the cause of the death; it was not an accident (*O'Neil* v. *City of Port Jervis* 1930; cited by Hart and Honoré 1959, p. 142).[1]

Job's Lament, Accidents, and
"Class-Consciousness"

The summary paragraphs above are set in a frame in which automobile crashes, at least a large percentage of them, are not perceived as "accidental" but as avoidable, controllable, and explainable. Those paragraphs, however, are addressed to an aggregate problem: Why are there automobile accidents? There is another level of "accident analysis" that is left unaddressed. It is Job's ancient problem of theodicy, the justification of God's goodness in an evil world. Job's question was not why is Mankind subject to disease and evil, but why is this happening to me? What did I do wrong? Why not others, who are less deserving?

Job's answer was a religious one: God's inscrutable will. For secular modernity, this is tantamount to "accident"; the answer is not an object of science and knowledge. However, Job's problem remains, and it leads me to distinguish an individualistic concern from an aggregate one. The

distinction can easily be observed in everyday examination of auto "accidents." When three deaths occur in one year at a grade crossing, public
demand and/or the response of officials will often involve a reassessment
of the crossing. Is the lighting adequate? Are stop signals needed? Are all
sides visible? The situation rather than the individual driver is assessed.
Job's question remains unanswered. Why, among thousands of people
who used that crossing, was I a victim, one of three?

The structure of consciousness in the summary statement of the 1968
report is about aggregates, not about individuals. It explains auto crashes
as determinable events in the aggregate; not as accidents but as natural,
explainable phenomena. The explanation, in this case, is in terms of
characteristics of individual motorists, but it is nevertheless *not* a matter
of randomness, of chance occurrences without blame or avoidability. It is
an explanation applicable to groups but not to specific situations. It is
about collectivities, not specific situations.

Clearly, automobile crashes have not gained an unalloyed status as
"accidents" in American life. If they had, it would be very difficult to
account for the development of elaborate and organized attempts to
prevent them. They occupy a social category in that a division of labor
and a complex institutional machinery exist to explain, prevent, and
deter them. As with other social problems, attributes of ownership and
causal and political responsibility are characteristic of how auto accidents are processed in this society. However—and this will prove to be
most important—such attributions are aimed toward explaining accident rates and magnitudes, toward reducing or maintaining rates and
magnitudes in the aggregate, as a public concern. They seldom provide
explanations for individual instances of accident in Job's sense.

Our consciousness of automobile accidents is akin in structure to that
most pervasive of sociolgical issues—"class-consciousness." A major
objective of Marxian thought has been the effort to shift thinking away
from explanations of inequality, poverty, and unemployment on the level
of individual traits, "luck," or particular problems of group and social
structures toward ones on the level of "class." Much of sociological
thought and practice, since Durkheim, has been marked by the distinctive
use of aggregate characteristics and aggregate concerns. (See the discussion of group rates as the distinctive data of sociology in Durkheim's
Suicide, chap. 1).

Accident, Disease, and Safety

The concept of "accident" used in the 1968 report represents a category
of thought about which rational principles and a body of fact are posited.

It would be absurd to maintain that automobile "accidents," in the context of the report, manifest the pristine sense of "accident" as a random, nonunderstandable, and uncontrollable event. Elaborate organized efforts to prevent accidents exist in the United States. Research attempts to frame a rational analysis of accidents belie the residual nonrational character which the word might imply.

We begin then with what the enterprise of accident prevention assumes. Without the assumption that accidents are objects of scientific understanding the activities studied in this book would have no point. As a sociological category, "accident" is a way of distinguishing certain events from others in a fashion which entails specific consequences. These consequences need consideration.

A glance at the annual report on "causes of death" shows "accidents" as a major category distinct from diseases (Monthly Vital Statistics Report, 1979; also Knowles 1977, pp. 60–61). They now account for approximately one-third of all deaths and are the largest category used to account for the deaths of persons below the age of forty. Regularly the ratio of death from automobile accidents to those of reported murder is approximately 10/1. In 1952, the year of the polio epidemic, the ratio of automobile deaths to deaths from polio was 25/1 (Haddon et al., 1964).[2]

For the sociologist it becomes important to ask what happens if one category, "accident," is used in a system of accountabilities rather than some other—"disease," for example. "Disease" places events into the jurisdiction of medical institutions and the province of the medical profession. There has been movement, at least since Gordon's classic 1949 paper, "The Epidemiology of Accidents" (Gordon 1949), to make the study of accidents a part of the medical curriculum. That movement has not had a wide acceptance. The major work on accident research, by William Haddon, Edward Suchman, and David Klein (1964) has even been out of print for a number of years. I will discuss this movement later in this chapter in examining an alternative consciousness of auto accidents in the context of public health.

A clue to the way in which accidents have been conceptualized in the United States can be found by looking at the areas where a concern for accident has arisen. The concept of accident prevention is connected with that of "safety." The modern safety movement in America emerged at the turn of the century. The Pure Food and Drug Law attempted to protect the consumer (Nadel 1971, chap. 1), while a concern for industrial accidents was manifested in union-management issues and in governmental regulation of safety measures at the workplace (Eastman 1910). The National Safety Council, which had a great bearing on automobile safety, was an outgrowth of industries concerned with prevention of workplace accident. Later, in 1922, it became a major source of automobile accident statistics deserving credit for their entry into the public consciousness.

It is among lawyers that the concept of accident has been a major occupational concern. Here the question of accident has been clearly associated with issues of responsibility for damage. The emphasis has been on distinguishing instances of "accident," where negligence is absent, from events that are nonaccidental. Thus responsibility is defined in both causal and political terms.[3]

The interests of lawyers has been in responsibility, not in accident prevention, although the question of how the event could have been prevented is implicit. Thus Friedman writes about nineteenth-century tort law: "Absolute liability might have strangled the economy altogether. If railroads, and enterprise generally, had to pay for all the damage done 'by accident,' lawsuits might drain them of their economic blood. So, ordinary caution became the standard" (Friedman 1973, p. 410). The legal discussion, and subsequent statute laws defining negligence and the responsibilities of business enterprise, are couched in a language that fixed responsibility in individual cases and "proximate causes" rather than in aggregate elements.

The assumption that automobile accidents are preventable is a selective assumption, making causal responsibility a major concern in the development of knowledge about auto accidents. That assumption is essential to the second aspect of thought about auto accidents represented in the 1966 report summation: the significance of the individual motorist as a crucial causal agent.

The Organization of Knowledge

Public and Private Knowledge

The phenomenon of the "auto accident" is neither esoteric nor unknown to Americans. Whether as an event we ourselves or others we know have been involved in, or as one we have witnessed, auto accidents are part of the personal, individual reality of the contemporary American. "Auto death" as a public event of problem status is a different matter; it is not part of the personal, experienced reality of individuals. The human being, except in the rare circumstances of wartime destruction from air, does not "experience" fifty thousand deaths. Such phenomena are not private knowledge.

The facts of auto death and drinking quoted in the 1966 report are public rather than private knowledge. They constitute a public reality in two senses. First, these are facts which are shared by many people in the society who have no, or very little, personal knowledge of individual cases making up the aggregated facts. As public facts, they are not peculiar to any particular class, cultural group, or educational stratum. Second, they compose a public reality in being an aggregated fact rather than the events involving particular people. They are not about anyone but about a society—the United States. In that sense they are akin to Durkheim's "social facts"—products of a collective entity and not of an individual actor or event (Durkheim 1951, pp. 46–53).

Because such facts are not records of individual events but are rather aggregations of data, amassed and presented, the "discovery" of public facts is a process of social organization. Someone must engage in monitoring, recording, aggregating, analyzing, and transmitting the separate and individual events into the public reality of "auto accidents and deaths." At every stage in this process human choices of selection and interpretation operate.

The Structure of Public Reality
and the Automobile

What facts are collected? By whom? How are they collected? How processed? How transmitted? Through whom and to whom? Here I will concentrate on two questions: (1) who are the aggregators and transmitters of the public reality of auto death and its corollary, auto safety? and (2) what is selected as the content of that public reality. The first is the question of social organization. The second is that of culture—the symbolic categories through which auto accidents and deaths are perceived.

A number of persons and agencies operate in the collection and dissemination of materials on auto safety, but they do not all have the same significance. At one level of knowledge stand (or lie) the experts and professionals. These are people who, like myself, have made it their "business" to collect and aggregate data. Their knowledge is close and detailed.[4] At another level are the journalists, writers, staff assistants, and teachers who transmit information and analysis to public and policymakers.

Who are the experts and the professionals who provide the aggregated facts about auto safety? What stands out in my interpretation of the formation of public reality is the dominance of private, nonindustry agencies in the field of automobile safety. Until the late 1960s neither state nor national government nor major industrial and financial industries played a major role in gathering, aggregating, analyzing, or transmitting public data on auto death and accident in the United States. While governmental health and safety agencies, police, and nongovernmental voluntary associations have been involved in various phases and projects of information gathering, the major source of continuous and publicly visible information on auto accidents and deaths has been the National Safety Council, a private, nongovernmental agency.

The relative absence of the major auto and insurance companies from the information gathering process is significant. Despite a seeming concern for decreasing the magnitude of auto accidents and deaths, none of the major auto manufacturing or life insurance corporations was very active in developing or supporting automobile safety research or in collecting and disseminating information. The passage of the National Highway Traffic Safety Act in 1966 produced the first major governmental agency devoted to auto safety. Since then there has been some change in the role of the auto and insurance companies.

The absence of insurance company interest in safety research has been difficult to explain since they have been involved in safety research in other areas, such as fire and marine loss. Ralph Nader has suggested that insurance companies had little interest in diminishing losses in auto crashes because, among other considerations, as long as insurance corporations can raise premiums, increased losses are balanced by increased premiums and a larger volume of funds is available for investment. It is from investment, not premiums that the companies derive their greatest source of income (Nader 1972, p. 219). Whatever the causal explanation, since 1968 the Insurance Institute for Highway Safety, now led by William Haddon and supported by a number of insurance companies, *has* played a highly important and innovative role in conducting research and disseminating information in the field.

The automobile industries have steered clear of safety information as well as research activities concerning safety. They have, from time to time, supported university research on specific safety issues, but they have not engaged in any continuous, long-range, or major research and development programs, at least before the passage of the National Highway Safety Act in 1966 and the consequent emergence of governmental impositions of standards.[5]

If the major industrial associations disowned responsibility for monitoring the accidents and deaths attributable to automobile travel, neither can government be said to have assumed significant responsibility in the field. The work of the Bureau of Roads has, during its history, been largely devoted to improving and extending highways so as to implement commercial and passenger travel, with safety an important element but not the major thrust of its work. Until the establishment of the National Highway Traffic Safety Administration there was no permanent, central agency at the national level which made auto safety its primary interest. The Public Health Service has been a significant source in supporting university and other safety research, and also, through gathering vital statistics, a major monitor of auto accidents. However, two considerations limit the role of that data in developing a public consciousness of auto accidents. First, the data are buried in the general data on mortality. Thus they are analyzed under medical categories rather than under a distinct category of their own. Second, and probably more important, the Public Health Service is not committed to use its data in educational or other campaigns. Consequently its product is not made the occasion for press releases or regular news coverage. Nevertheless these data constitute a significant source of information and will be examined later.

The absence of national involvement in auto safety research and information gathering has been one effect of the separation of state and federal powers, inherent in the U.S. Constitution. It has enabled states to retain and utilize control over policies toward the automobile. State administration and legislatures have resisted development of a national data gathering agency. In the early stages of public concern over auto safety (in the 1920s) state and national conferences reflected both state leadership and a self-conscious inhibition on the part of the federal government.[6]

Neither have consumer groups played more than a peripheral role in safety legislation and virtually none in information gathering. Unlike such associations in other countries, Sweden for example, the American Automobile Association has not been a leading source of information or research on auto safety.

The National Safety Council

The importance of the National Safety Council as a major generator of public reality about auto accidents stems from two considerations: its consistency in reporting nationally aggregated data on a regular basis, and its role in disseminating that information to public audiences as part of educational campaigns to diminish accidents. Since 1922 it has made, and published as *Accident Facts,* an annual audit of auto and other forms of industrial and domestic accidents. It prepares special reports and announcements for public release to communications media, especially in connection with holiday driving. Its news makes news and "good copy" for newspapers, radio, and television.

The National Safety Council was established well before the advent of mass automobile ownership in the United States. It began as an organization concerned with industrial accidents and supported by funds from major industries. It still performs a role in the field of industrial accidents, but its major focus is today on the automobile. While still supported by industries, the NSC also gets a significant amount of funds from both the auto industry and the U.S. Government.

As an association actively promulgating and supporting programs for effective safety measures, the NSC has largely devoted its attention to educational measures, such as persuading motorists to drive with care and less speed, and to law enforcement prods. Their publicity at holiday times is by now a familiar part of Americana. So too, the NSC has been one of the chief supporters of driver education in the schools. While they have also campaigned for safer roads, the big push of the NSC, as in so much of the social organization of safety associations, has been directed to the performance of the motorist.

The place of the National Safety Council in what Ralph Nader (1972) has labeled "the safety establishment" is accordingly one of major importance. Another study (Havelock 1971), investigating the problem solving system of highway decisionmakers and researchers in safety, found that more decisionmakers belonged to it than any other organization in the safety field.

While the National Safety Council is hardly the sole organization operating in the field of automobile safety, it has succeeded in becoming a major owner of the problem in public arenas. (For a general view of the safety organizations as of the mid-1960s, see Nader 1972.) In the collection and public transmission of automobile "facts" several major organized agencies have disowned the problem. Neither the insurance nor the automobile industry has provided, until recently, a significant input into automotive safety research or data collection (Nader 1972, p. 219). Neither has the federal government performed such a role until the early 1970s (O'Connell and Myers 1966, pp. 43–44). The implications of this social organization for the development of safety facts are seen when we examine the cultural categories utilized by the NSC.

The Cultural Organization of Automobile Facts

The character of perception and conceptualization inherent in the symbolic categories we utilize deeply influences our experience of reality and our actions. In the field of auto safety, the categories influence the data collected and the attribution of causal responsibility which emerges. The emphasis on driver attributes and driver performance in the attribution of responsibility for auto safety has been the characteristic and dominant mode in American solutions. It is illustrated in the statement of an engineering official of General Motors to a *New York Times* reporter: "The driver is the most important, we feel. If the drivers do everything they should, there wouldn't be accidents, would there?" (quoted in O'Connell and Myers 1966, p. 6).

This view of auto accidents as results of individual driver performance is the dominant theme in the cultural organization of accident reality in the United States. With some exceptions discussed below, not only the NSC but most of the traffic safety organizations have seen the driver as the major causal agent in auto accidents and championed improving driver abilities as the major policy in controlling them. Two leading accident analysts sum up the pervasive character of this impaired driver thesis:

> Although the moralistic view has largely disappeared in medicine and public health, it still prevails in many areas of highway safety . . . police, insurance companies and administrative authorities attribute the vast majority of crashes to "carelessness," "negligence," and other avoidable human behavior. . . . Police efforts . . . are most heavily concentrated on the determination of "guilt"; the entire court system, as it relates to traffic problems, is devoted to the identification and punishment of "fault" or "negligence." And both insurance companies and motor vehicle administrators have been more concerned with weeding out the "bad" driver than with other, and possibly more productive, ways of reducing fatalities, injuries, and property damage. [Klein and Waller 1970, p. 12]

Readily available data and some less easily available are significant in reinforcing the view of the automobile driver as the focus for control policies. The point is evidenced by a brief look at an annual publication of the National Safety Council, appropriately for this study entitled *Accident Facts*. The 1977 issue, reporting on accidents of 1976, is a ninety-six page document, largely made up of tables reporting accidents. While there are specific sections on particular types of accidents, such as home, farm, school, and work, the largest section is devoted to automobiles— almost half of the space is devoted to special types of auto accidents. While the authors make no attempt to analyze the data presented, they do provide a number of analytical tables in which total figures of deaths and accidents are seen in relation to specific facts, sometimes aggregated data and sometimes special studies reported in the literature of safety.

Thus a table presenting data on the sex of drivers in all accidents and in fatal accidents was compiled from information obtained from state motor vehicle departments and the Federal Highway Administration, while data on alcohol involvement were based on a 1975 report of the California highway patrol. A table listing pedestrian actions (walking on roadway, standing on roadway, etc.) by types of roadway is based on reports from eighteen state traffic authorities. The categories used, a number of them in cross-tabulations as well as singly, include collision type (pedestrian, with fixed objects, other vehicles, etc.); place (urban-rural); time (day, night, hour of day); motor vehicle mileage; accidents on turnpikes; type of road and place (size of city, state, road, county, etc.); directional analysis of accident (going straight, turning, etc.); pedacycle–motor vehicle collisions; driver action (improper driving, skidding, avoiding, etc.); use of alcohol and drugs; age; sex; pedestrians and pedestrian actions; speed; motor vehicle category (trucks, passenger cars, etc.); state residence; state; costs; nations. In cross-tabulating, the most frequently used categories are year, place (urban-rural), and age.

What is not presented reveals the general scheme of conceptualization with which facts are developed. Proponents of design standards for American autos have called attention to the failure of the NSC to report data on the vehicle and the proximate cause of injuries and death (Nader 1972; O'Connell and Myers 1966; Haddon 1972). Thus such data as age of vehicle, brand, and model (e.g., Dodge Polara), weight, and other matter describing the vehicle design do not appear. Nothing is collected or presented which would indicate the way in which death or injury was sustained, such as the shock entailed in striking ground after emission or the puncture resulting from collision of the body with a protruding object. The 1977 edition of *Accident Facts* contained a paragraph cautioning the motorist to use safety belts and indicating that twelve thousand lives could have been saved by their use, but no data were presented on their use in the accidents and deaths reported.

The NSC data on roads serve to place roads without giving their character (one- or two-way, number of lanes, etc.). The distance between deaths and nearest emergency medical facilities or the one-way or multiple direction of roads is not tabulated for accidents or deaths. The interstate highway system is discussed as an effective agent in reducing auto accident rates per mile driven.

A sociological account of auto accidents would utilize another conception of the automobile. It would make inquiries into the function of the auto and situation in which it was used. For example, where are motorists and pedestrians going? Nothing is presented by the NSC that bears on the journey to work, vacation usage, shopping, passengers, going home, or other data that place the automobile in a context of caution or risk except time of day. Neither are elements of social structure introduced that might relate income and information to automobile maintenance.

The purpose of mentioning alternative or possible data is to substantiate the selecting and compressing process by which automobile accident facts emerge. Some of the possible data are available, such as vehicle brand and model. These are collected routinely in police accident and death reports. Other data are collected indifferently if at all.[7] While data collection is, of course, limited by the practices of the reporting agencies, those practices are in turn influenced by the data that have come to be sought. Where insurance companies, law enforcement agents, and national monitoring organizations make little effort to obtain a kind of data, there is little incentive for the reporting agencies to report on it accurately. Insofar as the legal standards limit causal attribution to driver performance for criminal and civil cases, such data are emphasized and other data ignored. The very individualistic character of the law in automobile accident cases has made the collection of aggregate data on auto design a matter of indifference by reporting agencies.

Causal Attribution and Individual Responsibility

The designation of driver performance as the major "cause" of auto accidents has been a persistent facet of the public discussion of automobile safety in the United States. An examination of the coverage by the *New York Times* of news about auto safety since 1922 indicates the extent to which private safety organizations, automobile industry spokesmen, and insurance company officials "explained" auto accidents as the consequence of careless, incompetent, or impaired driver performance.[8]

Thus, since the early 1920s, the private safety organizations, especially the National Safety Council, and the major auto and life insurance companies pressed for programs and legislation to control and train the individual driver. The state licensing of automobile drivers, originally a device to raise revenue, quickly became attached to a system of examinations designed to screen drivers for minimal levels of competence. State legislation increasingly was passed providing for fixed speed maxima. Campaigns to establish driver training courses in the schools, and later to make these compulsory followed.[9]

Perhaps more pertinent than the existence of news of programs, legislation, and research is the absence of news of programs, legislation, and legislative demands based on different or on opposing theses of accident prevention. The role of specific makes of vehicles in auto accidents, the implications of various road building plans and materials, the possibility of alternative forms of transportation, the costs of mobility in auto travel, or any widespread movement to lower auto fatalities by means other than influencing driver performance is absent from the news accounts and major legislation until the middle 1960s. Department of Motor Vehicles policies are almost solely concerned with driver performance. With some exceptions, notably New York in the late 1950s, state departments of motor vehicles made no attempt to set standards for auto design, search for major design defects, or pressure for lessened auto traffic or for increased mass transportation. They provided no input into the planning of roads. They were less departments of motor vehicles than departments of motorists.

While the building of better roads, especially the interstate highway system, has had an effect in lowering auto deaths per miles driven, the demand for road building has not been prompted by perceptions of bad roads as a "cause" of accidents. Road building in the United States has been largely a response to the demands of farmers for means to transport crops, businesses to carry freight, and automobile manufacturers to increase sales to consumers (Baker 1971; Rae, 1971, pp. 76–77).

With accidents interpreted as results of "poor driving," the legal process easily becomes the agent bearing public responsibility for automobile safety. Since the problem was located within the personal attributes of the motorist, the solution lay in persuading the motorist to improve his or her driving skills and/or to exercise a greater standard of care in operating the vehicle. It is not strange that I can illustrate the fundamental doctrine of law as a solution to the public problem of auto safety through a public statement made in 1934 by the General Motors representative to the Convention of Highway Officials: "The average and not the drunken or defective driver is responsible for most of the traffic accidents, and therefore adequate policing and strict traffic courts are the best accident preventatives. *Most accidents are caused by doing things known to be wrong.* The answer is plenty of uniformed police in plain sight and inflexible courts" (*New York Times,* February 17, 1934, 23:1; emphasis added).

In the early history of auto safety in the United States, there was some reliance on private and nonpublic methods of control. In the 1920s there were even various forms of "traffic vigilantes." These were private groups organized to observe traffic and stop offending motorists and cite

them for offensive driving. (*New York Times* 1922, 1926, 1930). Educational campaigns, attempting to persuade the motorist to improve skills
or drive carefully, still are rife and claim much public attention. But they
are far from being major points of reliance for auto safety.

The theory of deterrence through criminal law enforcement has determined the major system of public responsibility for automobile safety
in the United States. Traffic laws and their regulation operate on the
theory that the individual motorist can be led to more diligence in driving
through the fear of police apprehension and legal punishment (Zimring
and Hawkins 1973). State laws hold the individual and not the auto
industry or the road or the locality "responsible" for accidents and search
for fault in the acts and attributes of the motorist.

Multiple Frameworks and Alternative Consciousness

The individualistic premises in conceiving of auto accidents and in
directing attention toward drinking-drivers as causal agents have dominated American thought and policy toward the dangers of the automobile. Holding the motorist politically responsible seemed "normal"
and "natural." It met prevailing concepts of fault traditional in American
law. It was congruent with the desires of the automobile industry to
avoid safety as a major consideration in the design of cars.[10] As I will
assert later (chap. 6) it made the world of accident one of moral understanding.

The unsafe motorist thesis couched the problem of auto accidents in
the language of Job and in a politics of individualism. An alternative
consciousness might conceive it as one of aggregate accidents and place
political responsibility at other levels. In the middle 1960s such an
alternative began to gain credence and support both as a mode of consciousness and as a political activity.

In making the "unsafe driver" the prime "causal agent" in automobile
accidents, agent, not scene, was the paramount object of attention.
Strategies to reduce the loss of life and the injuries resulting from auto
crashes concentrated on such programs as driver education, licensing
examinations, legislation, law enforcement, and maintenance of existing
cars. Over the period of automobile use in the United States emphases
within the theory of the "unsafe driver" have shifted from careless but
competent drivers to incompetent drivers to special categories of
"accident-prone" drivers including the young, the very old, and the
alcohol-impaired (Cloyd 1972).

By 1965 a very different conception of causal responsibility and of political obligation had begun to gain currency, especially among scholars, experts, and some political officials. The "unsafe car" thesis directed attention away from the motorist and toward the automobile, away from the accident and toward its effects, away from the driver and toward the manufacturer. It turned the headlights on the design of the car—its capacity to withstand impact, to protect the occupant after impact, and to eliminate the trauma connected with crashes.

William Haddon, Jr., one of the leading figures in the public health accident field and the first administrator of the National Highway Safety Administration, put the difference between the two conceptualizations in this fashion:

> The single most important and essential point in viewing the full range of energy-damage phenomena is that the emphasis, the priorities placed upon given loss-reduction countermeasures among the options available must be based on their effectiveness in reducing the end-results in damage—not necessarily on preventing the initiation of the events themselves. This frequently means that primary emphasis, if rationally selected, must be placed on other than pre-event countermeasures. For example, on a net for an acrobat rather than propaganda telling him to "perform safely" and never to fall; on better packaging of a postal shipment rather than equal expenditure directed at postal employees. [Haddon 1972, p. 4; also see Haddon 1970; Haddon, Suchman, Klein 1964, pp. 27–30]

In the context of the automobile this conceptualization has been associated with the movement to develop governmental safety standards in the design and manufacture of automobiles which culminated in the passage of the National Highway Traffic Safety Act of 1966 and the establishment of an agency to develop and enforce such standards, the National Highway Traffic Safety Administration. Beginning with the research of Hugh De Haven and the Cornell University research center in 1942, a series of investigations had developed the view that serious injuries in auto accidents were largely results of the design—protruding and pointed objects such as noncollapsible steering wheels and daggerlike dashboard equipment—and of the failure of the auto body to prevent the ejection of the rider. This concern for the "second collision"—the after-events of the initial crash—placed the emphasis in safety strategy on the character of the vehicle rather than its navigator. It was the major research supportive of the introduction of safety belts, padded dashboard, collapsible steering wheels, and better, less collapsible doors (U.S. Congress 1966, pp. 320–48; Haddon, Suchman, Klein 1964, pp. 537–83).

This shift in causal theory carries with it a potential shift in political responsibility. By putting the onus for accidents on the design of the auto, it emphasizes the role of the manufacturer as an agent of accidents. The movement toward imposition of design standards on the automobile industry generated a small degree of interest during the 1950s, picked up speed in some states in the late 1950s, and came to fruition with the Senate hearings on auto safety in 1965 and the enactment of the legislation of 1966.[11]

For this study, the significance of the alternative consciousness is in the political consequences which ensued. Not only does the new consciousness shift the focus of action from state and private associations to the federal government, but also replaces the motorist, drunk or sober, by the automobile industry as the bête noir of safety advocates. One witness at the U.S. Senate hearings on the national traffic safety bill said that the problem was not in the foolishness or drunkenness of the driver but in the failure of the auto industry to construct an automobile designed on the assumption that drivers would be foolish or drunk. In the legislative procedure during which the act was established the suggestion was made that the auto industry be mandated to produce an auto which would cut deaths to fifteen thousand per year (interview with William Haddon, Jr., Sept. 1973).

Accident, Risk, and Certainty

This chapter will not, I hope, be read as an argument for the virtues of the "unsafe car" thesis and an attack on the "unsafe driver" and the drinking-driver perspectives. Although the evocation of any alternative consciousness weakens the claim to naturalness and reality of the dominant mentality, I am not claiming that one is superior to the other as strategies to explain auto injuries. I will argue later that judging these frameworks as technical, means-ends schemes ignores the moral connotations which lend credence to either strategy. There is a dichotomy between the individualist stance, with its condemnation of the drinker, and the political ideology of liberal government, with its assumption that industrial corporations are evil. Both are systems of thought which locate foci of trouble. It is not that a theory of causal responsibility establishes a specific locus of political responsibility. It may be that the reverse is more frequent; a belief in the political reality lends credence to causal theories which sustain that locus. The relationship between the two is at least a two-way road.

Both theses are explanations of events as well as bases for strategies. Each places its priorities of policy in different places. The "unsafe driver" thesis considers accidents as separate events and seeks solutions for individual events, minimizing the aggregate character of accidents. The "unsafe car" thesis provides a consciousness of accidents in the aggregate and seeks solutions through aggregate policies. The movement to produce safer cars accepts accidents as given—as inevitable or probable, rather than as random or inexplicable, events. It attempts to heighten the public consciousness of the individual event as embedded in a collective and aggregate process.

Although the consumer movement has resulted in some regulation of the auto industry's design of autos, any conclusion as to its efficacy in reducing auto casualties is probably premature. The earliest standards were imposed in 1967 and 1968 and only on new automobiles coming off the line in 1968 and 1969. While auto deaths per miles driven and per cars owned have declined since the auto has been a common form of consumer equipment, the absolute number of deaths from auto accidents has continued to increase as have deaths per unit of population, with two exceptions (R. Baker 1971; NSC 1978). As figure 2 indicates, between 1942 and 1945 there was a sharp decline. These were years of war when automobiles and gasoline were less available than usual. The second time occurred in 1974/75, following the oil shortage of 1974 and continuous increases in the price of gas. Although the 1977 deaths were still fewer than in 1973, they had begun to climb. While a great debate persists in explanation of the 1970s decline, it is still too early to maintain, as have some authorities, that either decreased speed limits or the impact of national safety standards has produced the results (NSC 1976; Insurance Institute for Highway Safety, May 3, August 30, 1976).

It may be maintained that I am being misleading by referring to the "unsafe driver" and the "unsafe car" as alternative modes of consciousness (Rae 1971, pp. 347–48). These might be seen as different components of the auto safety problem, each an object of concurrent policy. Yet each has not played an equal role in the public arena. The "unsafe roads" hypothesis has not been dominant for much of the history of auto safety in the United States and the "unsafe car" is only a decade old. In the political arena, where legal and governmental responsibilities are argued about, the diverse explanations appear in conflict, as matters of where and how priorities will be placed. In the Senate hearings on the National Traffic and Motor Vehicle Safety Act of 1966, the president of the National Safety Council, Howard Pyle, made a strong argument against the imposition of federal standards of auto design by supporting the greater importance of driver competence than of design as a causal agent in auto accident (U.S. Congress 1966, pp. 133–81). From a different stance, the

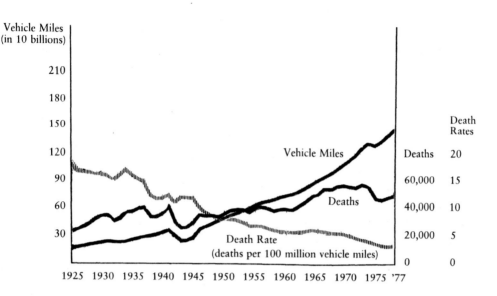

Figure 2. Motor Vehicle Travel, Deaths and Death Rates, 1925–1977.
Source: National Safety Council

chairman of the Senate committee, Senator Magnuson, pointed out the
practical implications of a strong adherence ot the "unsafe driver" perspective by the auto industry:

> But the committee met with disturbing evidence of the automobile
> industry's chronic subordination of safe design to promotional styling
> and of an overriding stress on power, acceleration, speed and "ride"
> to the relative neglect of safe performance or collision protection. The
> committee cannot judge the truth of the conviction that "safety
> doesn't sell" but it is a conviction widely held in industry that has
> plainly resulted in the inadequate allocation of resources to safety
> engineering. [U.S. Congress 1966, p. 14,221]

The diverse ways of conceiving of automobile accidents place the
events and phenomena under attention in diverse contexts. Causal
theories and political attributions of responsibility exist in a relationship
to each other. Such differing contexts provide a backdrop to understanding conflict or, in some instances, its absence. The "unsafe car"
movement became the opening activity of what has since grown into the
consumer movement and the environmental movement in national politics (Nadel 1971; Halpern 1972). It provided a public context which put
a new emphasis on old issues, such as accidents, pollution, and health.

The attention to the drinking-driver is set in a mode of categorizing that implicates individual motorists. As I will show, the implications of this approach for alcohol policy have been specific and congruent with that individualistic structure of thought.

There is another aspect to the analysis of consciousness about auto accidents. (This foreshadows my later analysis in part 2.) All the theories of auto accidents discussed above have been based on the presumption that accidents can be explained and prevented or their consequences diminished. Yet the history of auto casualties in the United States must also provide a basis for a less Enlightenment perspective. Even the largest drop in auto deaths, that of 1941–44, reduced the number of casualties only by forty percent, from approximately forty thousand to approximately twenty-four thousand. They still remained a major source of death and a risk that automobile users faced. Our exhilaration in reducing rates may make us lose sight of how an increase in driving brings about more casualties. It is not facetious to say that the greatest cause of automobile injuries and deaths is the driving of automobiles; the greatest cause of increasing automobile fatalities is increased driving.

To "see" accidents in such a perspective is to consider casualties as a cost of using the automobile. It is to consider accidents as being as much a problem of religious or philosophical thought as of scientific, as close to Job as to Nader. The parable of Professor Cohen's angel of benevolence and death is yet with us.

Such different ways of organizing the world of consciousness interact with strategies of action and expectation. There is a social organization which structures that world and a cultural system of meanings which makes it intelligible. Reality is *not* an unorganized entity only waiting to be discovered. How versions of reality take shape and gain consistency and acceptance is the topic of the next two chapters.

3

The Fiction and Drama of Public Reality

Creating the Drinking-Driver

We live in a forest of symbols on the edge of a jungle of fact. In understanding the world about us, we human beings are increasingly drawn into beliefs about that which we cannot experience or personally recognize. We have beliefs about "society" that are public in the sense both of being shared and of being about an aggregate of events which we do not and cannot experience personally. A great many people in the United States have had direct and personal experience with automobile crashes and collisions. These are personal facts. The total number of automobile fatalities is not. It is a public fact. No one observes all the automobile crashes. We are dependent upon an organization of special investigators for the factual world of automobile casualties.

Such public facts constitute an important part of the belief content of persons. Unemployment is rising or falling; the nation is threatened by or threatens a foreign nation; the use of hard drugs accounts for so many deaths per year. The "social problem" of the automobile accident is only one of those factual matters compounded out of a multiplicity of events and transmitted to the public arena by scientists, medical practitioners, experts, policymaking officials, and journalists who help to create what Walter Lippmann called "the pictures in our heads" that operate to direct and channel much public action (Lippmann 1922). The public world is made into a consistent reality by this process. In the previous chapter I described the structure of this reality. Given a cognitive framework, certain data appear relevant while other material is implicitly ignored as irrelevant. Even the "fact" of choice is not a matter of consciousness since the selectors are not aware of alternatives. The process is experienced as normal, natural, and self-evident. The factual world appears as unproblematic, certain, and devoid of ambiguity.

This chapter is concerned with how such finished and authentic facts are constituted from raw observations. Were a person to rely solely on his or her personal knowledge in forming a perception of the impact of alcohol and the automobile on American life, the shape of the problem and the demands for public action might be different than they are. But he also relies on public or societal knowledge, thus imputing both understandability and consistency to "society" as an organized and perceived entity. A "crime wave" is not a matter of personal, private experience. What is happening to "the community" or "society" enters into the assessment of the person about the public experience. What is "true" about society is more than a reflection of individual experiences; it is also a set of beliefs about the aggregated experience of others.

The style of the National Safety Council's annual compilation of statistics is indicative of the process. The title *Accident Facts* contains a ring of authority; there really is a consistent and valid body of data about auto accidents. The format of the report is that of tables and figures expressed in numbers, often to one decimal point or not rounded (1,123 rather than 1,120 or 1,100). What if it were called "Accident Estimates" or "Accident Guesses"? What if the format were a narrative instead of tables and figures, if all the numbers were rounded to the nearest tenth? To imagine such alternative styles is to reflect on that style which does convey believability and certainty. Such games of imagination make one conscious of the problem of how fact is created and certified in the public arena.

It has been typical of much social and political commentary to conceive of scientific work as standing outside the culture and society of its time. To be sure, the nature of scientific institutions and the impact of scientific theories and findings on technology and thereby on social change have been a major theme in much social analysis. However, the *content* of science, its method and its results, has traditionally been viewed, even by Marxists, as a process and a product that lie outside the deterministic and historicist conceptions of social scientists, as "base," not "superstructure." The sociology of science has generally avoided the analysis of the criteria and content, concentrating instead on either the insitutional frameworks underlying choice of subject matter or the impact of science as technology (Ben-David 1971). Scientific thought, the "culture" of science, has remained outside the sphere of analysis and study.

In recent years this "preferred status" of science has been under great criticism. Philosophers such as Michael Polanyi have stressed the tacit presuppositions which seemingly presuppositionless scientific method requires (Polanyi 1962, esp. pt. 2). Thomas Kuhn's *The Structure of Scientific Revolutions* has had a wide influence in directing attention to the historically specific character of paradigmatic assumptions (Kuhn 1962). Both social science and specifically Weber's concept of rationality and rationalization have been examined as ideologies of technicism by the "critical theorists" working within a neo-Marxist framework (Marcuse 1968; Habermas 1970, 1975). Others have more directly confronted the empirical study of how science is done, observing the acts of observation, presentation, and argument, emphasizing the interpretive acts and presuppositions necessary in the process.[1]

In this chapter I will show that the body of knowledge about drinking and driving begins as uncertain, inconsistent, and inaccurate. Almost from the moment of conception, it is fashioned into a public system of certain and consistent knowledge in ways which heighten its believability and its dramatic impact. A dramatic image of the drinking-driver as a person of evil and blame results. It is not my intention to criticize this process or hold it up to shame. It is my contention that such processes are necessary to develop policy actions in a world of limited and flawed knowledge.

Fiction as the Shape of Fact

In borrowing terms like "fiction" and "drama" from the world of literary art, I run the risk of seeming to attack the integrity and validity of "serious" scientific work, to hold it and its creators forth to ridicule and shame. Showing up imputed truth as falsity is not my intention, though that is probably one way of reading it. My message is both subtler and cruder; fiction and drama are deeply inherent in the way in which knowledge is presented at several levels of its development. Its presentation as fact is part of the process by which a real world of substance and significance is formed. Kenneth Burke, whose writings are a major source of ideas in this book, distinguishes between *semantic* and *poetic* meanings in human discourse. Semantic meanings are close to what is conventionally accepted as scientific; they have a neutral cast about them and designate what is clear and devoid of emotion. Poetic meanings involve a perspective; they take an attitude toward an object. They suggest "what to look for and what to look out for" (Burke 1957, pp. 121–44).

What I am engaged in doing in this chapter is part of an analysis of how semantic meaning is transformed into poetic meaning, into a real world of significance; how the "facts" about drinking-driving are converted into the public problem of drinking-driving. Such analysis is a phase of the kind of rhetorical analysis which the logician Perelman refers to as the "new rhetoric" (Perelman 1963, pp. 134–42). Thus I include the analysis of scientific documentation and method as itself a form of rhetoric under study: it is a system of proof and argument which, like other arguments, attempts to bring about the adherence of an audience to what is proposed. In seeing the materials of drinking-driving research as a species of rhetoric and poetry I am underlining the artistic or artful character in scientific argument and analysis. This perspective is in contrast to the imagery implicit and explicit in much conventional wisdom about knowledge as a source of authoritative pronouncements about the real world, an imagery of a world of fact as is covered and reported by a neutral, objective observer.

The Place of Fiction in Scientific Analysis

The world of facts, wrote William James, is a "big, buzzing, blooming confusion." To analyze it, human beings have frequently made use of imaginary situations and types. Mathematicians talk about infinity or negative numbers or zero as if such concepts had tangible references. The physicists and chemists use concepts of attraction, repulsion, and pressure as if the physical reality were animate. Sociologists reify ideal types like community, society, and capitalism as if they described an existing world. The use of fictions as a unifying and directing vocabulary has long been recognized as part of legal reasoning (Fuller 1967; Levi 1949; Hall 1952, chap. 1). Its use in scientific language has been overlooked.

In examining the corpus of research that constitutes the basis of drinking-driving policies there are two different kinds of fictions to which I allude. One is conceptual, as illustrated in the examples above. But there is another form of fiction, the one involved in reaching conclusions *as if* the model of a perfect methodology were applicable. Here my treatment exemplifies the approach to the understanding of legal and other thought in the much neglected work of the nineteenth-century German philosopher Hans Vaihinger, whose *The Philosophy of "As If"* contains the basic analytical framework of this chapter (Vaihinger 1924). Vaihinger recognized the great extent to which science and other forms of reasoning operated by analogy, treating the confusion of events and data "as if" they were analogous to already familiar and understood phenomena.[2] The materials I will describe and analyze operate on imperfect, inconsistent and ambiguous material. They produce an illusion of certainty, clarity, facticity and authority.

Ten Million Alcoholics:
The Social History of a Dramatic Fact

The morning that I sat down to begin a draft of this chapter, I had heard and seen the introduction to a television news commentary on the problems of teenage drinking. The announcer began his introduction by saying "It is *a fact* that there are ten million alcoholics in the United States" (italics mine). It was said with an air of gravity and in a context which made the problems of alcohol worthy of serious consideration by the audience. "Ten million" was used as a "large" number, accentuating significance and urgency.

The "fact" of ten million alcoholics in the United States appears in many places at a variety of levels of informed awareness of alcohol issues. Figure 3 is an advertisement for a group of community hospitals, part of outreach programs for alcoholics. Taking up a quarter of a page of the *Los Angeles Times,* it announces that "There Are More Than 9 Million Americans Being Destroyed by Alcoholism." A series of articles on alcoholism in the *Chicago Tribune* begins with the statement that more than nine million Americans are alcoholics (*Chicago Tribune,* Oct. 1, 1972, p. 1). A brochure for the Raleigh Hills Hospital refers to "the nine million estimated alcoholics in the United States" (Raleigh Hills Hospital, n.d.). Another brochure, this one from the AFL-CIO Community Service Activities in cooperation with the National Council on Alcoholism, refers to the alcoholic as "one of an estimated nine million Americans whose drinking interferes with his daily life" (AFL-CIO, n.d.). In none of these cases is any doubt expressed about the certainty of the figure claimed, although one does use the word "estimated." No sources or bases are claimed as justifications for statements. It seems to be assumed that the figures represent a "true" depiction of the magnitude of alcoholism, that there is nothing questionable about such a magnitude.

Even literature closer to "experts" in the field conveys the same impression of an unproblematic reality. A brochure published by the National Council on Alcoholism refers to the "nearly ten million alcoholics among our nation's drinkers" (National Council on Alcoholism 1976). Another brochure aimed at the public and put out by the National

Figure 3. "What is the Third Largest Killer In Our Country?" Advertisement, *Los Angeles Times,* June 2, 1975

Institute on Alcohol Abuse and Alcoholism (NIAAA) features a short article under the byline of the director which states that "the tragic *fact* remains that ten million persons in our country today have severe alcohol problems" (NIAAA 1976, p. 2; italics mine). *Newsweek* magazine, in a cover story about alcoholism, is more qualified in its language and in referring to "the fact gathered by NIAAA" states that "about one in ten of the ninety-five million Americans who drink is now either a full-fledged alcoholic or at least a problem-drinker (defined by NIAAA as one who drinks enough to cause trouble for himself or society" (*Newsweek*, April 22, 1974, p. 39).

Where does the fact of the number of alcoholics (and/or "problem drinkers") in the United States come from? If NIAAA has gathered the facts, where are they? The only census of the entire population of the United States is conducted by the U.S. government, and it does not contain questions about drinking habits. Several academic discussions of alcohol problems cite as the source for the fact of nine or ten million the widely distributed compendium of knowledge about alcohol problems, the NIAAA's *Alcohol and Health—New Knowledge.* The first of those reports was issued in 1971, the second in 1974, the third in 1978. The first paragraph of the 1974 issue contains this: "The number of Americans whose lives alcohol has adversely affected depends on definition; those under active treatment for alcoholism . . . are probably in the upper hundred of thousands but there *may* be as many as ten million people whose drinking has created some problem for themselves or their families or friends or employers, or with the police, within the past year" (NIAAA 1974, p. 1; italics mine). Even this highly guarded and qualified statement is not supported by any cited study or documentation.[3]

The Congressional hearings on the bill from which emerged the alcohol abuse and alcoholism legislation establishing the NIAAA are one clue to how the public reality of the magnitude of the alcohol problem took form and measurement. In his opening remarks the chairman of the Subcommittee on Public Health and Welfare of the House Committee on Interstate and Foreign Commerce referred to the "major health problem" represented by an estimate that "at the very least 5 million Americans, or one person in 40, can be considered as an alcoholic" (U.S. House of Representatives 1970, p. 1). By page 257, the "problem" has grown to eighteen million. There Representative Rogers of Florida argues that "with eighteen million people affected" there ought to be more funds and a larger staff devoted to the issue. Where had this new figure come from?

A few minutes earlier the committee had heard testimony from three experts: the assistant secretary for health and scientific affairs of HEW, the director of the National Institute of Mental Health (NIMH), and the acting director of the Division of Alcohol Abuse and Alcoholism. They were all physicians, and the latter was a leading authority on problems of alcoholism. The assistant secretary estimated the number of "alcoholics" at between six and seven million, maintaining that there had been an increase since an earlier study estimating five million.[4] He used the pronoun *we* to support the estimate and turned to the NIMH director for his view. The latter introduced the alcohol expert saying that "he has spent twenty years in the alcoholism field" and "can speak knowledgeably to this issue" (U.S. House of Representatives 1970, p. 224).

The remarks of the acting director illustrate how even casual and slight changes in nomenclature have unanticipated results. Though he pointed out that "the numbers game has been around for some time," he referred to a recently completed study by a social research unit showing that "the figure is closer to nine million people *with alcoholic problems*" (U.S. House of Representatives 1970, p. 224; italics mine). He then contended that since health care professionals do not make a diagnosis until late stages of the illness, the number could be safely doubled. Thus five million alcoholics had been supplemented by thirteen million in less than a day. With the addition of material presented, a picture was drawn of a problem of great magnitude and hence worthy of a new agency and increased funds.

But where did the nine million figure come from? At the hearings reference was made to the American Drinking Practices (ADP) study. This was the first major national survey of drinking habits, conducted by the Social Research Group at the School of Public Health of the University of California, Berkeley, in 1964–65. That survey was concerned with drinking practices not drinking problems or alcoholism (Cahalan, Cisin, Crossley 1969). However, the same group conducted another national survey in 1967 specifically devoted to the investigation of drinking problems, reported in two later publications (Cahalan 1970; Cahalan and Room 1974). The findings of the 1967 survey appear to be the basis for the figure of nine million.[5]

Treating the nine million figure as establishing the fact of nine million alcoholics involved a fiction in several ways. First, one category of analysis was substituted for another. The major thrust of the ADP surveys of drinking problems was to shift attention from chronic alcoholism, with a pattern of addiction, loss of control, and frequency of intoxication, to a more diffuse and differentiated concept of "problem drinking." The author of *Problem Drinkers* identified eleven types of drinking problems including binge drinking, frequent intoxication, job problems, spouse problems, and others (Cahalan 1970, chap. 2). One of them—

symptomatic drinking—was close to the traditional concept of the alcoholic, but even this is misleading since various patterns are possible.

The author of *Problem Drinkers* is quite explicit about the importance of the definition, describing his own as "rather arbitrary (but statistically useful)" (Cahalan 1970, p. 2). Alternative plausible definitions, he stated, yielded percentages of problem drinkers in the sample ranging from three percent to thirty percent, compared with nine percent reached by the author. Nor can these figures be used to estimate alcoholics: "comparing estimates of alcoholics and problem drinkers is a futile exercise, because the concepts of alcoholism and problem drinking are not very similar, do not necessarily apply to the same sufferers, and may have quite different implications for etiology and preventive public health measures and treatment" (Cahalan 1970, p. 3). Working with a male sample representing abstainers, Cahalan and Room found that the rate of classically defined cases of alcoholism was five percent in that population (Cahalan and Room 1974, p. 32).

A second source of the fictional character of public fact, the *as if* quality of certitude and authority, stems from using the material of these sample surveys as sources of conclusions on prevalence rates. The interest of the Social Research Group was not in prevalence but in process. Their focus was on such matters as correlations betwen problems, social backgrounds of problem drinkers, stability of problem drinking patterns over time, and the environmental elements affecting problem drinking. The sample used in the *Problem Drinkers* study was intentionally "light" on abstainers and light drinkers and "heavy" on heavy drinkers. It was necessary to weight the figures in order to make statements about the total population.

Further, as is often the case in panel studies, the sample acutally used was not a good one from which to make projections to the total national population. A subsample of the original National Drinking Survey sample was drawn three years later. In the original sample itself it had been impossible to get approximately 10 percent of those eligible actually interviewed. The subsample included 66 percent of those interviewed in stage 1. The sample actually interviewed was 49 percent of the stage 1 interviewees or 45 percent of the total who had been eligible for the original probablility sample. While for a panel study this is a fairly good return, that does not diminish its tenuous quality as a base for certainty about prevalence rates. Such ambiguities and qualifications are expressed, but then ignored as conclusions are drawn, and forgotten as they reach other arenas and other transmitters. A fact is not a near-fact, maybe-fact, or convenient fact. It becomes reality.

Cahalan and his group produced a series of studies whose thrust was to substitute a more "realistic" view of alcohol problems by distinguishing a variety of situations and conditions creative of problems associated with drinking. They were explicit in reading their materials as showing that problem drinkers were not subsumed in the stereotype of the "alcoholic." What resulted in the public arena was an increase in alcoholics—the very category they thought they were limiting.[6]

What is the point of all this? My concern is less with the "legitimacy" of the claim that there are or are not nine or ten million alcoholics. I am interested in the result of this process of expansion and dramatization for the character of the knowledge transmitted. At each step in the process, from data to interpretation to transmission, a more factually authoritative world was made. At each level the problem of alcohol grew. To present a world of indefiniteness, of interpretation and choice, of more or less and maybe would diminish the significance of the problem in a context of competing demands for attention, money, and commitment.

Let me illustrate the process with an example which indicates how it heightens drama and creates support. The following is from the House of Representatives report on the act establishing the NIAAA: "It is clear that alcohol abuse and alcoholism constitute one of the most serious health problems in the country. . . . Various spokesmen for the DHEW cited estimates showing that there are possibly eighteen million alcoholics in the United States" (U.S. House of Representatives 1970, p. 3). Such a statement of magnitudes, although it creates a factual world of order and certitude, is in another sense a statement of rhetoric—a way of saying: Look, this is an important problem; it deserves attention and priority. The two games, that of the scholar and that of the public official, the journalist, or the maker of opinion, are not the same. The game of the scholar is decontextualized, it is far removed from a setting in which it must compete with other demands for attention and commitment. The game of those of us who use knowledge to persuade to action is not the same. A former alcohol authority, then in a position of governmental activity, put it in this fashion: "When I was a professor I was critical of the view that alcohol is a drug. Now that I have to get up in public and speak to audiences, I always refer to alcohol as a drug" (from my notes on an informal meeting, 1973).

This two-sided conception of knowledge and reality must be kept in clear view as I describe the "state of the art" in drinking-driving research.

The "State of the Art" in Drinking-Driving Research

Although laws prohibiting drinking and driving came into the statute books almost simultaneously with the appearance of the automobile on highways, the systematic study of alcohol and traffic safety is a product of the past thirty years and especially of the past twenty. It is with the perfection of chemical-physical means for detecting and measuring the level of alcohol in the blood that a proliferation of studies was possible (Hoffman 1973). The first major papers appeared in the late 1930s in the *Journal of the American Medical Association* (Heise 1934; Holcomb 1938). Further work was postponed until the end of World War II.

In 1950 the section on alcoholism of the Swedish Karolinska Institute held the first international conference on alcohol and road safety in Stockholm. As was characteristic of the later conferences on this topic, it was organized by a research institute and focused on alcoholism rather than the automobile. This first conference was dominated by experimental studies of the impact of alcohol on physiological motor performance and on driving under simulated and experimental conditions (International Conference on Alcohol and Road Traffic 1950, esp. papers by Leonard Goldberg and coauthors). These and similar studies in the United States and other countries led to the conclusion that alcohol lowered driving performance and caused "poor driving."

During the 1960s three kinds of studies occupied the attention of researchers and policymakers. The most frequent were studies of the presence of alcohol in the blood of drivers and pedestrians killed or injured in automobile accidents. The studies of William Haddon and his associates were especially influential (Haddon and Bradess 1959; McCarroll and Haddon 1961).[7] This series of studies was the major source of statements about the significance and magnitude of the "drinking-driving problem." While some studies also reported on alcohol in passenger fatalities and/or pedestrian fatalities, the emphasis has been on the driver (Haddon and Bradess 1959; Freimuth et al. 1958; McCarroll and Haddon 1961; Waller and Turkel 1966). Although other studies in the 1960s and later also utilize the analysis of blood level alcohol among fatalities and/or accident participants, they are focused on other aspects of the problem in addition to alcohol involvement and utilize other types of evidence as data.[8]

A second series of studies concentrated on the drinking-driver and attempted to locate the demographic and other social, cultural, or medical characteristics which might differentiate him from the general population. These utilized police arrest records for driving under the influence of alcohol (DUIA) or fatalities data to compare with a general driver population (Hyman 1968a, b; Cosper and Mozersky 1968). A major concern of these studies was the role of the problem drinker or alcoholic as a possible source of disproportionately frequent drinking-driving and auto accidents (Waller 1967, 1968; Waller and Turkel 1966; Popham 1956; Schmidt, Smart, and Popham 1962). Other studies also analyzed the accident patterns of treated alcoholics (Selzer 1961, 1969; Selzer and Weiss 1966). It is this group of studies which formed the basis for the NHTSA assertion that "alcoholics and other problem drinkers . . . account for a very large part of the overall problem" (U.S. Dept. of Transportation 1968, p. 1).

It was recognized that most of the studies of drinking-driving lacked adequate control groups so that the population at risk—those actually drinking and driving—could not be ascertained. Thus the increased risk of accident due to alcohol could not be gauged. Roadside surveys of stopped vehicles were expensive and difficult to conduct. However, a major roadside survey was conducted in 1964. The Grand Rapids study became the most significant drinking-driving research of the decade (Borkenstein et al. 1964). That study compared blood alcohol levels. Data was collected on approximately nine thousand drivers involved in traffic accidents and from approximately eight thousand drivers in cars stopped at sites and times identical to those of the nine thousand accidents. This study has been the major source of statements about the magnitude of alcohol involvement, the degree to which risk is increased by alcohol use among drivers and the demographic character of drinking-drivers.

The research outlined above helped to draw attention to the magnitude of the problem. With the establishment of the NHTSA and its Office of Alcohol Countermeasures in 1968 (absorbed into the Office of Driver and Pedestrian Programs in 1973), there was a stable source of funds and programs. The establishment of the NIAAA in 1970 adds additional impetus to research and enforcement. These groups constitute the chief basis for research funding, programs, and publicity in the 1970s.

During the '70s, research on drinking and driving has deepened the general pattern of the 1960s. The NHTSA launched a program for increased enforcement of drinking-driving laws in thirty-five cities. In evaluating the laws, a number of roadside surveys were conducted (Voas, 1975; Wolfe 1975; Perrine et al. 1971). In general the studies of the 1970s have paid greater attention to controls and have compared groups, with less concern for the magnitude of alcohol involvement than for the nature of the drinking-driver as a causal agent (Perrine et al. 1971, 1974; Filkins et al. 1970). As part of this orientation there have been more careful studies of subgroups other than alcoholics. This is especially the case in relation to age as a factor in auto accidents (Pelz and Schuman 1974; Pelz and Williams 1975; Zylman 1973). Another concern of such research has been the issue of causal responsibility for accidents involving alcohol and driving (Sterling-Smith 1975).

The research of the 1970s has given greater attention to other factors associated with alcohol than was true of the 1960s research. This growing recognition of the multivariate perspective toward auto accidents and alcohol, while not typical of drinking-driving researches, is nevertheless an increasing characteristic of them. It forms a major basis for the developing critical literature of such researches (Zylman 1968, 1972, 1974, 1975; Hurst 1973; Cameron 1977).

The Isometric Fiction: Blood-Alcohol Levels

I will examine several common fictions in the literature of drinking-driving with two goals in mind: (1) to indicate the fragility, uncertainty, and inconsistency of data on which policies and pronouncements are made; and (2) to examine how, even at the level of primary scholarship, under the pressure of the need for usable knowledge a facade of certain and ascertained generalization and fact is built up, removed from the context of ambiguity and doubt.

My intent is not to excoriate either the materials or the authors, but rather to understand how a world of reality is constructed as the raw confusion of a real world takes shape in the arena of public actions. Having presented the dilemmas of being scientific in a world of unscientific data, I will turn later to how the conviction of fact is made dramatic and even more certain.

The object of drinking-driving research is to ascertain the effects of alcohol on the driver, but how can it be known that a driver is or is not *under the influence* of alcohol? Prior to the use of chromatographic methods for analyzing alcohol content of the blood and the introduction of the breathalyzer in 1950, both law enforcement agencies and scientists had to use direct, clinical observations to make that determination. That meant a morass of uncorroborated reports, individual judgments, and criteria difficult to apply to each case in the same manner. Both at law and in the research "laboratory," the technology of the blood level sample and the breathalyzer meant a definitive and easily validated measure of the amount of alcohol in the blood and, consequently, an accentuated law enforcement and a higher expectancy of convictions (Hoffman 1973; Holcomb 1938).

All research on drinking-driving of the past thirty years has used the blood level count as the indication of the fact that a person is or is not under the influence of alcohol. All legislation in the United States defines being under the influence in terms of a blood level count (referred to from now on as B.A.L.—blood-alcohol level). However, the object of concern is not alcohol in the blood but the effect of alcohol on driving ability. In other words, a physiological-chemical condition is transformed into a behavioral one. B.A.L. is considered isometric, similar in measure, to the psychic state of "being influenced." This imaginary construction is my first fiction.

Some description of the B.A.L. is necessary to provide setting. Briefly, alcohol is metabolized in the human body at a constant rate in the liver. The liver, even in a healthy state, can convert only so much alcohol into fat per time unit. The remaining alcohol is deposited in the blood prior to metabolism. This amount can be ascertained by present chemical procedures and expressed as a percentage. In the United States, it is stated in terms of milligrams of alcohol per milliliter of blood. Thus a blood-alcohol level of ten hundredths of one percent indicates that each 100 milliliters of blood contains 100 milligrams of alcohol. A B.A.L. of .10 percent or .10 is the most common legal definition in the United States of being under the influence of alcohol.[9]

The breathalyzer is an instrument for determining the B.A.L. indirectly, through a fixed ratio between alcohol in the breath and alcohol in the lungs. Urinalysis is a third method but not widely used in either research or law enforcement. Although not supplanting direct blood analysis, the breathalyzer has become the most widely used system for determining DUIA by researchers and police agencies.

I too am adopting a fiction: that scientific analysis of blood and breath gives a "true" measure of the B.A.L. I treat such test scores *as if* such methods yield one hundred percent accuracy one hundred percent of the time. I do so because I lack the knowledge to assess adequately the theory or experimental data on which they rest. However, I do recognize that the matter is by no means a closed question. The breathalyzer results are particularly under debate. The uniformity of the ratio between alcohol in the breath and alcohol in the blood is in doubt (see the papers by Curry, Dubowski, Levett and Karras, Robinson, and especially Harger in Israelstam and Lambert 1975). This fiction is in general useage. The breathalyzer is the common tool of roadside surveys, and the B.A.L. *the* operational definer of DUIA (Borkenstein et al. 1964; Voas 1975; Wolfe 1975).

Such fictions are essential if raw data are to be converted into consistent and organized argument toward the solution of significant questions. Without such fictions it would be difficult or impossible to reach conclusions which seem to carry conviction, both for the audience to whom they are addressed and to the investigator. The fiction that requires acceptance in the case of the B.A.L. is its diagnostic isometric quality, because the grounds for the assumption of that isometrism are weak in specific cases. The experience of the driver with drinking, of the drinker with driving, of the person with both—all of these influence the ability of the drinking-driver to conduct himself or herself at the wheel (Zylman 1968; Hurst 1973; Cameron 1977). The same amount of alcohol will have less influence on the driving of a healthy, middle-aged man who is a heavy drinker, has just finished a meal, is generally overweight and has been driving for many years than on that of a teenaged woman of average height and weight with only one year of driving experience, four hours after her last meal. What this means is that the B.A.L. is *not* fully isometric with behavior. There is an ever-present error because some may be *truly* DUIA with a B.A.L. below the fixed point and some not *truly* DUIA at levels above the fixed point. Legislation has attempted to get around this hurdle by setting the limits so high as to encompass many people and many situations, but we do not know how many escape the net at one end or are erroneously included at the other. Again, researchers and legislators must treat this problem *as if* it did not exist in order to determine if a given person or fatality is or is not DUIA.

Fiction is also involved when experimental data are projected onto natural settings. Police tell me (see chapter 5) that they sometimes "spot" drinking-drivers because they are driving too slowly or too "perfectly" for the conditions, displaying an anxiety resulting from the realization that they are DUIA and that there is a risk of accident or arrest. Such risk was not part of the design of the experiment; we do not know how people drive after drinking if they think there is danger of accident and arrest. Such studies have not been done, again because the frame of relevance of the experimenters excluded them. The projection of experimental data onto natural settings requires the fiction of isomorphism—that people behave the same under awareness of conditions as they would under natural conditions.

What the fiction of isometrism enables the investigator to do is illustrated in this excerpt from a recent article on roadside surveys:

> Almost half of the drivers interviewed said that they had drunk alcoholic beverages sometime on the day of the interview . . . and 22.6 percent registered a BAC [blood-alcohol count] of 0.02 percent. *About one-eighth of the drivers had been drinking to an extent great*

enough to impair their driving performance—0.05 percent BAC or higher—and one out of twenty was at a BAC considered illegal in every state (0.10 percent or higher). [Wolfe 1975, p. 46; italics mine]

The italicized sentence illustrates how fiction has become converted into fact. No direct evidence is gathered about driving performance. The inference is drawn that each case with a BAC above .05 involved drunkenness and driving impairment and each case below .05 percent did not. *What began as conjecture, as generalization, as a matter of practical application has been turned into a consistent and certain judgment.* The B.A.L. has been taken as the icon, the model, for the event—impaired driving.

Once again, this is not a critique of imperfect method. I understand that it is not possible to accomplish research of this nature otherwise. Research findings are embedded in the assumptions that enable conclusions to be drawn and generalizations to be made. To understand and recognize the blurred and ambiguous character of "fact" in this context is not the same as presenting a definitive and certain asertion of reliable and valid knowledge about the amount or frequency of impaired driving.

What I am asserting is the usage of the B.A.L. as a measure of impaired driving as created knowledge—as knowledge which has required the application of fictional techniques. The B.A.L. has been treated *as if* it were impaired driving. Even as I write this I treat the above quotation from a research document *as if* it, too, were isomorphic—similar, in shape, to other DUIA studies. It is not that such usages are poor method. Rather, it is the realization that fiction has been essential to the creation of an orderly world of fact.

The Universalistic Fiction: Collecting Data

You, my reader, may be impatient with me at this point. I am demanding too much of science: a complete census of all cases of alcohol impaired and unimpaired driving. That is not my intent. My aim is to understand how knowledge is possible and how it assumes different forms in different contexts.

Yet the impossiblility of studying the entire universe of relevant acts directly has provided the researcher in human behavior with one of the most troubling issues in social science: sampling. If to study the whole can be done only by studying the part, how is it possible to make assertions about the whole? The sampling answer has been that the scientist must be able to assume that the part is like the whole, that it represents the universe which is the object of concern. The part is taken—to use the literary term—as a synecdoche, a representation. How to obtain valid representations of a universe has been a major concern of research methods in sociological study.

Drinking-driving research is no exception. Here it is my assertion that the difficulties and limitations in collecting data representing the universe of drinking-driving events are glossed over by the fiction that the data collected are a "true" sample of the universe under examination. This is the second fiction studied here.

To begin with, what is to be studied? What are automobile crashes and how can information be collected about them? The complete universe of auto crashes would encompass everything from "fender-benders" to the mass carnage of multiple fatalities. Official reporting of accidents *as if* report and reality were fused—for example, in *Accident Facts* the number of accidents caused by alcohol—or in official statements poses great problems to the investigator.[10]

Another use of the synecdoche is in the fiction that arrests for drinking-driving indicate the extent or nature of the event of drinking-driving or characteristics of drinking-drivers. The variation in the manner of DUIA arrests from one jurisdiction to another and the diversity of prosecution policies in forming charges and seeking convictions are discussed and analyzed in detail in chapter 5. When, where, and whom officers arrest are as much a function of policy and discretion as of the event being accorded attention. Studies which make use of arrests and arrest records to gain knowledge about the phenomenon of drinking-driving are then operating *as if* this unrepresentative sample could be considered an appropriate representation.

These considerations are recognized by many who create the state of the art in drinking-driving research. For these and other reasons the great bulk and backbone of drinking-driver studies has been done with data reported on drivers and/or pedestrians who have been killed in automobile accidents. Ironically, dead men do tell more tales than live ones. They offer less resistance to the use of blood-alcohol-level analysis, and their accidents are almost always dutifully reported to authorities. Sadly, the fact of death, even in this era of biological continuation of "life," remains the supreme example of a factual condition among secular societies.

Here then is at last a land of certainty—where fact rules and fiction is relegated to the bookshelves? Of course not. To develop knowledge about the significance of alcohol in traffic fatalities the data derived from drivers must be treated *as if* they too represented a universe of drinking-driving events. At least three such fictions are involved here: (1) that being killed as a result of auto crash is a clearly ascertained event; (2) that the test of B.A.L. is equally performed on all cases of fatality or at least that limits do not affect judgments and conclusions; and (3) that all drivers are equally likely to be killed in similar circumstances of crash.

The Fact of Automobile Fatality

In gathering data on B.A.L. and auto deaths in San Diego County (described in chapter 6) I became aware of several matters. The coroner's office, the source of the data, considered any death reported to them as due to automobile crash to be an "automobile fatality." This included at least one death occurring two years after the initial accident, several occurring following accidents in other states, and even one in another country (Mexico being a half-hour away from San Diego). The location of the death, rather than the crash, was the criterion for the coroner, since the jurisdiction of that office is one of geography and not causal agents. When I asked the research unit of the NHTSA for the criterion they used in defining an auto casualty, the research personnel to whom I talked did not know for how long after a crash a death was presumed to be an auto fatality. We then discussed the issue with personnel closer to the actual coding of data and were told that they used one year as the cutoff point. European data reported by the United Nations use, according to a footnote, a period of no more than thirty days, although ten countries reporting use different time periods varying from scene of accident to one year afterward (United Nations 1974, pp. 86, 88). Whatever automobile fatalities are, they do not exist in pristine state, unrelated to the interaction of event with observer and the linguistic categories of the nomenclature used to clothe them.

In addition, attributing a fatality to the automobile requires an artful inference. Thus the coroner's sheets reporting auto deaths occasionally include statements that the body was found in or next to an auto, and, given the damaged character of the car, that the death was presumed to be due to auto crash. Such statements reveal the inferential and selective nature of the category. A number of studies have raised the distinct possibility that some auto accidents are results of suicidal intentions (S. Brown 1968; Tabachnik et al. 1973; D. Phillips 1977). Deliberate suicide and the less deliberate forms of intended "carelessness" are not considered in the practical act of naming events as automobile casualties, but they do introduce an ambiguity in coding or categorizing that is ignored or neglected as the concept of "automobile fatality" is constructed. Drinking-driving studies are complicated by the fact that the use of alcohol in connection with deliberate or semideliberate suicide is a distinct possibility.

Still another element in the complex naming of events as auto casualties is the possibility of natural death, occurring before or during auto crashes. The only study I know of to discuss this question held that thirty percent of the automobile deaths were also attributed to natural causes (Gerber et al. 1966). Again, my point is not that the use of "automobile fatality" is unwarranted but that it can be used only as a fiction. Reality is too ambiguous, uncertain, and inconsistent to correspond to categories which render it unambiguous, certain, and consistent. Data are not collected solely for research purposes; "automobile fatality" is not a natural category but a human one. We can only presume that auto deaths involving alcohol are as likely to be nondeliberative as are nonalcohol ones.

The Fiction of the Adequate Sample

The B.A.L. is used to determine the presence or absence of alcohol and the existence of DUIA, but only a portion of drivers are tested. Many reports, however, treat the tested population *as if* it is a representation of the total or the untested is similar to the tested, when there is no indication that this is so.

Reporting agencies, such as hospitals and morgues, habitually perform blood alcohol analysis only on corpses. Analysis of the blood is not reliable four to six hours after death—or the last drink. Even when death occurs within four to six hours, the possibility that a B.A.L. will be taken lessens with time. Thus B.A.L. is most likely to be taken where death occurs at time of accident or shortly thereafter. These are limitations to perfect research conditions. As a result, a portion of drivers who die as a result of automobile crashes are not tested. This is a significant limitation in research that attempts to assess the frequency of DUIA in automobile crashes resulting in death. Not only is it the case that the DUIA driver who has not been killed may not be tested but the driver who is killed may not be tested.

How large is the untested group? Cameron, in her 1977 review of DUIA studies, lists twenty-three U.S. traffic driver fatalities studies in which the percentage of drivers DUIA was reported (Cameron 1977, p. 133).[11] In sixteen of the studies, either only the number tested is reported and used as the base for percentages or, as in five studies, there is no information on the number untested although the base for calculating percentage is slightly less than the total number of accidents. In seven studies, the number of accidents and the number of fatalities tested and untested are all reported. In two of these latter cases, the total number of tested cases was less than fifty (Waller and Turkel 1966; Boston University Law–Medicine Institute 1969). In other words, in most cases the representative nature of the tested as synecdoche of the total universe of auto fatalities is assumed. In the two cases just mentioned, a small number is taken as representation of a larger array of deaths over a longer period.

In the five studies which report on both tested and untested fatalities, the highest percentage of total fatalities tested was 72 percent (Davis 1974). The lowest was 32 percent (Baker et al 1971). The others were 68 percent, 63 percent, and 35 percent (Baker and Spitz 1970; McBay et al. 1974; Filkins and Carlson 1973). In none of these studies, where the discrepancy between the total number of fatalities and the number on whom B.A.L. were collected was reported, is there *less* than 28 percent for whom a B.A.L. is unavailable. In my analysis of seventeen years of coroner's reports in San Diego County, I found that among the 2,616 driver fatalities reported by the coroner, B.A.L. scores were reported for 1,991 or 76 percent. In no one year was the percentage higher than 84 percent.

I will examine the presentation of three different studies of fatalities and show how they handled the problems posed by the insufficiency of data. In two of these, the population actually studied is presumed to be synecdochal to a larger universe. In the third, the issue is clearly recognized and retained. All of these are major studies in the field, cited often and utilized by Cameron in her review.

In a study reported to the NHTSA by the Highway Safety Research Institute of the University of Michigan, the authors summarize findings of a comparison between fatalities, alcoholics, arrested and convicted DUIAs, and other court-related offenders (Filkins et al. 1970). Considerable analysis of the driver fatalities is reported. The opening page (p. 5) refers to data from this study which "indicate that alcohol is a characteristic feature in *many* fatal accidents. Forty-five percent of the total population of 616 fatalities had blood alcohol levels of 0.10 or above" (italics mine). The next paragraph informs the reader that fifty-five percent of the 309 drivers were legally impaired. There is no mention of the total population of traffic fatalities or of driver fatalities. The impression is left that the universe of fatalities has been studied.[12] This is hard to believe in the light of all else known about studying B.A.L. of traffic fatalities. No treatment of this issue is presented.

A more complex fiction resulting from the sampling problem is found in a study of fatalities concerned with the driver fatality judged to be "most responsible" in different types of fatal accidents (Sterling-Smith 1975). The author tells the reader that "only six cases collected over the thirty-month period were found to have insufficient data" (p. 94). Two pages later, the reader is informed that BACs were available only for 37 percent of the driver fatalities. Presence of alcohol and the incidence of DUIA were clinically evaluated for the remaining 63 percent (pp. 95–96). Yet the summary states "122 (46 percent) of the operators [were] *influenced to some degree* by alcohol" (p. 105; italics mine). Here even sketchier (clinical) determinations of DUIA are taken as a "true" sample of the fatality cases.

The disposition to present qualified, imperfect data *as if* it were certain is perhaps inherent in the aesthetic needs for clarity and succinctness. Haddon and Bradess, in one of the earliest major studies, were acutely aware of the tested-untested issue (Haddon and Bradess 1959). They discuss the elements affecting testing in considerable detail. They made a decision, based on medical understanding of blood alcohol levels, to restrict their sample of drivers killed in single-vehicle accidents to those who had not survived the crash beyond four hours. Fortunately, as they remarked, the medical examiner of Westchester County (where the study was conducted) had a great interest in the alcohol-driving problem, and the authors had B.A.L. data on 95 percent of the 87 such fatalities; the summary reports that "postmortem blood levels were studied in a group of 83 drivers" of single-vehicle crashes. But their tabular data (p. 210) indicate that there were 117 single-vehicle-crash driver fatalities; thus their sample is only 70 percent of that universe. Yet when Haddon, Suchman, and Klein introduce the paper in their classic text, *Accident Research,* they state that the results of the study demonstrate "that alcohol was present in high concentrations in 70 percent of *the* drivers killed in single-vehicle automotive accidents" (Haddon, Suchman, Klein 1964, p. 208; italics mine).

What occurs in the fiction of universal representation is that the results are tested *as if* they were either the total universe discussed or *as if* they were an adequate representation. The flaws and ambiguities contained in the data are "dropped out" in the interests of clarity and certainty. Facts take on a hard, undeniable form and fit into a world of scientific accuracy and validity. Even though the researchers are aware of the doubts, imperfections, and limitations in the data, the results are stated as undeniable fact, as the authority of the external world—what Herbert Blumer refers to as "obdurate facts" (Blumer 1969).

The Fiction of Association:
Alcohol Involvement

The 1968 Alcohol and Highway Safety Report states, in its opening
sentence, that "the use of alcohol *leads to* some 25,000 deaths...each
year" (U.S. Congress 1968, p. 1; italics mine). Studies of alcohol and
driving are often much more cautious and refer to alcohol as "the largest
single factor involved in fatal crashes" (Perrine 1970, p. 43) or a
"characteristic feature in many fatal accidents" (Filkins et al. 1970, p. 5).
Nevertheless, as Zylman has pointed out, the number of driver fatalities
with B.A.L. above the legal maximum has been emphasized to reach
conclusions of a causal nature (Zylman 1974). The sampling difficulties
resulting from limits in testing, the high percentage of high B.A.L. in
single-vehicle crashes, and the lack of clear evidence from many studies of
who is "at fault" make such conclusions dangerous. All fatal accidents in
which the driver's B.A.L. is one of legal impairment are not cases in
which the driver can be presumed to have been responsible for the accident.[13] Nor are all, or even most, cases of fatality to alcohol using drivers
instances involving more than a single vehicle. Although studies of
alcohol-involved accidents find approximately two-thirds of them are
single-vehicle ones, such studies of responsibility as have been done study
only multiple-vehicle crashes. Thus they substitute an insurance oriented
view of responsibility for a research oriented one of "cause" (Sterling-
Smith 1975; Cameron 1977, pp. 179ff).

Studies of alcohol and driving, however, frequently present alcohol *as
if* it were the only, or the major, cause in drinking-driver accidents. Such
"single-cause" explanations are crucial to the focus on alcohol as a target
of social action. Much of the work on drinking-driving has been concerned to delineate the "fact" that alcohol increases the risk of accident in
driving. In focusing almost exclusively on the factor of alcohol, such
work necessarily turns one element in a complex pattern of "causes" into
a single major factor. Zylman, who has been most vocal in criticizing
such studies, puts it succinctly: "People experienced in the study of social
problems will not be surprised to hear that single-cause explanations and
simple one-target programs are inadequate. The slogan that 'alcohol
causes accidents' is just as misleading as the counterassertion that it does
not. To conclude that nothing can be done, however, violates our historical tradition" (Zylman 1968, p. 231).

The issues can be illustrated by the analysis of age as an element in
automobile accidents and fatalities. The disproportionately high frequency of young (16–25) and old (70 and older) drivers among accident

victims and fatalities is striking (Carlson 1973; Harrington 1972; Pelz and Schuman 1974; Zylman 1973). Higher B.A.L. is more frequently found in both accidents and fatalities among the middle-aged group (26–69), however. In understanding the role of alcohol in accidents and deaths in light of these age differences it is necessary to consider a variety of elements. Alcohol is associated with other characteristics or variables, so that its presence may lead to false inferences of its causative or monocausative effects. Thus the overinvolvement of young people in auto fatalities was seen in Carlson's study of age, exposure, and alcohol to be a function of the greater nighttime driving of youth as contrasted to older persons. Night driving increases the risks of driving and the possibility of drinking in the general population of drivers (Carlson 1973). In another set of studies, by Pelz and Schuman, the authors conclude that alienated and socially hostile youth are more prone to accident and also to drinking. Unalienated youth who drink and drive appear less vulnerable to fatality (Pelz and Schuman 1974).

This is not to maintain that alcohol is not an element, but that it often appears in association with other and necessary conditions. Cameron (1977, pp. 158–60) points out that although there are a higher percentage of DUIA fatalities among 25–69-year-olds than the young (16–25), the latter group accounts for more such fatalities than does the former. This is a result of the greater proportion of fatalities among the young than the old.

Sometimes alcohol becomes significant as it accentuates or catalyzes some other element in the pattern of driving. Zylman (1973) places great emphasis on the inexperience of the young in either drinking or driving. Thus at the same B.A.L., the "new" drinking-driver is affected more than is the "older" one (Carpenter, quoted in Zylman 1973, p. 220). Carlson (1973) suggests that the 18–19-year-old is involved in learning to drink and drive while the older driver has passed through this training experience. Many conditions are thus involved. The time of day (3–6 A.M.) in which the highest percentage of drivers with high B.A.L. have been found is also the "safest" period in terms of death and accident; the traffic density is then at its lowest.

The structure of presentation of studies makes it difficult to examine the role of alcohol and yet retain the multiple causal model. Borkenstein et al. (1964) conducted what has been the major roadside control study of the drinking-driver literature. It has been very frequently cited as evidence for the significant effect of alcohol in increasing the risk of accident. The authors point out, in the opening summary of the study, that "the summary of results presented is a convenience . . . for brevity the qualifications which must be made in the interpretation of this kind of data are omitted" (p. xvii). Even so, the text contains many summative sentences like, "Drivers with positive alcohol levels caused more than one-fifth of all the accidents observed in this study, while constituting about 11 percent of the driving population" (p. 169). Once alcohol has been singled out as the factor to be studied, the language of assertion and summation makes fictional creation possible and probable.

This is the third of the fictions, association is converted into causation. The discovery that alcohol is associated with an auto accident is turned into alcohol as *the* cause of accident. The rapidity with which alcohol is perceived as villain exemplifies the moral character of factual construction. Without that moral direction the transformation of data into policy directions is difficult. Multicausality weakens the capacity and purposefulness which make control seem possible. The assumption that alcohol is *always* at fault strengthens the certainty that there is a credible body of knowledge to support what seems only sensible.

An alternative method might well utilize a model of multivariate analysis (Hirschi and Selvin 1967). Such a model would presuppose a complex interaction of variables. It would assess the way in which each variable, such as time of day, age, road, age of automobile, etc., combines with every other variable; the addition each makes to predictability (the amount of the variance); and the amount predicted by each variable separately and together. Such results, however, may not be very useful because they are capable of neither persuading people to a specific action nor framing policies. "The major purpose of the study of accidents," wrote Borkenstein et al. (1964) in their classic study, "is eventually to develop methods of control" (p. 4).

Knowledge and Authority:
The Ring of Conviction

In *The New Rhetoric*, Perelman and Olbrechts-Tytecka (1969) distinguish between convincing and persuading (pp. 26–31). Both procedures are concerned with gaining adherence to an argument. Convincing is a process in which the validity of the argument is claimed for every rational human being, a universal audience. Persuasion is argumentation that claims validity for a particular audience. Logic and science are methods that purport to establish universal truths, ones that cannot be rendered matters of opinion. All rational people must reach the same conclusions. Persuasion, on the other hand, is in the realm of the probable, the opined: "To the person concerned with results, persuading surpasses conviction, since conviction is merely the first stage in progression toward action. . . . On the other hand, to someone concerned with the rational character of adherence to an argument, convincing is more crucial than persuading" (p. 27).

The distinction implies divergent audiences, as Perelman and Olbrechts-Tytecka point out. Convincing involves a form of argument in which agreement is a matter of the compelling character of reason, a timeless and absolute validity. The audience such argument assumes, as in mathematics, logic, or science, is a universal one, because it claims to be "valid for the reason of every man" (pp. 31ff). Persuasion is always an act assuming a special audience and identifying the character and position of the arguers. Where conviction demands objectivity, argument by persuasion demands impartiality but assumes that the persuader is also an actor in the events; thus he or she has a commitment: "For the very reason that argumentation aims at justifying choices, it cannot provide justifications that would tend to show that there is no choice, but that only one solution is open to those examining the problem" (p. 62).

The New Rhetoric teaches us to stress the importance of different contexts in assessing how data and information are used. The scientist presenting work to a scientific audience is not necessarily impelled toward the same kinds of significance as one attempting to find a solution to practical problems. The politician and the practitioner in turn operate within circles of conflict about action, of competing interests and goals, of differing values and beliefs. In the social history of facts about alcoholism described earlier, congressmen and bureaucrats are arguing for the importance and significance of the alcoholism issue against others for whom it has less salience and value. A set of already fixed beliefs about the phenomenon involve investments of emotion, time, aspirations, and money.

The knowledge of the scientist is knowledge in the abstract. Presupposing a universal audience, it need make little effort to wrest practical significance from data or conclusions. It need make no concessions toward persuasion. The knowledge of the practitioner, the political official, the bureaucrat, the journalist is knowledge-in-use. If not governed by such knowledge, we are at least influenced by its consequences. The political official and former professor quoted earlier who came to refer to alcohol as a drug, distinguished between how he had used knowledge in the academic context and how he had used it in the political context. These considerations of context are salient in understanding the transformations I describe below.

The distinction between conviction and persuasion which Perelman and Olbrechts-Tytecka draw fails to delineate how one is used in the other. My analysis of the "state of the art" in drinking-driving research has shown how persuasion enters into conviction when research is considered as if it too were a form of argument. Persuasion, however, makes use of an agreed upon "reality" in attempting to persuade. In the discussions about alcoholism, the persuader attempts to place some aspects of the discussion beyond choice. He refers to "facts" as if they compelled a universal audience to agree, as a basis for further choices about action to be taken toward alcoholism.

It is important to recognize that much of the public discussion of alcohol issues and of drinking-driving takes place in an atmosphere of assumed conflict in which one party is arguing *against* another, attempting to induce somebody to do something he is presumed not willing to do. The character of public dialogue is debate and not demonstration. The aim is less one of assent to propositions in the abstract than it is one of action and commitment.

In the remaining part of this chapter I will examine the public arena of knowledge-in-use: the "facts" of drinking-driving. Two aspects of the use of knowledge are emphasized. The first is the continuing transformation of partial, qualified, and fragile knowledge into certain and consistent fact. The second is the transformation of abstract fact into facts of dramatic significance, implying attitudes and commitments, arousing images and values, having poetic rather than semantic meaning. Both aspects are important in developing an image or persona of the drinking-driver that conveys the sense of a cognitive and a moral order in which causal and political responsibility can be fixed and determined.

The Dramatic Significance of Fact

What I am contending is that the apparatus of public media, official authorities, and professional practitioners acts to build up a sense of an orderly world in connection with drinking-driving. That world is both cognitively and morally definitive. It presents an image of authoritative and unimpeachable fact about drinking-driving which is grounded in knowledge gained by the scientific method, an image of a moral order in which the act of drinking-driving is condemned and the campaign against drinking-driving is a struggle to convince sinners to be virtuous—an image that claims authority. An institutional order of power is projected as one of consensus and legitimacy, *as if* it were compelling and beyond argument among rational people.

To write about the drinking-driver materials as dramatic is to treat
public events *as if* they are only dramas rather than real events. I am
treating the public presentation of drinking-driving as a drama in three
senses. These emphasize the "as if" or fictional character of this form of
public action (Burke 1968), and its mood of excitement and conflict—its
dramatic value. The dramaturgical is only one way of organizing
experience—in Goffman's term, one mode of framing (Goffman 1974,
chap. 1). I am not treating it as an alternative but as an addition to a
positivist analysis of action as means to end. It heightens less often recognized aspects of a complex and multifaceted situation.

The first sense in which a public action is dramatic is that, in keeping
with the metaphor of theater, it is a performance. As performance it is
not to be understood as a response to an objective, detached "reality." As
with a staged event, the observer utilizes conventions which enable him
or her to sustain an illusion of an orderly world. The performer acts *as if*
this is a true and actual event, and the observer suspends disbelief. The
actor on the stage is indeed the character represented: a middle-aged
Italian woman singing on a stage in New York City in 1977 *is* for two
hours Madame Butterfly, a young Japanese beauty in 1868. The performance is a fiction, an illusion of reality.[14]

The second sense in which a public action is dramatic is that it is
staged; it is a construction of the performers as authors. Plays are written
and planned. The *théâtre de vérité* attempts to break with the illusionist
nature of staged performances but runs the risk of being dull. The
"make-believe" character of the dramatic is not unexpected. Authors
suppress the circumlocutions, the misperceptions, the uncertainties and
ambiguities of daily conversation, the pauses and lengthy interludes of
natural action. The result is a more concentrated and unambiguous
presentation of experience: "A fundamental transcription practice of 'dis-
closive compensation' is sustained throughout the interaction. . . . Eaves-
droppers are thus destined to hear fragments of meaningful talk, not
streams of it. . . . The theater, however, stages interaction systematically
designed to be exposed to large audiences that can only be expected to
have very general knowledge in common with the play characters performing this interaction" (Goffman 1974, p. 142).

The third sense in which events are dramatic is that they take on a
greater excitement and interest. When people speak of "dramatizing" a
problem or idea, the connotation is that of compressing into a visible act
or experience a complex of ideas or events. Elections dramatize the conception of participatory democracy. A boxing match between citizens of

two different nations, races, or ethnic groups can dramatize intergroup conflict. The experience is rendered in such a way as to heighten emotional involvement and make complex ideas simpler.

I am asserting that as the raw data of knowledge about drinking-driving are processed through fictions of scientific research, a step is taken to convert ambiguity into certainty. That process is carried forward in the public arenas of government and the mass media. Knowledge about drinking-driving is dramatized as unambiguous fact in a way which justifies concentration of attention on the drinking-driver as a major "cause" of automobile accidents.

Richard Zylman has compiled a number of examples of how research findings have been "twisted," the numbers of drinking-drivers responsible for auto fatalities increased and reported as assured and certain "fact" (Zylman 1974a, b). Zylman has been engaged in a critique of such statements as "inadequate fact." From my perspective they are actions in a context of argument, attempts to persuade others to support a program, back a law, or refrain from drinking and driving. As Zylman puts it:

> Public relations agents, administrators and volunteer safety workers as well as researchers and action program functionaries engage in these semantic gynmastics regularly. Words are used that mean different things to different people. Findings regarding specific and unique segments of the traffic crash problem are applied across the board as though they applied to the whole problem, and some research findings are ignored while others are distorted. [Zylman 1974a, p. 8]

Two of Zylman's examples are taken from a Congressional hearing and from a public information brochure of the Alcohol Safety Action Projects (ASAP). In the first, the director of the National Highway Traffic Safety Administration in 1972, justifying the large expenditure in the alcohol countermeasure field, took the official position that "alcohol is involved in 50 percent of all highway fatalities" and cited several studies to support this position (Zylman 1974b, pp. 165–66). In the second, a brochure on the countermeasures program cites the 1968 *Alcohol and Highway Safety* as authority, for "*as a matter of fact . . .* drinking drivers contributed directly to more than half of all traffic deaths and injuries" (italics mine). As Zylman points out, even that 1968 report said that "almost half the drivers" rather than "more than half" (Zylman 1974b, p. 164). In both cases the illusion of certainty is conveyed in the effort to persuade.

These "semantic gymnastics," as Zylman calls them, are common usage in public materials. One frequent fiction is to use the 50 percent "involved" figure to dramatize drinking as a "cause" of many accidents without reference to the different proportions of DUIAs among drivers in single-car and multiple-car crashes or driver-pedestrian crashes. Even so "factual" appearing an item as an article used in the drinking-driver course for convicted DUIAs of the University Extension of the University of California at San Diego and entitled "The Facts about Drinking and Accidents" leaves the impression that it is unambiguously the case that fifty percent of auto fatalities are due to drinking and driving: "Many studies reveal drinking to be a factor in a great number of traffic accidents. Studies in Wisconsin and California of accidents causing fatalities show that drinking *was involved* in more than 50 percent of those accidents" (*Traffic Safety Magazine*, n.d., p. 1; italics mine).

The same fiction, sometimes with the term "alcohol-related" instead of "involved," occurs in Alcohol Safety Action Project public brochures with studies quoted or cited. A public information pamphlet of the Addiction Research Foundation of Canada, one of the world's leading research organizations in this field, even blurs the distinction between "accidents" (in which one or two drivers are by definition involved) and deaths, which include pedestrians and passengers as well. "Traffic deaths make up 43 percent of all accidental deaths in Ontario. According to recent studies, about 50 percent of such deaths involved 'more than a trace' of alcohol" (Addiction Research Foundation 1975).

The implications of this body of constructed fact are found in the easy slippage from the drinking-driver to the "drunk driver," as newspapers frequently refer to him. The conclusion is readily drawn in public discussion as seen in the following letter to a metropolitan newspaper: "Your article (Oct. 1) on highway deaths failed to mention the principal cause of highway deaths—the drunken driver. If the drunken driver could be removed from the highway, the number of traffic deaths would decline by 50 percent" (*Los Angeles Times*, Oct. 16, 1973, pt. 2, p. 7).

But my point is not a critique, as Zylman's is. The various statements alleged as "fact," as certain knowledge, have a status also as rhetoric. They attest to the serious character of the issue through its facticity. They command attention and require the listener to accept the significance of the DUIA problem both because the magnitudes are high and because there is an authoritative account of an orderly world in which it is possible to say that alcohol is a cause of many fatal accidents. In the effort to persuade skeptical, recalcitrant, and indifferent people to a way of action involving cost, inconvenience, and displeasure, the appearance of certainty is an essential rhetorical device. The numbers dramatize concern. Summarizing research in ways which eliminate qualifications and uncertainties maintains the smoothness of the story line. The world of objective reality is, like much of natural behavior, confused, ambiguous, and unobtainable; it must be organized, interpreted, and compressed to create a clear message, to form an understandable but objective reality.

The image of the world of science is not that of the world of action. The seminar constitutes the arena of science as the factory does the arena of industrialization. The scientist faces an audience whose hostility is presumed neutral, whose skepticism is not partisan but Olympian. Scientists, it is presumed, do not have a passionate commitment to one or another conclusion. Qualifications and partial results, gaps in knowledge and areas of ignorance can be admitted. This image is, to be sure, also far from an exact description of a real world of acting scientists. It does, however, underscore the contrast with the arena of an audience already committed to a line of action and needing to be persuaded to an opposite line.

The argument in drinking-driving cannot utilize the language and atmosphere of the seminar. Facing a hostile audience whose behavior is to be controlled, the argument must present a state of affairs beyond dispute. To admit to the audience that the "facts" are not clear, that choice is necessary to translate them into certainty, is to shore up the target that the speaker is passionately devoted to knocking down. One must not look too closely at the referee while trying to punch the opponent. The public approach to drinking and driving is not a report on research; it is a call to action. Even the reports on research, I have been asserting, are not unaffected by the arena in which they will eventually star. Such considerations however shift the sources of compelling authority and conviction away from scientific method and toward moral or political interest or both.

The Moral Drama of the Drinking-Driver

Is it "accident" that I have used the language of conflict and combat to describe public campaigns, laws, and information on the problem of alcohol? My intent is to bring out the way in which the presentation of the issue takes the form of a dramatic confrontation between the informed and the ignorant. In this section I want to describe that confrontation as a confrontation between good and evil. The drinking-driver is the leading protagonist in the moral drama of automobile accidents. He supplies a major explanation for a source of death and destruction. To

convert him from sin to virtue is a salient element in the public drama of
the auto and American society.

What I am doing in this analysis of the drinking-driver as public presentation is treating public pronouncements as forms of drama similar
to those in other situations and historical periods. Following Kenneth
Burke's provocative analysis I look for a sacrificial principle as a dramatic
theme in creating social order. That is, when an image of social order is
conveyed, its opposite—disorder—is also portrayed. The drama consists
in seeing some players as victims, others as villains. Order is obtained
through sacrifice so that unity is derived. This universal theme is not
absent from modern life.[15] In the drama of drinking-driving the drinker is
portrayed as villain and others, including himself, as victims. The "accident" is not a result of random, blind fate but of human beings who fail
to observe the moral order of sober work.

The very fictive facticity described above enables the drama to be
performed. It renders the events closer to the imagined model of villainy,
and in this fashion serves to organize attitudes of condemnation. Burke
again is pertinent:

> The "perfection" of a secular enemy is the clearest observable in-
> stance of ways whereby the intermediate absolutizing step is involved.
> Given the vast complexities of the modern world, it would be hard to
> find a "perfect" material victim for any of our ills. ... [people] are
> eager to tell themselves of victims so thoroughgoing that the sacrifice
> of such offerings would bring about a correspondingly thoroughgoing
> cure. The "fragmentary" nature of the enemy thus comes to take on
> the attributes of an absolute. [Burke 1954, p. 293]

Consider the following headlines from news stories: "CHP Plans
Drunk Driver Crackdown" (Los Angeles Times, Nov. 27, 1977, pt. 1, p.
23); "Stronger Laws Are Needed to Curb Drunken Drivers" (Los
Angeles Times, Oct. 27, 1973, pt. 2, p. 1); "Crackdown on Drunk Drivers in L.A. Begins" (Los Angeles Times, July 2, 1976, pt. 2, p. 1); "Study
Defends Drinking Drivers" (San Diego Union, Sept. 1, 1974, B1–5). Such
terminology carries with it the sense of battle, of a conflict in which
drinking-driving is one side: the enemy. "You'll Be the Death of Me
Yet! ... If You're a Drunken Driver," proclaims an ASAP information
borchure on its cover (Greater Tampa Alcohol Safety Action Project,
n.d.). It portrays the drinking-driver as an active agent whose actions are
socially hostile and irresponsible. Another ASAP brochure quotes from a
Congressional message of then-President Nixon: "Our highway death
toll is a tragedy and an outrage of unspeakable proportions. It is all the
more shameful since half of these deaths involved drivers or pedestrians

under the influence of alcohol" (U.S. Department of Transportation, National Highway Traffic Safety Administration, n.d.).

Two aspects of these presentations, and others already described, need comment. First, the drinking-driver is portrayed as "drunk." The "sin" of drinking and driving is almost a microcosmic and symbolic enactment of the sources of disorder, the unwillingness to respect controls and boundaries in social life (this is discussed at length in chap. 6). Drunkenness has its own imagery and definition varying from group to group. I have shown above that while some drinking-drivers are "drunk," many do not demonstrate the loss of ability to drive or of self- or motor control to the degree that such a term implies.

The second aspect of the presentation needing comment is the term "drunken driver." Here the implication, examined in greater detail in the next chapter, is that of a permanent attribute of the person. Not the event "drinking-driving" but the person "drunken driver" is described. The personalization of the event keeps alive the sense of a drama of conflict against disordered persons, a performance of deviance. It is a drama of agents in which the individual is prime mover.

These same dramatic attributes occur as well in the personification of automobile design as "villain." In Ralph Nader's presentation, it is the auto industry that serves as "victim" of sacrificial rites. Just opening *Unsafe at Any Speed* "at random" I find: "For decades the conventional explanation preferred by the traffic safety establishment and insinuated into laws, with the backing of the auto industry and its allies, was that most accidents are caused by wayward drivers" (Nader 1972, p. xiii). Here, too, a possible drama of scene, of environment, is converted into one of agent, of auto industry directors as villains, by such expressions as "explanation preferred," and "insinuated into."

All the presentations put together into a concentrated image of drinking-driving add up to a drama of morality and order in the explanation of auto accidents and deaths. They are not random inescapable events before which we must bow, sacrifices made to the avenging angel for the gift of technological Progress. It is not the natural order that is largely "responsible" for the tragedy and destruction wreaked by the auto. It is the irrationality, venality, and even greed of humans; evil people who do evil to themselves and to others. "In contrast to scientific communication, which attempts to find an hypothesis that fits a situation, dramatization creates a situation that predetermines the hypothesis" (Young 1965, p. 151).

4

The Literary Art of Science Comedy and Pathos in Drinking-Driver Research

Prologue

It has been customary to distinguish efforts to persuade through language—the activity of the artist—from those through logic, the activity of the scientist. Albert Hofstadter has made this difference between scientific and literary uses of language the crux of his distinction between the two functions of art and science. The literary artist, maintains Hofstadter (1955), uses language as a significant vehicle for his or her activity. *How* objects and events are described or explained is more important than the subject matter of the narrative or poem. For the scientist this is not the case. Language is only a medium by which the external world is reported. That which is described and analyzed is not itself affected by the language through which it is reported.

Put generally, the scientist searches for *items involved with each other in patterns of dependence* . . . the scientist's language is not one of these items . . . he must not allow his language to become part of the content of his assertion.

The character of the imaginative object achieved by the artist depends on the character of the language he employs, whereas the language of the scientist does not operate within the involvement pattern he formulates. [Hofstadter 1955, pp. 294–95]

This is what I call the "windowpane" theory.

It insists on the intrinsic irrelevance of language to the enterprise of science. The aim of presenting ideas and data is to enable the audience to see the external world as it is. In keeping with the normative prescriptions of scientific method, language and style must be chosen which will approximate, as closely as possible, a pane of clear glass. The normative order of science is thus approximated. Scientists express their procedures, findings, and generalizations in "neutral" language. Their words do not create or construct the very reality they seek to describe and analyze.

From another standpoint, such a neutralized use of language is an impossibility. Idealist philosophy has generally insisted on the important role of the observer to what is observed, but seldom has attention been drawn away from theories and concepts to the language of presentation, to scientific documents as communicating devices and cultural products. For that we have to go to the literary analysts. A viewpoint directly opposite to Hofstadter's is given by Northrop Frye: "Anything which makes a functional use of words will always be involved in all the technical problems of words, including rhetorical problems. The only road from grammar to logic, then, runs through the intermediate territory of rhetoric" (Frye 1957, p. 331).

Frye's analysis of scientific work comes at the end of a major analysis of literature and is confined to general discussion. Literary critics have generally limited their art to the analysis of literature. With some major qualifications, discussed below, the literary analysis of scientific knowledge does not exist. Yet if words, sentences, paragraphs, and larger units are a major tool for reporting and therefore persuading, an analysis of the way in which scientific knowledge leads to practical actions cannot ignore the language and literary style of science as an object of study (White 1976).

That is just what I am going to do in this chapter. It is presented in the form of a staged play in order to make the metaphor of literature more obvious. My assertion is not that Science *is* Literature, but rather that we can treat Science *as if* it were Literature and that this metaphorical conceit will be productive. It will increase your and my understanding of the product and its implications for practical action. In this process I may lead both of us to a better understanding of where the metaphor is both applicable and inapplicable (R. Brown 1977; Turbayne 1962). But let us continue the prologue.

The distinction between Science and Literature seems to me to be capable of two dimensions, to each of which I address this chapter.

The Literary Style of Science
(The Substance of Act I)

The passage from philosopher Hofstadter is testimony to the intuitive hypothesis I have alluded to above. That passage implies that to be scientific is to give a definite form to the language in use, to write in a particular way which shows the audience that the writer is "doing science." The writer must persuade the audience that the results of the research are *not* literature, are *not* a product of the style of presentation. The style of nonstyle is itself the style of science. What I assert is that there is a literary art involved in scientific presentation.

The Literary Art in Science
(The Substance of Act II)

In this act I will look at the content of Science. Frye (1957, p. 74) maintains that in literary unlike nonliterary prose, the "sign-values of symbols are subordinated to their importance as a structure of interconnected motifs." Yet if there is a literary character to Science, efforts to be evocative, interesting, aesthetically pleasing and to make the work relevant and significant will contrast with the "windowpane" functions described by Hofstadter. The content of the research will itself be, in part, a result of its presentation. If all communication entails both an assertive, descriptive level and an aesthetic, artistic level then the windowpane is never completely clear; there is always a streak of stained glass to capture our imagination and wonder.

The Relevance of Art in Science
(The Substance of Act III)

While there is an aesthetic joy in the game of analysis, my intentions are not so purely artful. They also include the assertion that such analysis makes a difference, that the artistic side of Science is a significant part of the scientist's display of the external world. Not only will I show the artistic side of Science but I will use that exposition to understand the product—the theory, generalization, or conclusion to which the work of the scientist has led. Most importantly, I will use it to shed light on the practical actions which emerge as prescriptive through this process of artful Science.

My attention is not fixed on *the* Scientific Enterprise. It is both more modest and more searching. I narrow my vision to one set of windows:

the research studies in the area of "driving while under the influence of alcohol."

While I will allude to several papers in this area, one report has been chosen for a more thorough analysis. My method, treating papers as narratives and analyzing their frameworks, is such that I need to analyze the paper as a unit. Accordingly, I have resorted to a literary device common in science: the synecdoche, a device of representation in which a part substitutes for the whole. I selected one article for thorough examination, to represent the system of literary analysis applied to a scientific document. The paper, "Identification of Problem-Drinking among Drunken Drivers" (Waller 1967), was chosen for two conscious reasons: (1) it has been influential, frequently cited by other research persons and in government documents as a base for advocating particular policies; and (2) it represents a number of studies and papers which, in recent years, have operated as persuasive elements in a transformation of strategy toward the control of auto accidents associated with alcohol use. This too is fictional since each study and each interpretation has its uniqueness.

At the end of the 1960s and in the early 1970s, the view that drinking-drivers are very often alcoholics and problem drinkers gained much ground. As a diagnosis it was a significant source in the development of drinking-driving schools and treatment programs for convicted DUIA offenders. By the late 1970s, new studies led to much criticism of this view, and the feasibility of such diversionary programs was beginning to be called in doubt (Cameron 1977; Room 1979, pp. 189–90).

Enough procrastination. On with the play!

Act I. Scientific Style: The Rhetoric of Method

How does the scientist proceed to establish his claim to be "doing science" and thus to be read in a "scientific" way by the audience? In the frame of the windowpane, the scientist does not ask for that "willing suspension of disbelief" with which Coleridge maintained that the theater audience accepted a stage in London as the Italian balcony of Romeo and Juliet. How does the scientist, however, act as dramatist, setting a stage and persuading his readers to treat his work as one type of production rather than another?

In this act of my play, I am developing the literary *genre* of the scientific report, and my topic is not its content but its form. I will make use of two literary modes of analysis. Following Kenneth Burke (1945), I will examine the *dramatistic keys* in use: scene, act, agent, agency, and purpose. The objective here is to "uncover" the placement of responsibility for describing the action. With analysts of narrative fiction such as Henry James, Percy Lubbock (1957), and Wayne Booth (1961), I will then utilize the concept of *voice* to explicate the relation of observer to observed and observer to audience which influences the point-of-view or stance of the writer toward his subject and audience.

The Keys of Dramatism

What is the scenic surrounding of the paper? Scientific papers are not published randomly; they appear in a setting. The paper, "Identification of Problem-Drinking among Drunken Drivers," did not appear in *Playboy* magazine, in a collection of American short stories, or in a work on freshman composition. It is "placed" in the *Journal of the American Medical Association.* That setting establishes a claim for the paper to be taken as authoritative fact and not as fiction or imaginative writing. All of the drinking-driving studies in this book were like this one in being found in settings dedicated to research rather than art. Most are in medical journals, some in journals devoted to automobile safety or safety in general. A substantial segment are found in the *Journal of Studies on Alcohol,* and still another group are found in the proceedings of scholarly conferences on alcohol problems or specifically on the problem of drinking and driving. The *Journal of the American Medical Association* is not primarily an organ of news or professional advice. It contains accounts of new research in areas of physiology and medical science. In order to play in the game, the scientist must pick the proper field.

Act

What is the action of the paper? I want to show it as a form of narrative, a "story" which has movement with a beginning and an end involving change. The article begins with a title that describes a category, "drunken drivers," and an attribute, "problem drinking," which is to involve an action, "identification." Following the title appears a summary of the paper to follow. It presents the paper in a capsule form—the methods used and "findings," such as, "high correlation was found between two or more arrests involving drinking and an impression of problem drinking" (Waller 1967, p. 124). This summary presentation establishes the inference that what is significant about the paper can be separated from the larger body of language. The audience, if it so wishes, can get the crux of the play from the program. The stage production has a quality of embellishment.

Like a narrative, the first paragraph sets up a tension which the paper will proceed to resolve. The audience is told that "it is becoming increasingly apparent that a substantial proportion of drivers who get into accidents after drinking or who are arrested for drunken driving are not social drinkers but rather persons with a long-standing drinking problem" (p. 124). This assertion sets up a tension between this newer perspective on drinking-drivers and and older, conventional one in which drinking-drivers are representative of the general population of drinkers—the social drinkers.

Unlike a short story or poem, the paper reaches out for its material beyond the self-contained confines of its own product. It refers to other studies, including some of the author's as grounds for some of the assertions. Unlike the artistic, the author also gives his denouement in the beginning. "This finding necessitates the reevaluation of current methods for preventing driving after drinking" (p. 124).

It is in the unfolding of the story that the action of the paper occurs. Having foreshadowed the final comment in the first paragraph, the author does not presume to leave the matter unexplicated. He follows a pattern: first, the description of the methods used to identify problem drinking among drinking-drivers; second, the results or findings of this method; last, the comment, explaining the significance of the results. This sequential arrangement places policy significance, what is to be done, as the outcome of methods which generate results. The activity supported and/or rejected appears as the culmination of method. This centrality of method and externality of data is the major key to the story. The method is the ground, the rationale for persuading the reader to think differently and/or to act differently. The resolution of the conflict or tension set up in the first paragraph involves a change from a conventional perspective on drinking-drivers to a new perspective both in cognitive understanding and in policies to be espoused. In this sense the flow, or action, of the paper is dramatic.

Agent

What is salient here and in our fuller discussion of the agent under the rubric *voice* below is the hidden and unassuming posture of the observer. As the theory of the "windowpane" would suggest, the author must not intrude into the product. Yet the observer must also be trusted in a way not called for in artistic works. If the artist does not claim to be a reporter of the factual world but a constructor of imaginative and pleasurable products, his claim to veracity is not an essential part of the claim to artistic acceptance. We need not accept James Joyce as a reliable producer of accounts of Dublin in the early 1900s in order to appreciate *A Portrait of the Artist as a Young Man*. The reader need not even know who the author is in order to appreciate the novel. But where the author attests to a world of real properties, his integrity and competence to report are a question.

The dilemma of whether to personalize or to remove the agent seems to be solved in most drinking-driver studies by a device of identification through role. In this paper, following the title, appear the name and credentials of the author: Julian A. Waller, M.D., M.P.H. At the bottom of the page, in footnote form, the author is described as someone connected with an organization: "From the Bureau of Occupational Health, California Department of Health. Dr. Waller is now with the Bureau of Chronic Diseases" (p. 124). Thus the agent is described in a role (medical and public health) and in an organization.

Having told the audience about his professional competence and acceptance, the author must now move out of the limelight if the document is to be untainted by the obvious presence of the observer. The language chosen performs this function through an emphasis on the externality of the source of action and through the passive character of the agent. Viz: "It was decided to use this latter method" (Schmidt and Smart 1959, p. 632), not "We decided . . ." Or, "The test indicates there is a significant difference" (Borkenstein et al. 1964, p. 188), not "Based on the test, we concluded . . ." Other examples I culled from a variety of papers studied are: "Data . . . confirm a self-evident fact" (Holcomb 1938, p. 1034) and "Recent reports have suggested . . ." (Waller 1966, p. 532).

In Waller's 1967 paper (nota bene: I have taken to personalizing the product), such circumlocutions are frequent. The active voice is absent. In the lead sentence the author (by inference) writes: "It is increasingly becoming apparent . . ." But to whom? Throughout the paper the conclusion or result is portrayed as emerging from an external world of data or tables. "Differences were found . . ." "This finding necessitates the reevaluation . . ."

Agency

What this pattern of rejection of personal terms or active voice does is to place the source of action in the agency or method. Waller's paper creates a style consistent with "windowpane" theory by establishing a reality outside the observer. The style reinforces this externality and provides the basic epistemological assumption; by use of the same method different observers much reach the same conclusions.[1] Language and style follow philosophy.

Both the identification of the author in the beginning and the passivity of the style support the portrayal of a procedure in which the observer is governed by a method and by the rules of scientific integrity in relation to the method. He continues to make this point throughout the paper by following a regimen of meticulous attention to details, thereby avoiding a judgment by the reader that he has been less than scrupulous in following the method. Thus the percentages are given in decimals, such as 19.3 percent or 6.1 percent for samples ranging from 160 to 19 (table I, p. 125). Where discretion had to be used, the event is meticulously described to avoid the implication of whimsy or bias: "One nondrinking driver involved in an accident also appeared in the drunken-driver sample. *For purposes of analysis* he was considered as a separate person in each group" (p. 125; italics mine).

Purpose

That the author means to convince his audience of certain conclusions is both evident and explicit. The importance of method substantiates the overall style of detachment. He means to convince, but not to persuade, by presenting an external world to the audience and allowing that external reality to do the convincing. Thus the language must be emptied of feeling and emotion. The tone must be clinical, detached, depersonalized. His language must not be "interesting," his descriptions colorful, or his words a clue to any emotion which might be aroused in the audience. Beginning with the title, "Identification of Problem-Drinking among Drunken Drivers," the language is flat, prosaic, and descriptive without imagery. The title describes an object ("drunken drivers") and a set of attributes (problem-drinking), along with a process to be performed—identification. The title is not flamboyant, puzzling, or funny. Contrast a more journalistic title, "He Couldn't Help Himself," or a more literary one, at once ambiguous and intriguing, "The End of the Road." (The term "drunken driver" seems a violation of this style and will be discussed in considerable detail below.)

Let me pull these strands of analysis together. The style of the paper and its setting in a medical journal make it recognizable not as Art but as claiming to be Science. The language is deliberate, nonevocative, meticulous, and limited in imagery. It informs the reader that conviction is to come from an external reality—not from the author or his use of language. The description is minimally metaphorical. Jakobson suggests that the fundamental trope (figure of speech) of science is metonymy, a relationship of contiguity, while that of poetry is metaphor, a relationship of similarity (Jakobson 1966). However, as I stress in this chapter, the metaphorical element is nonetheless crucial to Science (also see Turbayne 1962; Sapir 1977). The intent is made to seem cognitive and logical rather than affective or emotional. We, the audience, are to think and not to feel. Although the author is not anonymous and is identified as a scientist in a governmental organization, the style of writing grounds the action of the paper in the agency of methodological procedures of data collection and analysis. The agent is minimized, and the drama of the paper is presented as flowing from the unfolding of the procedures of method, not from the interests, biases, or language of the author.

Voice and Viewpoint

Literary criticism has been filled in recent decades with the problem of point-of-view, especially in analyses of novels (Freidman 1969). Since Flaubert and James, novelists have self-consciously attempted to place themselves less and less into their novels, hoping to persuade the reader not by *telling* him or her about the characters but by *showing* through action (Booth 1961, chap. 1). When the novelist characterizes the protagonists through description of them, he is *telling*. When he presents the action and lets the audience infer character, then he is *showing*. "I am a camera," wrote Christopher Isherwood in the first sentence of *The Berlin Stories*, "with its shutter open, quite passive, recording, not thinking."

The author of a scientific paper may be considered as a narrator with a specific presentation of his point-of-view: "Whether or not they are involved in the action as agents, narrators and third-person reflectors differ markedly according to the degree and kind of *distance* that separates them from the author, the reader and the other characters of the story they relate or reflect" (Booth 1969, p. 180).

Audience-Author Ratios

In emphasizing the passive voice of the author and his absence as a significant mover of events and conclusions, I described the observer as presenting himself as a "windowpane" if not a camera. In that sense, the author does not claim a special vantage point or viewpoint as compared to his audience. He is in the same seat, showing the observations which lead to conclusions. The audience knows as much and as little as the author. They are on an equal plane.

One frequently used device to achieve equality is, of course, the regal or editorial "we." I did not find this in Waller's paper. The consistent absence of any designation of the author is also reinforced by the passive voice by which action is described: "Information was obtained . . ."; "An impression was ventured . . ." Although I did not find it in Waller, other authors use the inclusive "we" to put themselves into the audience: "In accident research *we* are now past the stage . . ." (Hyman 1968b, p. 53; italics mine).

The style of Waller's paper implies a ratio of equivalence between author and audience. The mode of writing reduces distance and avoids claims of authority or superior judgment on the part of the author. He seems to say: "I will give you, the reader, all the knowledge and factual information that I have. We will reason together and achieve a consensus through fact and reason. You, as a rational person, cannot but reach the same conclusion as I."

This ratio of author to audience can, of course, be distinguished from others of more or less than unitary equivalence. When the author tells instead of showing, he claims the authority and distance of someone with a viewpoint above the reader, in command of greater skill or special knowledge, like a scientist addressing a lay public or Henry Fielding writing his novels. When the opposite is the case, the author shows the reader and leaves to him or her to make of it what he or she wishes, as in a Pirandello play or in some contemporary forms of ethnography. Even in my reading of research papers, I found one or two instances where the author presented a set of findings and would not interpret or order them into a set of conclusions (Gerber 1963).

Distance and Subject

Who is the author in relation to the subjects he studies? Is he one of them? Is he decidedly not among those he describes? What is his stance toward and distance from the object of study? The endless discussions of objectivity and political morality in science since Marx have continually posed the question of point-of-view as a major one for the ethics of the scientist. Robert Merton has posed this question in spatial terms by referring to "insiders" and "outsiders" (Merton 1972). The problem is analogous to that of distance in literary analysis.

The clinical style of Waller's paper preserves the stance of the outsider by looking at drinking-drivers as a group of whom the author, and thus the audience, is not a part. He has neither loyalty nor economic interest in them. They are "objects of study" and not members of the audience. His paper is not addressed to drinking-drivers. Nowhere are any of the sampled groups referred to as including the author or the audience. Both author and audience are presented as "outsiders"; not drinking-drivers themselves, they take the stance of observers of the nonself.

Is the stance one of equivalence? In the first paragraph, the author speaks of the need to reevaluate "current methods for preventing driving after drinking" (p. 124). Throughout the paper there is no doubt whose "side" he is on; nor is there any evidence of an effort to persuade the audience of the wisdom of this "side." It is taken for granted. The author, and inferentially the audience, are superior to the subjects in that they are distant from and above the behavior of drinking and driving.

The stance or viewpoint of the author is one of equivalence with his audience but superiority to his subjects. As an appeal to the persuasive power of reason, it is the style of Science to minimize Rhetoric, to negate and downplay evidence of viewpoint. Wayne Booth's characterization of fiction is inconsistent with the "windowpane" theory of Science: "In short, the author's judgment is always evident to anyone who knows how to look for it. . . . As we begin to deal with this question, we must never forget that though the author can to some extent choose his disguises, he can never choose to disappear" (Booth 1961, p. 20).

You, the reader, and I are now at the endpoint of Act I, where the playwright reveals his dialectical hand. By now you have probably suspected what is the case. I will begin to assert that A is non-A, that what Wayne Booth has written about Fiction, I will assert about Fact. Art and Rhetoric have not been sent into perpetual exile to live outside the walls of Science and Knowledge. With or without passport, they steal back into the havens of clinical and antiseptic scholarship and operate from underground stations to lead forays into the headquarters of the enemy.

CURTAIN

End of Act I

Act II. Literary Art: The Rhetoric of Substance

I have shown you the stage. It is time to produce the play itself, to attend to contents after having seen the package. The first act has been the rhetoric of method—the style of Science. The second act is the rhetoric of substance—the presentation of the phenomenon revealed by the study.

To facilitate the discussion of Waller's paper, I reproduce the summary which is placed at the beginning of the article. It is a "quick and dirty" overview:

> Information about previous contact with community agencies, particularly contact involving drinking problems, was compared for 150 drunken drivers, 33 accident-involved drivers who had been drinking but were not arrested, 117 sober drivers involved in accidents, 131 drivers with moving violations, 19 drivers with citations plus arrest warrants, and 150 incident-free drivers. Screening criteria for problem-drinkers were two or more previous arrests involving drinking or identification by a community agency as a problem drinker. These criteria were met by the following: drunken drivers, 63 percent; drivers with an accident after drinking, 50 percent; drivers with warrants, 30 percent; non-drinking drivers with an accident, 14 percent; persons with driving violations, 8 percent; and drivers with no incidents, 3 percent. High correlation was found between two or more arrests involving drinking and an impression of problem drinking. Eighty-seven percent of the drunken drivers were known to community agencies, most with multiple contacts starting before age 30. [p. 124]

Reduction to Substance: The Whatness of the
Object

Let me begin at the beginning—the title and the first sentence. What is the object of study as it is described by the author? The title contains a significant term which contrasts with the nonemotive and clinical character of the paper and the general tone of the title: "drunken." This term conveys a specific image, far more concrete than the weaker and more general term "drinking." A "drunken driver" is not only a more opprobrious figure than a "drinking-driver," but "drunken" conveys a more visual image because of the commonsense experience of the audience with drunkenness. "Drunken" may, as it does to me, convey the sense of a reeling, incoherent, unreasonable, and thus unpredictable and dangerous person. Yet the first sentence shows the reader a somewhat different object, with a less specific and less visual image. What was studied were "drivers who get into accidents after drinking or who are arrested for drunken driving" (p. 124). While Waller consistently refers to "drunken drivers," what he studied were persons arrested for violating legal restrictions against "driving under the influence of alcohol," as evidenced by their blood-alcohol count. Arrests with or without accidents are *not* evidence of "drunkenness" in a commonsense or lay conception.

With the first sentence and the title, the author has already converted "fact" into imagery; he has changed or reduced the data to something else. He has determined which aspects of the events of accidents after drinking shall be highlighted. The issue of reductionism is crucial, both to Science and to this paper. It is a major way in which the research scientist makes sense or draws relevance out of his work. "Metonymy," writes Kenneth Burke, "is a device of 'poetic realism'" (Burke 1945, p. 506). The terms in which the object is described have, in Waller's paper, already involved a reduction in one dirction by the rejection of other terms. He has used the part ("drunken") for the whole ("drinking")—the literary device of synecdoche again.

The description of the object involves other issues besides reduction whose analysis is significant for the ultimate conclusions and policy advised. Here Waller's usage is similar to that of most of the work in the field of "drinking-driving." He attempts to uncover permanent personality components and/or social habits of the drinking-driver. In defining and analyzing the "drinking-driver" Waller, like others, narrows the range of matters connected with the events being studied. The language used leads toward one particular formulation of the object and away from others.

The concept of the "drinking-driver" emphasizes the agent and minimizes the scene or the act or the agency as possible elements in accidents. "Drinking" becomes an attribute of the self; there are drinking drivers and nondrinking drivers as there are male and female drivers, old and young drivers, competent and incompetent drivers. Both "drinking-driver" and "drunken driver" lead to the search for attributes of the person which exist before, during, and after the action of driving. Other terms in use, though less frequent, direct attention toward aspects of the driving situation. The terms "alcohol-impaired driver" or "intoxicated driver" place the driver in a context and place the attribute in interaction with a situation; give it a temporal rather than a permanent character.

It is possible also to dispense with "driver" and to describe the same phenomenon in terms which emphasize placement or scene or act. The phrase "persons engaged in drinking-driving" or even "drinking-driving" contrasts with "drinking-driver" by underlining the situational character of the event being examined.

These differences between "driver" and "driving" are not merely ones of grammar. They reflect the significant perspectives of psychology and sociology, respectively—the difference between a drama of agent and a drama of scene. By choosing "driver" in his title and in his opening sentence, Waller has pulled the audience into the perspective of psychology and into a search for abiding characteristics of the personalities of persons rather than that of sociology which emphasizes context as scene.

Metaphor:
The Transformation of the Drinking-Driver

Waller's paper is one of several major research studies which resulted in a transformed perspective on the drinking-driver in governmental and legal circles. His study design influences which of two major perspectives should be utilized in thinking about drinking-drivers and in developing policies to minimize drinking-driving. These perspectives are expressed through two central terms or metaphors: the *social drinker* and the *problem drinker*. What is happening in this paper can be expressed as the dramatic reconceptualization of the drinking-driver from social drinker to problem drinker.

I refer to these terms as "metaphors" because they are used to extend the meaning of primary data. They are not descriptions of the factual information collected but are instead presentations of that data in a form which creates linkages to something already known by the audience. They heighten perception by extending the primary data into another realm. Utilizing Max Black's interaction theory of metaphor (Black 1962), Mary Hesse has stated the view of metaphor I use here: "The metaphor works by transferring the associated ideas and implications of the secondary to the primary system. These select, emphasize or suppress features of the primary; new slants on the primary are illuminated; the primary is seen through the frame of the secondary" (Hesse 1966, p. 232).[2]

It is the major conclusion of Waller's paper that, contrary to the then conventionally held view, "a substantial proportion" of drinking-drivers are problem drinkers and not, as formerly believed, social drinkers. A "large" number of drinking-drivers also had arrest records involving the use of alcohol or had been diagnosed by one or more community service agencies as having a problem involving alcohol use. Such records and/or diagnoses were found only among a "small" proportion of the non-drinking drivers.

It is again the first paragraph in which the author tells his audience the nature of the two types found among drinking-drivers: the drinking-driver qua social drinker and the drinking-driver qua problem drinker.

Present methods for diminishing drinking-driving assume, he says, that
"the erring driver has committed his act rationally but foolishly" (p.
124). In contrast, the behavior of the opposite type, the problem drinker
as drinking-driver, is characterized as "psychosocial *pathology* rather
than social misjudgment" (italics mine).

In this paragraph and throughout the paper, Waller touches the central
issue of knowledge and policy toward drinking-driving: Are such drivers
who threaten to cause accidents to be seen as ordinary citizens whose
habits of alcohol use are "normal" for American life? Or are they extra-
ordinary people whose drinking habits are "abnormal" for American
life? If the former is the case, then the drinking-driver can be seen as a
generally conforming person whose occasional lapse is not a sign of a
basic attribute connected with antisocial behavior. He or she is not a
deviant person. Insofar as the latter is the case, the drinking-driver is less
controllable, more compulsive, and less amenable to change through
reason and persuasion.

The contrast is continued in the manner of description. The actions of
the ordinary citizen are merely venal. He is "social"—conforming and
not compulsive. He may act foolishly, but there is a basic attribute of
rational capacity and attitude. He is "not likely to repeat his indiscretion" (p. 126), unlike the problem drinking-driver who "does not learn
from a punitive experience" (p. 129). He is "engulfed in the deluge of
alcohol-related problems" (p. 12).

The "root metaphor"—the basic metaphorical system around which
the distinctions are drawn—is essentially organic-medical (Bruyn 1966,
p. 137). The population of drinking-drivers is seen through the lenses of
medical language. Some are "normal" and others are "pathological."
Both terms are repeated in describing, respectively, the two types of
drivers and the two types of drinkers in the society. Social drinkers are
normal citizens and their drinking-driving is not symptomatic of devia-
tion from attributes of the *healthy* person. Problem drinkers are *unhealthy* and their drinking-driving emanates from a flawed and unhealthy
personality.

Myth and Archetype:
The Production of the Morality Play

Literary critics have frequently pointed out the recurrent use of certain
stock characters and types as the basis for themes and patterns in contemporary literature. Such archetypes constitute a major device by which
the artist enables the reader to identify the new through the form of the

old. Sociologists, using a literary metaphor, have expressed the same idea in concepts of "social role," "social types," and "ideal typology." Northrop Frye refers to such common patterns of typology as "myths" in that they draw upon already shared images, stories, and events: "Realism, or the art of verisimilitude, evokes the response 'How like that is to what we know.' When what is written is *like* what is known, we have an art of extended or implied simile. And as realism is an art of implicit simile, myth is an art of implicit metaphorical identity" (Frye 1957, p. 136).

In order to create theoretical and generalizable knowledge, the author must liken the specific objects of his study to more universal categories of persons and events with which the audience is already familiar. Unless he chooses such types, the knowledge will exist at the level of history or ethnography descriptive of a particular time, place, and set of people. Social roles, such as "the father," or literary myths, such as the story of Oedipus, become conventionalized forms through which the objects can be described. Such myths and archetypes bear a distinct relation to scientific models. The model of a frictionless system enables physicists to "talk about" motion; the model of a "primary group" enables the sociologist to "talk about" human relationships. The similartiy between the products of this analogical process in science and in literature led Max Black (1962, p. 241), in his discussion of models, to refer to them as "conceptual archetypes" and Vaihinger to consider them "fictions."

It is in the light of types seen as myths that we can again analyze the major contrasts in Waller's paper between drinking-drivers and non-drinking drivers and between "social drinkers" and "problem drinkers." All of these are types with which there is familiarity, in actual or vicarious experience, or both. They constitute stock themes in popular literature and drama as well as in news and common talk. The idea of the "killer drunk" is one such character whose irresponsibility and commitment to a hedonistic style of life creates tragedy for others. The use of the term "drunken" in the title constitutes an invocation of a stock theme in an official context of persons who have come to attention through arrest for drinking-driving or through accidents in which the offense is uncovered. So, too, the usage "social drinker" implies a contrast to "drunken." Suppose Waller had referred to "problem drinkers" and "social drunks"? In this alternative usage, he would have referred to that category of persons who, on occasion, drink to drunkenness but whose action does not express an addictive problem. This behavior is quite common in a large segment of Americans (Cahalan et al. 1969).

The typology thus operates to label and stigmatize the drinking-drivers as "problem drinkers" and to label and exonerate the "social drinkers" as responsible citizens who have slipped but whose derelection is not a reflection of a personal flaw. The root terms of "normal" and "pathological" continue to cast these groups in the image of the archetypal forms. The drinking-drivers are analogized to the problem drinkers and characterized within the terms of the myth of the drinker as deviant, outcast, and stigmatized. "Engulfed in the deluge of alcohol-related problems," they are described in the following way: "The central theme in the lives of the drunken drivers seems to be alcohol. Almost three quarters of their many arrests involved drinking. Their marriages often were in a state of dissolution because of excessive drinking. Among drunken drivers, arrest reports commonly observed that the person had been arrested for assaulting his wife when he arrived home intoxicated and she began scolding him for his alcoholic pattern" (p. 129).

Waller has given the audience a strong depiction of the stock figure of the drinker as deviant. Agency workers, whose records Waller utilized, had found drinking problems in only one-fourth of the cases and made a medical judgment of alcoholism in only one-tenth. Waller explained this contradiction to his findings by saying that the agency workers had used the stock image of gross intoxication and the "skid row bum." Nevertheless, his portrayal comes close to that stock figure. Writing of the sample of persons with arrest warrants out for failing to answer citations for nondrinking moving violations, Waller says that they "*also* represent a population with profound psychosocial pathology" (p. 129; italics mine).

If the problem drinker has been stigmatized as responsible for drinking-driving and the drinking-driver stigmatized as a deviant drinker, in this process the "social drinker," the convivial "solid citizen," has been "taken off the hook" and absolved from deviance. The contrasting archetype—the social drinker—is an "erring driver" when he strays. He is a man of rationality and basic good will who "can be dissuaded." Such a man is not very likely to be a drinking-driver: a "social drinker *might* err once in the excessive use of alcohol sufficient to result in his arrest but he would not be likely to repeat his indiscretion" (p. 126; italics mine). If not exactly heroic, the social drinker is neither villainous nor venal.

The implicit use of stock forms has enabled the author to produce a morality play in which drinking-driving is a stage for the expression of personal and moral character. The social drinker is Everyman—rational, socially responsible, given to occasional and human lapses of conduct but basically law-abiding, controllable and controlling, and responsive to norms of social cooperation and control. The Boy Scout of the highways, he can be trusted to carry out the dictates of a rational and interdepending society with a minimum of guidance and force to keep him from going off the road. Not so the problem drinker. He is the juvenile delinquent of traffic. Irresponsible, compulsive, and irrational, his drinking is part of his social defiance and deviance.

The Rhetoric of Action

The author is not content to stop before the open window. After *showing* the audience, Waller also *tells* them how the study changes proscribed behavior. Assuming a shared interest between himself and his audience in minimizing the phenomenon of drinking-driving, he draws implications for how the audience should now formulate policies to that end. His message is directed to an audience of policymakers or advisors to policymakers and not to drinking-drivers or to persons who may be drinking-drivers. "This finding necessitates the reevaluation of current methods for preventing driving after drinking" (p. 124).

The policy argument of "Identification of Problem Drinking among Drunken Drivers" is that the apparatus of law enforcement cannot control drinking-driving effectively because the drinking-driver is usually a medical and not a legal problem. The assumptions of law, according to Waller, are based on the image of the "social drinker"; they expect that the delinquent or potential delinquent is a rationally motivated person whose behavior and future behavior can be influenced by fear of punishment. Instead the drinking-driver problem must confront the "problem drinker" who cannot exercise sufficient self-control to permit rational considerations to operate. The central paragraph reads as follows:

> Among the drunken drivers, the 971 previous arrests, 694 of which were due to drinking, represent a pathetic monument to the failure of the punitive approach to prevent further difficulty with drinking. With the current availability of more appropriate methods to treat and rehabilitate those with a drinking problem, we must look with utter amazement at the determined employment of techniques that have so completely proven their futility. Current methods for treating alcoholism are highly successful in a quarter to a third of patients and at least partially successful in a substantial proportion of the remainder [p. 124]

In Burke's terms, Waller has produced a transformation of scene, from the law courts to the hospital or clinic. Having reconceptualized the drinking-driver from a delinquent to a patient, he has diminished the significance of legal measures as appropriate policy and increased the importance of medical practice for solving the problem of drinking and driving. The audience must now look to themselves—doctors, alcohol treatment personnel, experts on alcoholism—rather than to lawyers and police as the effective agents of social policy in this arena.

It is noteworthy that as the author proceeds to draw action implications, the "measured cadence" of the scientific style gives way to a brisker pace and a more emotive, imperative language. Phrases like "patent failure," "pathetic monument," "look with utter amazement" appear. As Frye pointed out, when the author moves to persuade the audience to action, the "strategic withdrawal from action" which characterized the reporting of methods and findings gives way to a faster rhythm and a more emotive style (Frye 1957, p. 327). Most of the imagery alluded to in this paper has come from the introduction and the final section labeled "Comment."

So we bring the second act to an end on an upbeat. The courts have moved off center and to the side. In their place the medical and paramedical practitioners of alcoholism treatment have taken the starring roles. The audience of the *Journal of the American Medical Association* can paraphrase Pogo and say, "We have found the solution and the solution is us."

CURTAIN

End of Act II

Act III. The Rhetoric of Social Hierarchies

The drama of drinking-driver research, especially as exemplified in Waller's study, may now be seen as a dialectical process in which the main actor—the drinking-driver—has been transformed from acceptable social drinker to stigmatized problem drinker. In what follows, I assert that this transformation also involved the disestablishment of one form of social hierarchy and its replacement by another. Through the medium of research as drama, the phenomenon of hierarchy is itself re-presented and emerges as something different from its appearance at the opening curtain.

The Hierarchy of Drinkers as Social Hierarchy

The analysis of drinking-drivers and their drinking patterns, as illustrated by Waller's study, has provided the audience with a shift in the hierarchical character of the major actors. In this shift the social drinker has been "upgraded" by being exonerated from the charge of responsibility for auto accidents. The "drinking-driver" has been "degraded" by being equated with the "problem drinker." That very equation further stigmatizes the already labeled deviant status of the "problem drinker." As the play has been acted out, what was down has come up and what was up has come down. The social drinker regains the aura of Everyman while the drinking-driver is now "pathological"—marginal and deviant. In this fashion the gap between law-abider and law-avoider has been widened. The social drinker has moved up the hierarchy of deserved esteem while the drinking-driver has, in a veritable *double entendre*, been "put down" (Burke 1945; Duncan 1962, pt. 6).

This distinction, and its correlative hierarchy, are also congruent to social structure. They correspond to the hierarchies of class, race, and ethnic background. Like many recent students of drinking-driving, Waller does more than locate the drinking-driver on a spectrum of drinkers. He also locates the drinking-driver qua problem drinker, in the social structure of American society. Waller supports the view of drinking-drivers and problem drinkers as resident in the lowest income and status levels. He reports that blacks comprised forty-nine percent of the drunken drivers but only twenty-five percent of the driver population of Oakland, site of the study. Drivers of Mexican or American Indian descent were eleven percent of the drunken drivers, but two to four percent of the total population of drivers. Even though qualified, the image of the low status of the drinking-driver emerges. In discussing information about arrest records, Waller writes: "Nonwhite drivers consistently had larger proportions with arrests, and had more arrests per person. However the differences were not significant at $P \leq 0.05$ except for drivers of Mexican or Indian extraction with violations" (p. 128).

In an earlier companion study (Waller and Turkel 1966), the authors found a statistically significant difference based on race. Among auto fatalities, blacks were more likely to have had alcohol present in the blood than were whites and were also more likely to have evidence of cirrhosis of the liver, or a record of arrests for public intoxication or both. Blood-alcohol levels were higher among drinking whites than among drinking blacks, however. Commenting on these findings the authors remarked: "There is reason to believe that the predominant subculture among American Negroes is fairly tolerant toward the use of alcohol, explaining the observed differences. However, heavy drinking is not over-represented among Negro fatalities" (Waller and Turkel 1966, p. 535).

Note that in both papers the image of the black as problem drinker is introduced and then qualified, rather than being presented directly as a qualified or ambiguous image. What has happened is that the problem drinking-driving has now been located at the bottom of the social structure. Other scholars have been less emphatic about class differences. As one research report states it (Cosper and Mozersky 1968, p. 110), "class differences, although present, are not great except for the marked disparity between the poorest, least educated persons and the rest of the population." The equation of social structure and problem drinker is not supported by all investigators (religious and ethnic differences are also viewed as significant).[3]

The emergence of the problem drinker as drinking-driver and the location of one major source of problem drinkers in the lowest categories of the social hierarchy in Waller's paper does place the problem outside the scene of the solid citizen. As long as the social drinker was the potential source of the problem of auto accidents due to drink, a prevalent style of stable middle-. and working-class drinking habits was under impeachment. Caught between the pressures and self-imposed demands for "tough" enforcement, and the perception of drinking-driving as a "normal" crime of "normal" people, police and courts have had difficulty in response. The findings in Waller's paper provide a happy solution to the moral dilemma posed at the beginning of the paper by the imputation of dereliction to ordinary, lawful people. The problem has been shifted to people who are "sick" and quite likely morally suspect anyway. Thus the social structure and the legitimacy of social hierarchy are reinforced, and the possibility of degradation is dispelled.[4]

Comedy and Tragedy in Social Structures

If this is a literary analysis of a document, what is the mood of the writing? Is it comedy, tragedy, tragicomedy, or farce? I look for the answer in the final character of the main protagonists—the social drinker and the problem drinker. The importance of the question goes beyond completion of a literary analysis. To determine the mood of the writing will help you and me to understand the kind and quality of emotive response which the writer of the document may attempt to elicit in the reader.

Whatever the status of the social drinker in the original scene, at the conclusion, I assert, he has been cast as a comic figure. He is the classic comic drunk: a figure of stability and established position who has temporarily lost his balance. He is *not* portrayed as being inherently and through personal makeup a menace to the community, either on the

road, in his familial life, or in his roles as worker and citizen. His drinking, and even his driving after drinking, become comic. They are neither
venal, "sociopathic," "pathological," nor recurrent and threatening to
the audience. Drunkenness as an unusual episodic event in the life of a
stable person is a comic event, classically introduced in comedic scenes in
drama. Only when the drunken behavior is perceived as a constant,
compulsive event, filled with recurrent threat to self and others, does it
become frightening and "tragic."

But the drinking driver qua problem drinker is not the tragic figure of
literary history. Victim of his own incapacity to control his drinking and
possibly socialized to a life-style which prevents a change in his habits of
leisure, he cannot change himself even under the sanction of legal
punishment and the fear of death through accident. Yet his is not the
story of the great man fallen from high places and powerless to regain the
seat of power. No Oedipus he! The source of his own and others' destruction, he is a powerless figure whose stigmata are not offset by any
ribbons of glory.

The Descent into Pathos and Therapy

Neither major figure of Waller's drama is heroic or villainous. The social
drinker is at worst foolish, at best the rational man. Neither he nor the
problem drinker, his contrasting image, is a heroic man caught in large,
indifferent, or malevolent forces which shape their destinies, rough hew
them though they may. If the problem drinker is tragic, his is a low
mimetic tragedy, that of a pathetic soul rather than a tragic one. In his
lowly status and his compulsive drives, he is a figure of pathos, impossible for the audience of readers and the author to identify with. His
troubles stem from his indulgence and lack even the dignity of being the
outcome of his having carried otherwise laudable motives to excess, as
Macbeth "o'erleaps" his own ambitiousness.

What deeply distinguishes this drama from many literary tragedies is
its "deus ex machina" —the intervention of the author, the audience, and
the profession of alcoholism treatment. An array of hope, in the form of
counselors, screeners, and practitioners, is available to redeem the pathetic drinker through the vehicle of therapy. The utopian strain of social
engineering lifts the drama above the mood of despair and finality which
high mimetic tragedy entails. No agency for the blind can help Oedipus
nor can old age assistance restore Lear.

Scientific Feeling:
The Union of Form and Substance

I have now pushed myself into a patent contradiction. The style of a
nonemotive language has created a whole bucketful of emotions—comic,
tragic, pathetic. But the language of Science is not quite that of Literature,
and the arousal of feeling is much more ambiguous here than on the
stage. While Waller describes the problem drinker he does not tell us, the
audience, how we are to feel toward that central character. When I call
the drinking-driver "pathetic," I do so by reference to feelings aroused in
me by the paper and those I expect the "ordinary" reader would have.
This expectation is reinforced by my experience with how such people
as those likely to read Waller's paper have responded to the problem
drinker in other contexts and other places.

It is significant that the language through which the writer has tried to
describe his characters is couched in the nonemotive forms already described above, rather than the more direct phrases with which a novelist
or playwright might try to arouse feeling. The drinking-driver stands as
an object outside the emotional ambit of the writer and the reader. For
this reason, pathos is to be checked, limited, and even obliterated as a
reaction of the audience.

It is important that the only clear use of emotional language appears
in the paper when the author describes not the actors—the drinking-
drivers—but those officials who create policy toward the actors. In the
quotation above, the author emerges from hiding to score past policy as
a "pathetic monument" and to view it with "utter amazement." Here is
anger, scorn, and irony.

The avoidance or limitation of identification with the drinking-driver
allows the writer, and therefore attempts to persuade the reader, to identify with the "society" as victim. To see the "problem drinker" in highly
differentiated or individual terms or to view him as an object of emotional concern would make the problem of drinking-driving less clear and
the objective of social control more problematic. To be punitive, as the
law has been according to Waller, or benevolent, as an "underdog
sociology" might entail (Becker 1967; Gouldner 1968), would be to
adopt a very different stance: less functional, less efficient, less concerned
with rational maximization of benefits and minimization of costs. Waller's critique of law and his support of medical therapy is an argument
based on effectiveness for social functioning. The drinking-driver is
neither villain nor hero. He must be helped because he creates "trouble"
for other folks, such as his readers.

Form and substance combine. In placing the drinking-driver down-
ward in the social structure and in constructing him as a neutral object,
control is enhanced. In order to consider the social costs and benefits,
the reader and the policymaker are cautioned to mute their feelings toward the specific and particular qualities—loathsome or appealing—of
drinking-drivers and see them as types from the stance of the organization and the society. Both language and feeling, imagery and emotion,
are those of Olympian hierarchy and organizational logic—*sans passion,
sans anger.*

CURTAIN

End of Act III

When I first presented some of the ideas in this chapter before a faculty
seminar at Goldsmiths College, University of London, the question was
raised: Am I not also utilizing the devices of Art in my analysis? Is not my
critical stance toward the author misplaced since I too might similarly
"put down" my own performance? This criticism invites me to provide
an analysis and a rationale for the status of the scientific document as
something worthy to be accepted as a "true" account. By invoking a
description of Science as Art, have I now diminished or effaced the claim
of Science to be doing Science and not Art?

These critics ask me to go beyond *showing* that scientific documents
can be examined as if they were works of art. They want me to *tell*
readers what I conclude from the performance: to produce a policy. I will
try to do that in this final section.

One possible response is that Waller has been deficient as a scientist.
Indeed, my critics at Goldsmiths felt that I myself had, through irony,
taken a tone of moral and intellectual superiority toward him: that I had
been a "smartass." Unfortunately, there is no denying it. The transformation of the author from competence to unawareness is implicit in
criticism. But that "deficiency" is not a personal failing, a breach in the
author's operation within the standards and canon of scientific method.
It is implicit and inherent in the enterprise of defining, describing, and
interpreting data through verbal or written communication insofar as
conclusions and generalizations imply meanings for action. That is what
I mean by having a culture.

My concern is with the conversion of statements of fact into statements
of policy, exactly the procedure used to produce conclusions of action
from descriptions of knowledge. It is precisely in the acts of developing
and presenting particular data as classified into general categories, the

very nub of theorizing and/or conclusionmaking, that acts of selection, of nomenclature, of artistic presentation and language emerge. Waller is not accused of "bad" science. His procedure is a normal part of the effort of scientific procedures to make sense out of the world and to couch that sense in language that will lead to activity.

To be relevant or significant, data must not only be selected, they have to be typified and interpreted. In doing this, language and thought are themselves the vehicles through which such relevance is conveyed. In Burke's terms they are "modes of action" (Burke 1950; 1945, p. xxii). They lead us to conclusions and thus to new perspectives. It is not that Science is "reduced" to Rhetoric and thus rendered corrupt and useless. It is rather that the rhetorical component is unavoidable if the work is to have a theoretical or a policy relevance. Thus an analysis of scientific work *should* include its rhetorical as well as its empirical component. Science is thus a form of action with meanings derived from its Art as well as its Science (White 1976). "Rhetoric *persuades;* it engages the active intellectual attention, as well as the emotive responses of the listener ... figurative language does not just *express* the pertinence of certain cultural axioms, it provides the semantic condition through which actors deal with that reality" (Crocker 1977, p. 46).

This analysis of Science as Literature is by no means inconsistent with "normal" science as a truth-begetting instrument. It points, however, to the multiple realities in which and through which Science may be construed. Some years ago I was driving across the country with a friend who was then employed as a radio announcer. On hearing a news broadcast with a stirring news event, I remarked, "Did you hear that?" My friend answered, "Yes. His diction is terrible." As Schutz (1970, pp. 245–62) and more recently Goffman (1974) have both shown and told, there are multiple realities possible in granting meaning to events and objects. What is important and significant, at least in the analysis of the drinking-driver literature presented here, is that such an analysis heightens our recognition of the ways in which the objects—in this case drinkers and drivers—are being transformed in a dramatic presentation.

But at another level, represented by my sections analyzing the transformations of meaning in the objects of policy, the dramaturgical and artistic components of Science are not so consistent with the view of Science as positive knowledge. When I examine them, my own words carry a ring of skepticism toward the claim that the policies presented by Waller flow from an objective body of knowledge. It is not that the author is "wrong" in concluding that drinking-drivers can be seen as problem drinkers. It is that his interpretation involves theater—it involves a performance and a presentation which contain an element of choice and which both enlist and generate a context, a set of meanings which give content and imagery to his data. The analysis of the document as a literary performance has revealed the human actions through which the transformation of the social drinker into the problem drinker has ocurred. It is not that the data are challenged. What is at stake, however, is the necessity of the interpretation and the close connection between that interpretation and its form of presentation, its artistic element. It is in underlining the tenuousness and ambiguity of conclusions that I cannot blink at having called into question the certainty and stability of scientific interpretation.

The Hidden Agenda of Moral Authority

What I am asserting may now be clearer. The process by which authority is established in the area of drinking-driving serves to hide from its users and from those toward whom it is used that there are moral choices by which selection and adherence are developed. The policy of attention to the impaired driver and of excoriation of drinking and driving is not alone the solution to a practical, technical problem of automobile safety. It cannot be defended only on grounds of practical, technical cognitions. That is what I have asserted in this part of my book. Alongside the technical, instrumental reasoning of the scientist there is the moral choice of the practical philosopher and the aesthetic creativity of the artist. The culture of instrumental reason does not operate apart from the culture of public problems.

I am therefore in agreement with Jurgen Habermas: "The new ideology is distinguished from its predecessor in that it severs the criteria for justifying the organization of social life from any normative regulation of interaction, thus depoliticizing them. It anchors them instead in functions of a putative system of purposive-rational action" (Habermas 1970).

If it cannot be defended on grounds of absolute scientific certainty, what then are the grounds of policy? What the scientific quest for absolute grounds has done is to hide the conflicts of sentiments and interests which are embedded in the admonition "If you drive, don't drink; if you drink, don't drive." It is not that this is a foolish admonition. My contention is that it also is a conclusion about moral values—an assertion of modes of behavior supported by some sentiments and interests but in conflict with others.

I turn now to the legal system and its definition of the drinking-driving phenomenon as a way of exploring that moral dimension of illusory authority.

Part Two   The Ritual of
                    Law: Creating a
                    Moral Order

On November 8, 1919, Glenn Townsend took Agnes Thorne for a ride on Lover's Lane in Kalamazoo, Michigan, in the course of which his Cadillac Eight roadster left the road and struck a tree near the fence line. A side of the auto caved in, injuring Mrs. Thorne so that some time later she died in the hospital of blood poisoning resulting from the wounds. Townsend was uninjured. After the crash he crawled out of the car and produced a bottle from which he drank and offered drinks to spectators. He was so drunk that he did not realize what had happened to the car or to Agnes.

Townsend was charged with and convicted of involuntary manslaughter. On appeal to the Michigan Supreme Court, Townsend's attorney claimed that though the intoxication while driving was a criminal act in itself, it should not, without further evidence of recklessness, be converted into manslaughter following a fatal accident. The court thought otherwise. (People v. Townsend, 214 Mich. 267, 1921; 183 NW 177; 16 A.L.R. 902).

> the purpose of the statute is to prevent accidents and preserve persons from injury, and the reason for it is that an intoxicated person has so befuddled and deranged and obscured his faculties of perception, judgment and recognition of obligation toward his fellows, as to be a menace in guiding an instrumen-

tality so speedy and high-powered as a modern automobile. *Such a man* is barred from the highway because he has committed the wrong of getting drunk and thereby has rendered himself unfit and unsafe to propel and guide a vehicle capable of the speed of an express train and requiring the operator to be in possession of his faculties.

....

It is gross and culpable negligence for a drunken man to guide and operate an automobile upon a public highway, and one doing so and occasioning injuries to another, causing death, is guilty of manslaughter . . . it was criminal carelessness to do so. [People v. Townsend, 16 A.L.R. 905, 906 (1921); italics mine]

The language of Justice Wiest is the language of condemnation. Townsend is more than a casual violator of the traffic rules; he has "obscured . . . obligation," "rendered himself unfit and unsafe," perpetrated an act of "gross and culpable negligence." He is "such a man," antisocial and dangerous, whether or not accident and injuries were incurred. He is a "menace."

This description of the drinking-driver as "killer-drunk" has been presented a number of times in this book. It forms the substance of much of newspaper and popular public statements. It has been the public attitude toward the drinking-driver continuously since the early 1900s when states began passing such legislation. The drinking-driver is a serious malfeasant; he is not the average citizen, the "natural man" who sometimes speeds, makes a left turn against a prohibiting sign, or otherwise acts in the foolish or perverse manner of you and me. He is epitomized in *People* v. *Townsend*. This decision and the set of attitudes embodied in it constitute the myth of the drinking-driver.

The myth of the "killer-drunk," stated in *People* v. *Townsend*, is both cognitive and moral. It builds on a view of the reality of alcohol and driving already analyzed in part 1. But it also builds on the moral premise of the flawed character of the drinker. In the language of the court, echoed and reechoed in the public condemnation of drinking-drivers, the driver who enters traffic under the influence of alcohol is a sinner against others. He is not the ordinary driver but one who has failed to live up to moral obligations. There is more to his offense than there is to that of the ordinary motorist who commits a traffic violation.

The myth of the "killer-drunk" organizes the cognitive and moral order of the world into a form which can be utilized to make sense out of the incidence of auto accidents and fatalities. As model, as iconic metaphor, it presents a narrative which constitutes a guide to understanding other events. As Mircea Eliade suggests, myths reiterated in ritual helped "primitive man to hold to the real." The myth of "killer-drunk," embedded in contemporary law, provides a similar "paradigmatic act": "By virtue of the continual repetition of a paradigmatic act, something shows itself to be *fixed* and *enduring* in the universal flux" (Eliade 1963, p. 140).

My intention in this and the next chapter is to describe and analyze the law of drinking-driving as a system of communications, not only in its manifest language but also in the metaphorical symbolism of its latent meanings. It is as seen semiotically, as part of a set of verbal and nonverbal signs and symbols, that law possesses a mythical property and its promulgation becomes public ritual (Barthes 1967, pt. 3; Hawkes 1977, chap. 5). As part of a system of law, the contrast between drinking-driving and other traffic offenses is essential to the communicative status of the "killer-drunk" message.

The Criminal Metaphor
and the Ambiguity of Traffic Law

The automobile drove through the opening of the twentieth century carrying a new force for violence and danger. It pushed aside the slower moving horse and the leisurely boat and ran a victorious race against the still competing railroad. In its pervasive and profound impact on American life the auto became the source of new public problems and new issues in the regulation of behavior. A law that had arisen to govern the greed of a laissez-faire rail industry had a difficult time when Everyman became his own locomotorist. The emergence of traffic law and its enforcement by police are the most visible signs of the automobile revolution in American daily life. The "traffic offense" has by no means a clear or unambiguous legal status. If the offense is definite its "criminality" is less so. The illegality of drinking-driving is even more ambiguous and puzzling in the scales of criminal justice and in the hands of courts, police, attorneys, and defendants. That perplexing ambiguity is the occasion of this part of the book. What is the significance of having a harsh and punitive attitude toward drinking-driving yet a lenient and accepting one toward other traffic offenses?

I want to examine law as a mechanism in the definition and solution of public problems. Much social study of law is directed to its possible utilitarian effects, directly in diminishing the behavior of DUIA (Driving Under the Influence of Alcohol) and indirectly in decreasing damage, injury, and death from automobile accidents. I am more attendant to the

less utilitarian but cultural attributes of law as an embodiment of meanings, a way to think about the phenomenon of drinking-driving or the
character of the drinking-driver. The utilitarian attributes are very often
discussed in social science and legal scholarship as the problem of deterrence or impact; the cultural are less often studied but are sometimes
defined as the symbolic properties of law.

In this chapter I shall examine the meaning of "criminal within the
law" as applied to traffic offense and the place of the drinking-driver
"within the law." My arena of study is law as an abstract but public set
of rules—opinions and decisions to which judges, lawyers, police, law
students, and professors may refer in the context of legal work. It is Law
with a capital L; the legislation and law of the legislatures and the appellate courts, the stuff of legal hornbooks and law review articles. But I will
also consider "the law" with a lower case l—its *impact* on behavior, on
what the police, lawyers, judges, and defendants do. In the next chapter I
will bring these two together and examine the relationship between the
cultural and the utilitarian dimensions of law on the one hand and the
judicial and courtroom levels of law on the other.

The Utilitarian Metaphor in American Law

Traffic law, like any branch of law, is a set of assertions from which can
be drawn implications about human behavior and human responsibility.
It is not only a set of orders or commands about what to do but also a
group of images of factual and moral character from which liability is
deduced. Analyzing traffic law, and drinking-driving as a legal issue,
carries me into the discussion of the conceptions of causation and liability
in American law and their applicability to traffic ordinances.

In part 1 of this work, I have used the analysis of metaphorical reasoning as a way of examining how social science research is presented
and the consequent way in which the research on drinking-driving has
yielded policy impacts. In many areas of symbol usage the idea of a "root
metaphor" is useful as a tool for clarifying and contrasting. This concept,
first developed by Stephen Pepper, recognizes that the structure of
thought in many areas reflects an analogy between the subject matter and
something already known, explored, and utilized as a model for understanding the new.

> The method in principle seems to be this: A man desiring to under-
> stand the world looks about for a clue to its comprehension. He
> pitches upon some area of common-sense fact and tries if he cannot
> understand other areas in terms of this one. The original area be-

comes then his basic analogy or root metaphor. . . . In terms of these
categories, he proceeds to study all other areas of fact. . . . He under-
takes to interpret all facts in terms of these categories. [Pepper 1966,
p. 91]

Whole bodies of thought can be made clearer and illuminated by utilizing
such metaphors to characterize the underlying structure of thought and
the assumptions on which specific studies and conclusions are based.[1]
Root metaphors lead to an understanding of the assumed reality on
which the perception of events depends (Auerbach 1953).

In earlier papers several sociologists, including myself, have made use
of metaphorical reasoning to examine types of nonconforming behavior
in the history of American institutions (Gusfield 1963a, Chap. 3; 1963b;
Aubert and Messinger 1958; Stoll 1975). Over the past hundred and fifty
years of American life, institutional responses to drunkenness and
drinking have proceeded from changing images of the deviant drinker. In
the early ears of the temperance movement, he was seen through the
metaphor of the *repentant sinner*. Defining his own behavior as immoral,
illegal, or both, he desired his own salvation. Like a repentant sinner he
accepted the institutional definition of his behavior as sinful or criminal
and thus a result of his personal choice and his fault. The responsibility
for mending his erring ways rested with the sinner.

Repentant sin has not been the only analogy. The metaphor of illness
has also been one of the root metaphors, especially in recent decades. The
perception of the drunkard as a *"sick"* person who has succumbed to the
"disease" of alcoholism has been a major form of analogical reasoning of
the period since Repeal. In this imagery of illness the resolution of the
problem, and the responsibility for it, pass from the sufferer to the professional medical practitioner. I shall analyze the development and consequences of the medical metaphor in alcohol policy in detail in a study
now in process (see also Room 1979; Schneider 1979).

Still a third metaphor has been that of the *"enemy."* Here the underlying consensus between the putative "deviant" and official agents that the
phenomenon is unfortunate, painful, and demanding of change is itself
absent. The distinction between conforming and nonconforming, deviant
and normal is in jeopardy and in conflict. The parties to the action, in the
past sinners and saved, sick and healthy, are now enemies. The current
"revolt" of homosexuals against their definition as "problem people" is
illustrative. They do not seek to be cured or absolved but to have their
practices recognized as legitimate, one among the varieties of sexually
permissible behavior. Here movements for normalizing or decriminaliz-
ing behavior formerly seen as "deviant" convert a religious, legal, or

medical problem into a political one. The application of the metaphor of deviance, with its implications of disapproval and immorality, is itself contested.

The metaphorical structure of reasoning in the legal process takes on political and social implications through the manner in which responsibility is imputed. Legal doctrines of fault and of strict liability carry divergent assessments of the elements of fact or reality; it is these assessments which really govern the imposition of sanctions and the attributions of a moral character. Traffic law is no less the embodiment of such metaphors.

Fault and Absolute Liability

The doctrine of the intentional act as the sine qua non of responsible legal behavior has been salient in Anglo-Saxon civil and criminal law for the past hundred and fifty years. Although often under attack, qualified, and changing, it continues as the major premise of much legal response to behavior. It implies that human action can be likened to that of a metaphorical model of rationality and utilitarian method. That model becomes the basis for attributions of crime or fault.

In the criminal law of Anglo-Saxon countries the doctrine of *mens rea* ("subjective element") and in torts the doctrine of fault as a basis for liability both presuppose an image of the human actor as a rational, foresightful individual who is responsible for the reasonably foreseeable consequences of his actions and who can be significantly influenced in action by the knowledge of and fear of punishment (Hart and Honoré 1959, chaps. 3, 9; Hart 1968, chap. 2; Friedman 1973, pt. 2, chap. 10, pt. 3; Gregory 1951). The idea that a negligent act is essential to tort liability makes judicial liability a consequence of fault—of utilizing a standard of care and foresight below that of the reasonable and prudent human being. It also presupposes that the actor is capable of reason and prudence and should have recognized the appropriate action. In criminal cases the requirement of a *mens rea* implies intentionality. People are required to act in accordance with a standard derived from the model of a rational and utilitarian human being; they are responsible for intended action and for harmful consequences which are their fault—deviations from such standards. As rational, utilitarian persons they can be dissuaded from non-conformity by knowledge and fear of punishments.

That an opposite view has appeared and even dominated Anglo-Saxon law at various times is indicative of the historical status of the metaphor of utilitarian behavior. Strict, or absolute, liability is not concerned with the motives, condition, or intentions of the actors but only with the character of their actions. In the dramatic pentad of Kenneth Burke (cf. chap. 4) doctrines of fault and intention highlight Person while those of strict liability highlight Acts. In other periods of legal history pre-adolescent children, mentally defective persons, physically handicapped people, and even animals and inanimate objects have been held guilty of crimes and punished in the same manner as "normal" adults.[2] The current debate over "no-fault" insurance is certainly evidence that absolute liability is far from a dead doctrine and that its existence has great pertinence for traffic law (Calabresi 1970; Blum and Kalven 1967; O'Connell 1971).

Whatever the status of strict liability in criminal or civil law, since the nineteenth century the conception of fault or intentionality as essential to responsibility has had great power in legislative and legal reasoning.[3] Action and behavior per se are not illegal; harm per se is not a matter for judicial punishment or financial redistribution. Excuses, mitigating circumstances abound. "Hence the self-willed deviant is morally reprehensible, while the unintentional wrong-doer is merely unattractive" (Stoll 1975, p. 195).

This utilitarian view of human behavior necessarily leads to punishment and reward as major springs which the law can use in inducing action or inaction in the potential lawbreaker. Punishment can deter; lack of punishment will generate law violations. As a principle of human behavior, the view that action is or should be influenced and governed by rational decision lies at the base of the deterrence doctrine and punishment as a "solution" to public problems. It is part of the popular and lay attitude that punishment deters and more punishment deters even more.

It must be emphasized that doctrines of limited liability, fault, negligence, and *mens rea* are far from being entirely matters of pragmatic instruction. They are also moral principles, influencing designations of moral character, deciding what is reprehensible and what is not. As H. L. A. Hart writes, "even though the Ming vase is just as broken by accident, by carelessness or by vandalism each is a different level of venality. The first is not a matter of liability and the latter is criminal" (Hart 1968, p. 136). They specify in what ways the good man is expected to act and justify the punishment and liability visited upon the criminal and the negligent. They constitute the stated standards of public morality. Doctrines of strict or absolute liability, in avoiding the distinction between good and bad intentions, appear less moralistic and more forgiving in tone even though they create a wider scope of responsibility.

The doctrine of fault and negligence provides a moral argument which rests on the character of the actor: he failed to meet a standard of right conduct. He did what he should not have done and is thus a person of lesser value and liable for damages. Doctrines which classify negligent acts and dangerous or riskful acts as normal and typical remove the onus of guilt and the determination of the moral character of the defendant. The doctrine of *mens rea* requires that the accused must be shown to have "intended to do the act or bring about the consequences" which constitute the crime (G. Williams 1961, p. 218). From this perspective, unintended consequences are not criminal.[4] The negligence which might make someone liable at civil law for damages is not sufficient to establish crime. Mere carelessness (with the exceptions that constitute gross disregard for consequences in reckless acts, manslaughter, and gross negligence) is not criminal even though people are hurt and property destroyed.

Yet here too the doctrine is breached and strict liability rears its head once again. The cases of statutory rape are dramatic and instructive. It is no defense to claim that the defendant was unaware of or mistaken about the minor age of the woman. Indeed, legislative action has often taken activities which were liable under tort law and turned them into crimes. For example, regulatory statutes concerning the sale of commodities generally carry criminal sanctions. Friedman uses as illustrative of this an 1898 New York State statute declaring it a misdemeanor for a silver merchant to represent as sterling objects containing less than a specified percentage of silver. While the "victim" might have sued at civil law, the matter and cost were not an appropriate remedy. The state assumed a duty as surrogate consumer. "The states and the federal government were invoking criminal law in one of its historic functions—a low-level, low-paid administrative aid" (Friedman 1973, p. 510).

Two points emerge from this analysis of torts and crime in American law. First, normatively there has been an underlying emphasis on the moral character of the individual actor as the determining element in construction of justice. Emphasis has been on the distribution of guilt rather than the distribution of loss; on "criminals" rather than "victims." This emphasis has been tempered, however, by the continuous use and increasing development of doctrines of stricter liability, which emphasize the distribution of loss and minimize the moral guilt of the individual actor. There has been some transition from stigma to insurance.

The second point is more sociological than legal. It is that legislatures and juries rather than judges have been responsible for stricter liability. From another standpoint, this has been a disposition to throw support behind the "victim" and to enjoin collective entities, such as corporations, governments, and organizations, to carry losses. The wide development of large-scale enterprise, of national and regional economic units and markets, and the interdependence of transportation has tempered common law conceptions of individual moral fault with more collective conceptions of insurance, loss distribution and administration.

This is the background to the emergence of traffic law. The size of the danger represented by the automobile, because of the speed at which vehicles are operated and the large number of them on the streets and highways, creates a problem of regulating and controlling traffic. The character of that body of law seems anomalous; it is criminal and comes from state action, and yet it is unlike the rest of criminal law in the very high magnitude of violations. How can its position in American law be understood? What is the justification for laws of traffic regulation?

Traffic Offenses and DUIA:
Ordinary Violations and Crimes

In a famous statement in 1915, Woodrow Wilson predicted that the automobile was sure to bring socialism to the United States. The poor and the middle classes would both see so marvelous and so convenient a mechanism available only to the wealthy, a situation which was bound to magnify their envy and resentment (Flink 1977; Rae 1971, p. 43). That the auto has not remained the plaything of the rich is a crucial part of the story of driving in America. If traffic laws may not fall with equal weight on rich and poor alike, they do bestow their curse on each with great bounty.

The possible violation of auto traffic law constitutes the most frequent form of contact between the police and citizens at all class levels. Auto theft is the most prevalent form of juvenile and adult reported crime. Police apprehend far fewer people for prostitution, indecent exposure, and assault and battery combined than for traffic violations. In 1976–77, there were approximately 4.8 million citations for traffic code violations in California municipal courts and approximately 8.7 million parking violations (Judicial Council of California 1978, p. 100). In 1976, there were about 116,000 arrests involving police custody for violation of a traffic offense, making it the third largest source of misdemeanor arrests. The largest violation was drinking-driving, with about 258,000 arrests, and the second was public drunkenness, with about 213,000 (California Department of Justice 1976, pp. 20–23). All together these three violations accounted for seventy-five percent of all the misdemeanor arrests. In 1976, traffic arrests involving custody and drinking-driver violations exceeded the total for *all* juvenile and adult felony arrests in California. When the central significance of auto accidents in civil suits and civil law is considered (Friedman 1973, chap. 7; McRuer 1963, pp. 54–55), it might well appear reasonable for an observer to see alcohol, the automobile, and the intersection of the two as the focus of contemporary American legal institutions.

But numbers alone do not generate significance, and the place and meaning of traffic violations in American culture and society are *not* given by count. If Everyman is a motorist and Everywoman equally so, then both are also traffic offenders, so ubiquitous is the lawbreaking indicated by such magnitudes. In most American states traffic offenses are criminal offenses, but a motorist apprehended for speeding, making a left turn improperly, or running a stoplight is seldom accorded the punishment at law or elsewhere given to the "common criminal." Failure to stop at a stop sign is not the act of a potential "killer." Within legal doctrine a difference is made even between the "ordinary violator" and the "criminal."[5] Some violations are more serious than others. Where within this frame of deviance and criminality is the drinking-driver to be found?

In 1900, long after the saga of the covered wagons had ended and the great golden spike of the Union Pacific had been hammered into the ground, the first automobile appeared in California. In 1901 local authorities moved in and were permitted by the state legislature to license autos. Despite their scarcity in 1905 the state of California passed legislation requiring a state registration fee of $1.00 and the display of a license number. By 1906 there were 6,248 registered automobiles.

Traffic laws came with growth. A 1905 law set speed limits of 10 mph in built up areas and 20 mph outside of towns (Nida 1971). By 1920 there were more than 600,000 registered vehicles; by 1930, more than 2 million; by 1950, more than 5 million; and by 1977, almost 17 million cars were licensed. California, like the rest of the United States, had seen the automobile change from an item of luxury in the equipment of the rich to a commodity of necessity in the living standards of most Americans at most income levels.[6]

The conflict between rich and poor which Woodrow Wilson feared the auto would produce in the United States never occurred. There are hints of it in early laws which regulated the auto, but by 1910 the mass market potential of the auto in America was evident, and the coming popularity of the auto for consumers was apparent (Flink 1977, chap. 1–2). A struggle between motorists of social position and income, who could afford the automobile, and populistic legislatures determined to limit the dangerous sport of the idling rich and to protect the plebeian horse is more apparent in British history than in American. The British motorists began to protect themselves against traffic legislation which placed fixed miles per hour rather than "reasonable and prudent" limits on speed, required licenses to be displayed, and otherwise sought to brake the individualism of the driver. In 1903 motorists formed the first of the major national automobile owners' associations which have continued to be a significant political factor in traffic politics in England (Plowden 1971, chap. 1; Cressey 1975), in clear contrast to the American Automobile Association with its largely insurance nature.

The railroad was a major symbol of the nineteenth century in the United States. It expressed the expansion of a people across the continent as well as into an industrial civilization. The automobile proclaimed a new style of life, one of personal control, power, and speed. As symbols, the collective, producing, capitalistic business enterprises of the railroad contrasted with the individualistic, familial, and consuming image of the automobile. Jesse James could attack the railroad as a gouging, plutocratic Devil, reaping unjust profits from its exploitation of the poor, the powerless farmer and the widows and orphans pauperized by accidental death. No such hero defended the horse against its remorseless replacement. The auto industry could serve as political target, but the individual owner and the motor car could not. The filmmaker could use ownership of an auto as a sign of wealth in the early twentieth century, as Orson Welles did in *The Magnificent Ambersons*, but that was soon pointless. In that compelling novel of poverty in the 1930s, John Steinbeck's *The Grapes of Wrath*, the truck even became a symbol of poverty through its dilapidated condition. The fact of ownership of an auto was not an occasion to depict wealth or even middle class existence.

The legislation governing the railroads was chiefly business law. It limited or liberated the industry. The traffic laws that govern the use of the auto are regulations which bear on most adolescent and adult Americans. Approximately 84 percent of American households in 1974 owned one or more cars, and 144 million Americans were licensed to drive (U.S. Department of Commerce 1978, pp. 650, 656). Studies may differ on whether or not white collar or blue collar workers, minorities or dominant groups are more likely to be apprehended for traffic offenses. Compared with other "criminal" offenders, traffic law violators seem more like the aggregate population than do any other category of arrested or apprehended offenders (Ross 1960; Cressey 1975).

The Ambiguity of Traffic Violation
as Criminal Behavior

I have put quotation marks around the word "criminal" in the sentence above as a way of indicating the ambiguity of referring to traffic offenses as crimes. Even applications and personal histories that ask about arrests and convictions exempt traffic offenses from scrutiny. For just that reason they should be of interest to the sociologist and the criminologist who attempt to understand more readily agreed upon phenomena like murder or failing to renew a fishing license.[7]

Arguing for a distinction between "wicked" and "errant" motorists, the British jurist Lord Devlin advocated reserving prison for "people who do what public opinion accepts as disgraceful or for those who defy the law." He added that respect for law has been lost because "we failed to distinguish between what was sinful and disgraceful and what was a failure to measure up to a required standard of conduct" (*Times* [London], October 21, 1960, in Hood 1972, p. 106n).

"Sinful and disgraceful" and "failure to measure up to a required standard of conduct"—that is a good beginning for the issue of traffic laws as crimes. Sociologists have spent much good time and foundation funds trying to define "crime," and I shall not try to duplicate that discussion.

The ubiquitousness of traffic offenses constitutes a part of the issue of their possible venality; the representative character of the traffic offender turns abnormality into the norm. The enormous magnitude of traffic violations as part of the total administration of justice has been evidenced above, by comparison with other offenses which meet clearer public judgments of "disgrace and sin," as Lord Devlin might see it. Even petty theft arrests are fewer than those for traffic offenses excluding drinking-driving.

The Legal Perspective

Considering traffic violations as criminal acts is difficult in three respects: as an issue at law, as a matter of police enforcement, and as an object of "citizen" perception. In law, traffic violations are criminal violations rather than civil wrongs. They involve an action of the governing body—state, township, municipality—against the individual offender. This includes a range of violations, such as improper turns, disregarding stoplights, improper passing, reckless driving, improper lane changes, speeding, drinking-driving, leaving the scene of an accident, and driving without a license or after license has been suspended. All of these, and other traffic violations, are contained in state vehicle codes. The bulk of traffic offenses are misdemeanors, although some, such as drinking-driving, hit and run, or reckless driving, are punishable by jail sentences. Our attention here is focused on misdemeanors rather than on felonies, such as drinking-driving involved in an accident and personal injury, gross negligence, and manslaughter with an automobile. Here the criminal status is less questionable and the defining term "felony" already presents a resolution of the problem (see Hood 1972, pp. 103ff).

In what sense are traffic offenses criminal acts? If the demand is made that a *mens rea* be shown, then the traffic offender is hardly a criminal. Intention to speed, to make a wrong turn, to pass in a nonpassing zone is not essential to commission of the wrong. Some states take the car by the horn and specifically exempt most traffic offenses from the criminal definition by referring to them as something other than misdemeanors or felonies. New York uses the term "traffic infraction" and declares that the offense should not be construed as a "crime" (Ross 1960, p. 239). In most states, however, traffic offenses are misdemeanors and punishable by fine—in some by jail sentences. Traffic law, however, represents one form of strict liability law. The action alone is sufficient to create the violation. Absence of intent is no excuse.

There is another aspect of the ambiguity of traffic laws that further deepens the difficulty in defining their violation as "criminal behavior." Unlike much criminal law, traffic violations involve no victims. No one has been hurt by acts of speeding, wrong turns, reckless driving, and drinking-driving unless an accident occurs, which places the act in another legal category. Neither are traffic offenses comparable to that category of "crimes without victims" about which so much sociology has been developed in recent years (Schur 1965). Such crimes generally include activities in which a supplier and a customer are engaged in illegal activity, such as gambling, prostitution, drug peddling, and abortion. An economic or sexual service is supplied or two people engage in behavior which the state, as third party, finds illegal. This analogy is not continued in traffic offenses. The manifest aim of traffic laws is to prevent the occurrence of actions which, assumedly, public policy deplores. The accidental injury, death, and/or property damage incurred in auto accidents is not a positive gain for anyone involved in the accidents. It is not intended and is not the usual outcome of traffic offenses. Traffic law is a form of administrative activity—the regulation of the flow of automobile traffic in a convenient and safe form.

Police Perspectives

From the standpoint of police, as Donald Cressey points out, traffic enforcement is proactive rather than reactive (Cressey 1975). Police discover motoring offenses by themselves. More traditional crimes are reported to them by victims or by citizens who are morally outraged. Traffic enforcement is either wholly administrative and regulatory, as in the case of the traffic police directly regulating traffic, or dependent on the initiative and direction of the police, unassisted by citizens. It is exemplified in the state highway patrols that drive up and down the highways, regulating traffic by their presence and by their observation of offenders. Essential to the traffic offense is visibility. If not observed by police, it is not acted upon. There is no victim to report it.

A second consideration in traffic enforcement is the social status of offenders. As I pointed out above, the automobile constitutes the major source of official contact between police and both working class and middle class citizens. Since many more traffic violations occur than are acted upon by police, the action of the police involves discretion, direction, observation, and chance. This leaves the police open to frequent charges of harassment of the citizen, and favoritism toward some and discrimination toward others (Gardiner 1969).[8]

> The discretion demanded of the police by motorists and openly granted the police in traffic affairs, has put the policeman in a game he cannot win. If he enforces the law in a routine and efficient way . . . he is damned for being inhumanly overzealous. But, if he exercises discretion . . . he is damned for operationalizing discriminatory attitudes. [Cressey 1975, p. 234]

The Citizen's Perspective

An American police expert, V. A. Leonard, writes that "traffic violators are not criminals and, obviously, do not fall into the same category as burglars, pickpockets and other members of the criminal gentry" (Cressey 1975, p. 217). Employers seldom construe traffic offenses as "crimes" and do not utilize them as barriers to consideration of an applicant for a position, even if the offenses are multiple (B. Johnson 1974). Unlike other misdemeanors, such as sex offenses, they are not deemed discrediting acts; they do not carry a stigma. Almost universally, citizens, and even often police and courts, take a benign view of the traffic offender. He is not seen as "criminal" in the sense of "sinful and disgraceful," as Lord Devlin put it. Hence the occurrence of traffic offenses in an otherwise unblemished career is not the occasion for opprobrium or moral condemnation. They are acts of ordinary people and not of ordinary criminals. In H. Laurence Ross's term, traffic violations are "folk crimes": "As opposed to 'ordinary criminals' folk criminals are relatively numerous, unstigmatized, and differentially treated in the legal process" (Ross 1960, p. 237). Drivers and their friends do not believe that they are criminals when they commit traffic offenses, do not act toward each other as if they were, and do not expect the police and the courts to do so either.

Such responses to traffic law are not a repetition of the early years of the automobile, when the law was seen as unfairly regulating the motorist by curbing his individual discretion. The citizen may resent paying for his minor sins of the road, but he does not expect to fall from grace by the turn of a wheel.

The common law on search and seizure during traffic stops makes the same point. The distinction between "ordinary violators" and "criminals" has provided a basis for determining when a police officer may search the person and/or the car of a motorist stopped for a traffic offense (Alwin 1976). Although courts differ on the rationale behind such a distinction, important criteria involve reasonable belief that the police may be under risk of violence. Thus there are underlying shared beliefs between the judge and the police about the character of "ordinary violators" and other stopped motorists. As one reviewer of traffic stop cases said, "a person would have to be a 'genius' to traverse the highways without violating some regulation of a state's motor vehicle code" (J. Hart quoted in Alwin 1976, p. 854). The "ordinary violator," without other evidence, gives no cause for an inference that he is dangerous. Traffic offenses, in usual circumstances, are small sins, minor delicts, and afford no basis for stigma, deviance, or abnormality, let alone crime.

Perhaps another useful way to think about traffic violations is as analogous to insurance payments. Making insurance payments is not a stigmatized act, carrying the hint of sin and incompetence for the motorist who is, by insurance, betting on the possibility that he may be "at fault" in an accident. Insurance has become the recognized accompaniment of driving, a necessary part of the costs of using the automobile on the American road. Most drivers do violate traffic laws from time to time and, from time to time, are apprehended and fined. These fines too are part of the anticipated costs of doing motoring in the United States, at all social levels.

The commission of a traffic offense, while a sign of improper driving, is not the action of a faulty person. Even the reasonable and prudent citizen occasionally lapses from the standards of reasonableness and prudence.

While such lapses may leave the driver "at fault" in a negligence case, they do not make him or her a "faulty person." Driving an automobile is not perceived, by law or by custom, as the act of perfect beings. That would demand too much of "normal" people. We must live in a world of imperfect beings, and we cannot demand more than a reasonable amount of rationality and prudence. Traffic violations are acts of reasonable people.

Criminal Law and the Drinking-Driver

In his searching discussion of search and seizure cases involving traffic stops, Ronald Alwin remarks that "unusual circumstance" can reasonably lead to the police officer's assumption that the instant case is an exception to the ordinary run of traffic violators. Such exceptions justify a "frisk" of the motorist and a search of the car. "Another exception, of course, occurs where there is reasonable cause to believe that the driver is intoxicated" (Alwin 1976, p. 367). That "of course" is the occasion, of course, for the sociologist to stop and examine that which is taken for granted.

Every state in the United States has a statute under which driving under the influence of alcohol is declared a criminal offense. In all of them the violation of the statute is punishable by a fine, imprisonment, and suspension or revocation of the driver's license. In most states license revocation is mandatory and jail also mandatory on second offense within a stated time period. In all states today further statutes define DUIA or "intoxication" in terms of a measure of the concentration of alcohol in the blood at the time of detention, usually between .10 and .15 miligrams of alcohol per 100 milliliters of blood.[9]

The California statute of 1971 is typical:

Section 23102. Misdemeanor drunk driving
(a) It is unlawful for any person who is under the influence of intoxicating liquor, or under the combined influence of intoxicating liquor and any drug, to drive a vehicle upon any highway. Any person convicted under this section shall be punished upon a first conviction by imprisonment in the county jail for not less than 30 days nor more than six months or by fine of not less than two hundred fifty dollars ($250) nor more than five hundred dollars ($500) or by both such fine and imprisonment and upon a second or any subsequent conviction, within seven years of a prior conviction, by imprisonment in the county jail for not less than five days nor more than one year and by a fine of not less than two hundred fifty dollars ($250) nor more than one thousand dollars ($1,000). A conviction

under this section shall be deemed a second conviction if the person has previously been convicted of a violation of Section 23101 of this code.

(b) If any person is convicted of a second or subsequent offense under this section within seven years of a prior conviction and is granted probation, it must be a condition of probation that such person be confined in jail for at least five days but not more than one year and pay a fine of at least two hundred fifty dollars ($250) but not more than one thousand dollars ($1,000).

(c) If the person convicted under this section is under the age of 21 years·and the vehicle used in any such violation is registered to such person, the vehicle may be impounded at the owner's expense for not less than one day nor more than 30 days. [*West's Annotated California Codes* 1971, Stats. 1959, c. 3, p. 1707, Section 23102, amended by Stats. 1959, c. 1282, p. 3433, Section 1; Stats. 1963, c. 177, p. 910, Section 1; Stats. 1963, c. 1990, p. 4072, Section 2; Stats. 1965, c. 1662, p. 3771, Section 1]

There were several amendments following 1971, but in 1977 and 1978 the state legislature passed a trial law involving recognition of diversionary programs and coupling drug use-driving legislation and drinking-driving legislation.

Two aspects of DUIA legislation will prompt my initial comments. First, drinking-driving is (except for driving under the influence of drugs) the only condition of the motorist specifically declared to be a legal offense. The state of "under the influence" is singular and special in its relation to automobile accidents. Other conditions of the person, although often viewed as increasing risk of accident, are not designated as legal offenses. Driving while sleepy, after ingestion of sedatives, during periods of acute depression, or following intense emotional trauma is not per se a declared misdemeaner. Such conditions may be significant items in civil law, where negligence is a question, or become matters of importance in determinations of recklessness in driving, but they are not categorically crimes or otherwise traffic offenses. Legislatures have not assayed statutes which even fix appropriate standards of the physical and/or mental condition required at all times for driving. While age has been shown in a number of studies to be associated with accidents (Zylman 1973; Carlson 1973), only some states have made special qualifications for licenses for persons over seventy and none limits licenses among the high-accident-prone age group of adolescents and young adults (16–25). Although age differences are reflected in insurance rates, traffic laws make no distinctions based on age, sex, or any of the conditions associated with higher accident risk other than drinking and the use of drugs.

The second matter of comment is the higher punishment prescribed for drinking and driving as compared with other traffic offenses. License suspension is mandatory. The fines are higher and the jail sentences longer and more often mandatory than those permissible for the "ordinary violation" of traffic laws. The drinking-driver is arrested and placed in custody; the traffic violator is cited and permitted to return to traffic. The boundary between the two "crimes" is made explicit when the DUIA offender is apprehended, put in the back seat of a squad car in which the inside door handles have been removed, read his rights, and possibly handcuffed. If he has not committed murder he has visibly done something more heinous and more "serious" than make an improper left turn, run a stop light, or drive sixty-five miles an hour in a fifty miles-per-hour zone. If he is not yet a full-fledged "criminal" neither is he "just a traffic offender." Both he and the police stage a dramatization of his moral failing (Manning 1977).

The use of alcohol in the case of the DUIA offense heightens rather than lessens the response of law. In torts and common law drinking is not in itself proof of negligent conduct.[10] In DUIA it is not only an offense per se under conditions of driving, but it makes the offense more than "ordinary."[11]

Yet there is much that is similar in the DUIA laws to those of other traffic offenses. The issue of *mens rea* is excluded, as it is in other traffic violations. The intent of the motorist to have become intoxicated need not be shown. Even awareness of being under the influence is not essential to establish the criminality of the offense. The frequent claim of the driver—"But, officer, I know I'm not drunk"—has no legal standing beside the intoxicometer score of .10 or more. Neither does the motorist's "defense" that he didn't realize this was a no-turns zone. Like other traffic legislation, driving while under the influence of intoxicating liquor is strict liability, *malum prohibitum.*

Like traffic laws, the DUIA legislation is administrative in character. It acts to regulate an orderly and safe flow of automobile transportation, to administer traffic, to prevent accident. A California case illustrates the argument. Robert Chatham drove his automobile while under the influence of alcohol and struck a motorcycle, inflicting severe injuries on the rider. Evidence established that Chatham's driving had been negligent. He was convicted in a lower court of felony DUIA, since the DUIA was a misdemeanor that resulted in injury. Chatham sought to have the offense declared a misdemeanor. His lawyer argued that had the same negligent driving occurred while Chatham was sober, it would have been only a misdemeanor of reckless driving. Evidence had not established any relation between the condition of being under the influence and the negligent acts. The court reaffirmed the lower court's judgment: "It is not the receiving of the injury that concerns the state, but the causing of such injuries which the state seeks to minimize" (People v. Chatham, 43 Ca. App. 2d ser. 298 [1941]).

But there is another sense in which DUIA legislation is unlike traffic legislation and more like crimes without victims. In the distinction between "ordinary violators" and "criminals," crimes like prostitution, abortion, drug use, and gambling occupy an ambiguous place. The "victim" is as much a consumer as a person damaged. He or she is not a complainant. It is the behavior per se that is reprehensible. DUIA shares much of this status. There is no specific victim, as there is none in other traffic violations. It is the behavior itself which is singled out for greater disapproval than are other driving offenses. In the Chatham case, Justice Pullen wrote that the legislature is "doing all it can to discourage such a *menace*" (italics mine).

Embedded in the DUIA legislation is the image of the "killer-drunk" and the hostile, antisocial menace. DUIA is presented as something more than a "folk crime," more heinous than exceeding the speed limit or passing in a no-passing zone. Like crimes without victims, DUIA is deviant behavior. The enforcement of drinking-driving legislation, from this perspective, is as much a matter of public morality as it is of public convenience and safety. The drinking-driver is a public criminal and a faulty person.

Law, Alcohol, and Traffic Policy

The automobile is inherently a risk taking machine, given the current nature of its construction and the state of the highways. The driver, other drivers, and pedestrians are all aware of the dangers which exist in each lane and around each curve. Perfect driving is a standard meant for angels on some heavenly highway. The "normal citizen," the "average driver," the "reasonable and prudent man" takes chances every day as he or she sits behind the wheel and makes quick decisions in the face of oncoming traffic. Risk is gauged and action taken. Traffic laws are broken every minute, sometimes with intent and sometimes without it. Neither the courts, the police, nor drivers see speeding as abnormal, lane changing without signaling as heinous, or taking an improper left turn as criminal. (They do not result in arrest and custody.) The relation of these to auto safety and the risk of collision is well known, but these offenses are accorded only minor status as crimes and none of the moral condemnation of drinking and driving. What Willett found in England, interviewing offenders in "serious" motoring offenses (which included not only DUIA but such offenses as driving recklessly and failing to stop after an accident), is the case today in the United States: those who also had criminal records for nonmotoring offenses distinguished between motoring offenses and "real crimes" which they defined as "breaking, burglary, and assault" (Willett 1964, p. 302).

Traffic enforcement is administrative regulation. Its rationale is deterrence. It is believed that unless the standard of care is upheld, motorists will lose the added and needed goad of punishment to take adequate care and avoid known risks. The belief exists among many police that just "showing the flag" by driving along the highway or the streets will diminish risk taking behavior, and thus "accidents."[12]

In the arena of traffic the law does not appear as an agent of public morality. The police are not the champions of goodness against public indecency. The law presents itself as the regulator of convenient and safe public intercourse, a neutral instrument of a rationalized, technologically interdependent society.

Are traffic offenses "crimes"? The ambiguity of the status may be explained in a variety of ways (Hood 1972, chap. 5). Marxists might reason that the "leniency" of traffic punishment is class justice. Since traffic offenses are the crime of both white collar and blue collar workers, they are responded to as those of "our kind" and given less significance. While studies indicate the greater representation of the middle classes in motoring than in other "typical" crimes, traffic offenses, including drinking-driving, are not "white collar" crimes (Willett 1964; Hood 1972; Ross 1960). From another viewpoint the "folk crime" character of traffic "crimes" stems from the random nature of apprehension, including the lack of *mens rea* itself. This gives the conviction or citation the appearance of a chance event, not a matter of intent or of uniform enforcement (Hood 1972, pp. 97–98, esp. fn.3). The enormous magnitude of traffic violations, as they occur in daily driving, and the chance elements of risk in driving make the process of damage and injury from the use of automobiles a matter of "accident" rather than intentionality. Why then should the driver see his or her normal lapse from perfect driving as peculiarly menacing to public safety?

The motorist and the law are engaged here in a game of fictional outrage. Occasional apprehension and fine for driving delinquency are part of the costs of driving an automobile, a gentle reminder to an otherwise adequate taker of risks. As long as all the parties to the infraction treat its criminal status as a fiction, the resulting apprehension, citation, and fine can be seen as one of the hazards of driving, not as the encounter between a criminal and an upholder of public morality. There is an analogy, in some respects, to the prostitute who pays her periodic fine and returns, like the motorist, to cruise the streets. It becomes a game whose legitimacy is understood by drivers, police, and the courts.

Experience with traffic violations and with being a traffic offender is so ubiquitous among the American population that I can assume it among my readers. Not so with drinking-driving. A great many of you have probably been apprehended, cited, and fined for some traffic offense some time in your life. Whether or not you have ever driven while under the influence, arrest and punishment for DUIA cannot be assumed a part of your experience. The legal position of the DUIA offense is in the ambiguous zone of criminality and moral offense.

Is DUIA acted on as if it were traffic offense or Lord Devlin's "sin and disgrace"? One offender, being interviewed by a probation officer in a San Diego County jurisdiction, objected to the condition of probation that required his attendance at a class on drinking and driving. He asked to be given a fine without all this attention. That attitude takes DUIA, like other offenses of traffic, as an accepted risk of driving. At the other pole of attitudes is the remark, though rhetorical, of former attorney general Ramsey Clark, opposing the suggestion following the Martin Luther King riots that police shoot at looters. With some sarcasm, he called for the shooting of drunken drivers: "What is it that causes some to call for shooting looters when no one is heard to suggest the same treatment for a *far deadlier* and less controllable *crime*?" (*Los Angeles Times,* Jan. 19, 1975, pt. V, p. 6; italics mine).

Turning from the law of the books to the law of the courts and the streets, we ask which is the legal status of DUIA?

The Ambiguity of Drinking-Driving: Fault without Censure

In the Gilbert and Sullivan operetta it was a fictional and musical Mikado who sought to make "the punishment fit the crime." A more workaday and utilitarian legal institution has had less aesthetic purposes— attempting to make punishment prevent crime. The results of such efforts have not seemed sufficiently successful to warrant a continued belief in the efficacy of punishment as a universal strategy to bring about licit behavior.

The observer in an American courtroom looks at a daily ceremony which celebrates the majesty and authority of the law. The black-robed judge, the American flag, the armed police officer, and the clerk's call to bring the audience to their feet on the judge's entrance—these are the outward signs of an imputed inward power and respect. Such impressions of majestic omnipotence dissolve when the same observer contemplates the continued occurrence of illegal actions, the large number of persons who continue to commit and recommit the same or allied offenses, the high number of crimes unreported, undetected and unsolved, and the limited efficacy of the criminal punishment system in reducing either crime or recidivism.[13] Surely my fictional observer can conclude that while the majesty of the law is very real, it is nevertheless an emperor without clothes. That mood of skepticism and disillusion is a premise for me in the remainder of this chapter.

The jurist studying law finds its embodiment in the norms and precepts of judge-made opinions or the carefully worded substance of legislative enactments. The law student may look around at the thousands of volumes of appellate decisions, government statutes, municipal ordinances, and legal summations on the shelves and conclude that here, in this book lined library, is "the law" for his or her case. Such is the view of law as a system of rules, a normative order which is learned and learnable.[14]

For sociologists, as for legal realists in general, the library is a misleading place to spend all of one's time in studying the law. As in most institutional areas, the sociologist does not take the "official" or the public statements of an institution as a working blueprint of its behavior. From the perspective of the sociologist, law includes the day-to-day activities of judges, police, prosecutors and defense attorneys, and clients and disputants. It is found in courtrooms, offices, on the streets, and wherever legal personnel use the rules of law and act with reference to them.[15]

The Negotiated Reality of DUIA

This dichotomy between law as a normative order and law as the behavior of courts and law enforcement agents is very much part of the standard fare of social science menus. On the one hand there are general rules of behavior and punishment entailed by infractions; on the other there is the recognition that infractions often go unreported, undetected, and unpunished. At the level of public attention there is the persistent and shrill cry for more punishment; at the level of daily events there is the negotiation between lawbreakers and law enforcers and the continued occurrence of prohibited acts. The drinking-driving phenomenon clearly replays this scenario. On the public level of law and the media of public communications it is criminal behavior—easily perceived to be like other crimes; on the working level of daily routine it is mostly undetected and unapprehended. When drinking-driving becomes a matter of enforcement attention, its existence is ambiguous and a matter of policy and social construction, largely responded to by fine. The effectiveness of enforcement in deterring accidents and death is likewise ambiguous and uncertain. As a matter of Law, drinking-driving is a criminal offense; as a matter of law it is not more than a traffic violation.

From one standpoint, "the law" has a universalistic character; it represents a judgment of a situation irrespective of the persons involved in the individual case; its subject is rules, not persons. Thus, as John Noonan has complained, even the language of legal decisions "hides" the personal facts of the protagonists; whether the defendant is rich or poor, male or female, black or white, thin or fat (Noonan 1976). Yet in the routine actions of daily life, such considerations are by no means absent; they are part of the way in which a rough justice is meted out and a sense of fairness maintained. So too, despite the existence of legislative or judicial norms, common behavior may adhere to other standards, other values. All of these facts and values seem to be at work in the ways in which practical contingencies, accepted social norms, interests, and powers operate in daily life. The idea of law as a statement of a moral reality, a consensus about acceptable and unacceptable behavior, is seemingly contradicted in the process by which the drinking-driving event becomes a "fact" in judicial practice. Here it is a negotiated reality, not a clear and consistently discovered event. It is a result of values, organizational constraints, pragmatic contingencies, and bargaining between the relevant parties, considerations that make it a matter of the choice, discretion, and power of the several parties interacting in the process of law. It is in this sense that "driving while under the influence of alcohol"is a social construction—a creation of human beings and not a direct representation of an objective fact.

The dichotomy between these two realms of law as normative order and law as behavior is not the same as that often described as causing the difficulty of applying rules, or generalizations, to specific cases—what H. L. A. Hart refers to as the "open texture" of legal rules (Hart 1961, pp. 120–32). Hart's problem is how a given case can logically be fitted under a variety of rubrics and rules. What I am pointing to is how general rules of legislation or of common law become open to new sets of political and moral considerations not involved in or present in their original creation. A new, less formal set of rules, a different realm of law is thus constituted.

At each stage human beings make decisions arrived at through a variety of factors. The final product—a specific sentence for DUIA—is not a mechanical process, a direct one-to-one response to unambiguous events.

The social organization of the police, the court, the local judicial bar, and even the distribution pattern of drinking establishments and of drinking habits must be taken account of in order to understand how DUIA becomes reality.

The Decision to Arrest

There are two beliefs about drinking-driving that are significant to my interpretation. One is the recognition that there are neither victims nor beneficiaries involved in the misdemeanor of DUIA. No one reports the "crime" to the police. Secondly, drivers arrested for DUIA constitute a very small tip of a very large iceberg of all drinking-drivers. As one police officer said to me, "There are a helluva lot of them out there."[16]

In both ways DUIA is like a traffic offense. No one is injured by the offense per se: its rationale is wholly preventive. Like a "folk crime" it is committed by a large segment of the population and understood as something of lesser public offense than other crimes.[17]

The legal offense of DUIA (California Vehicle Code Section 23102A) shares with both "victimless crimes" and other traffic offenses the quality of arising from police observation rather than from reports of victims. Unlike most arrests these are proactive rather than reactive; they are observed by police rather than reported to them by others (D. Black 1971; LaFave 1965, chap. 1; Rubinstein 1973). In the routine round of activities, arrest is not the typical outcome of police-citizen encounters. Whether or not a motorist is suspected of DUIA and arrested on a charge of DUIA are decisions almost entirely dependent on police initiation and interpretation. The officer must observe the event, decide it merits investigation, interpret behavior as establishing a presumption of DUIA and decide to arrest, place the citizen in custody, and initiate the procedure for establishing a blood-alcohol count.

The observation of DUIA differs from that of the ordinary traffic action. DUIA is less directly observable. A speeding car is "clocked"; an illegal left turn is perceived. DUIA is a condition of the motorist, not an action. It may be inferred from two sets of data; the driving behavior of the motorist and/or the condition of the motorist—his or her physical appearance, breath odor, speech and/or performance on a Field Examination in which routine motor acts are demanded, such as touching the tip of the nose with one's index finger. Ultimately the inference of DUIA is given support or rejection by the breathalyzer, blood or urine test taken after arrest.[18]

The condition of the motorist is not observable in a moving car. The distances between moving cars are too wide to permit the police officer to scrutinize the physical appearance of the driver. What can be observed are the driving patterns of the motorist, such as weaving between lanes, and the situation or context in which the motorist is driving, such as emerging from the area of a party or the parking lot of a bar. But these only establish suspicions. Under the legal constraints of "probable cause" the officer cannot stop cars at random (Wilson 1976, pp. 54–55; LaFave 1965, chaps. 11, 12). He must be able to demonstrate that there was adequate reason to suspect a felony was being committed or show that a misdemeanor had been observed "in his presence" and therefore there was no possible time for a warrant to be issued. Any routine traffic offense, even a broken light, can be the occasion for a command to "pull over and stop" and intoxication then perceived. The observation of DUIA might also be made as incident to an accident which the officer is investigating. But there must be an opportunity to make a closer inspection than given by driving alone. Such considerations indicate some of the reasons for the second characteristic of the drinking-driving offense—the very small number of arrests in ratio to the high incidence of the event itself. In general, arrest is a process in which police discretion is of great importance and deeply affected by the social organization of the police, local policies, social characteristics of potential arestees, and the cultural categories and beliefs of police (Skolnick 1966; Rubinstein 1973; Cicourel 1968; Reiss 1971; Wilson 1978; Manning 1977). Elements of selectivity, chance, local arrangements, and police organization are even more significant in the case of drinking-driving than in either reactive crimes or events more directly observable. Like traffic offenses DUIA depends on the proactive selection and judgment of the officer, especially his facility in being in the place at the time and his willingness to assess the driver as possibly DUIA. The process of negotiation, the understanding of observed behavior in ambiguous situations, and the acts of discretion in police action are illustrated in the following two cases from observations of a police drinking-driving squad action:

1. Travelling northeast on Rosecrans Avenue [a large business and shopping avenue with a major thoroughfare] we observed a late model Datsun pickup truck weaving from one side to another but within its own [curb] lane. At an intersection with a side street, the officer turned on the overhead light and the driver pulled to the curb. In conversation, he explained his poor driving by the fact that he was "tired" after the end of his work as a bartender. He was going home to get some sleep before going to work on another job. He denied that he had been drinking and offered, without prompting, to take a

field sobriety test. The officer did not smell any alcohol on his breath. He [the officer] explained why the driver had been stopped on the basis of the weaving, admonished him to drive more carefully and waved him on without a traffic citation. Afterwards, the police officer told me that the man had staggered when he got out of the truck, and he [the officer] thought he had a "deuce" until he noticed that the man had one leg that was shorter than the other. (Paraphrased from field notes, October 1971)

2. Travelling northward on Midway Drive [A major throughfare and an area of many bars] the officer observed a vehicle leaving a parking lot of a bar just ahead of us. It came out at a high speed, spinning the rear tires and "fishtailing" [the rear end of the car weaving from side to side] as it turned left and into the parking lot of a motel, without signalling for a turn. At his first observation of a traffic offense, the officer turned on the overhead light on the car roof and then the siren. Even when he got within six feet of the car, by then parked in the motel lot, the driver still seemed unaware of his presence. After some preliminary conversation, and the odor of alcohol on the suspect's breath, the officer asked him to take the field sobriety test, which the motorist failed. He was arrested, taken into custody and scored above .15 on the breathalyzer. [Gusfield 1972; paraphrased from field notes, November 1971]

The decision to arrest on a DUIA citation is by no means a clear-cut response to an unambiguous set of circumstances. Not only must the police officer reach a factual conclusion, often with the negotiating "story" of the driver as one interpretation of the events. He must also decide that the offense "warrants" the charge; that the breathaliser will sustain the inference of drinking beyond the legal limit; that the time entailed in apprehending, testing, and filing the reports is worth it. He can interpret the action as proper, cite the motorist for a "routine" traffic offense, or arrest him on a DUIA citation. Organizational features enter into the decision as well. The policies of the department, the previous arrests for DUIA, the general or special character of the police all influence such actions.[19]

Steps along the Way to Being an Offender

The decision to arrest is only the first in a series of acts through which the legal process comes to define and describe a motorist as a "drinking-driver," duly charged, arraigned, tried, and convicted of violating Vehicle Code Section 23102A in California. The stages that lead to a conviction are summarized in figure 4. There is no automatic or clear designation of

Figure 4   Stages and Alternatives in the Generation of a DUIA Conviction

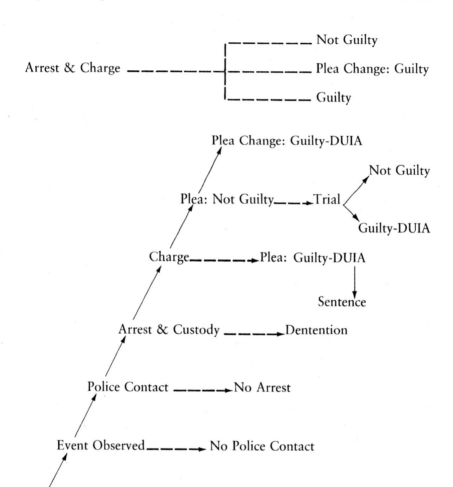

what will happen at each stage. Instead negotiation between defendants, attorneys, judges, and police officials determine what will occur— whether or not the case will proceed and, if so, under what designation. In the San Diego County study, there were considerable differences among the various courts about the policy of plea bargaining. In the San Diego City court more than half of those arrested were charged with something other than DUIA, usually "reckless driving." In other courts in the county this was less often the case, but in none were more than eighty per cent charged as arrested. In all of the courts more than ninety per cent eventually pleaded "guilty." Again the negotiations between defending and prosecuting attorneys operate to create a judgment-of-fact DUIA or none (Rosett and Cressey 1976; Blumberg 1967a, chaps. 5, 8).

What appears on a record as a matter of fact has not been a result of unambiguous actions and clear legal direction. The plea bargaining process is itself a form of political negotiation in which such matters as possibility of proof, inconvenience and expense of trial, degree of intoxication (the blood-alcohol level), the character, family status, and past legal record of the defender all operate along with the policy of judges toward DUIA.

The justice and wisdom of plea bargaining have been much debated and discussed. Its frequent use in American courts is undeniable (Rosett and Cressey 1976; Mileski 1971; Cloyd 1975). Both practical exigencies of courtroom organization and operation and considerations of justice are at work in influencing prosecuting attorneys and defense attorneys to bargain and judges to accept the procedure. It is, however, a description of American law and legal process that stands in contrast to the adversarial arrangements which the model of the trial would have us believe to be the reality of American justice. Instead of attorneys attacking each other at arm's length in defense of their clients there are legal personnel cooperating with mutuality and agreeing to maintain the fictional event of combat as if it were reality. Instead of a legal response to an event there is a negotiated settlement to decide what event will be described (Blumberg 1967a, b).

The judicial process operates with a more graduated definition of the reality of driving while intoxicated than the legislation describes. The process of justice in this instance is one of negotiation between the various interested parties. It is bargaining that depends upon a variety of situational factors and is a matter of policy. It is important to stress this, since it means that the conviction for DUIA is, as with arrest, a function of a process of interaction between parties. It makes the records of persons ambiguous and the use of convictions to indicate the total number of events of drinking-driving that have been detected in the past a dubious procedure. What is at issue between negotiating parties is not so much the question, Was the motorist involved in driving the automobile under the influence of alcohol? but rather, What kind of punishment shall be brought to bear upon him? and consequently, What shall be the consequences to the motorist for his act? The evidentiary question, Is he guilty of drinking-driving? is not really at stake. The process is a defining of crime and punishment, not a stating of facts (Sudnow 1965). In the beginning was the Word; shortly after came the Record.

Crime and Punishment

The problem of negotiation and plea bargaining is that of fitting punishments and crimes. The object is neither sublime nor ridiculous. The sentence is the point of contention not only in bargaining but in public displays of dismay over the alleged leniency of judicial processes in drinking-driving cases. "If only the courts were tougher" is a constant plaint in public denunciations of drinking-driving. The following is an example from the *Buffalo Evening News* castigating the courts for "judicial mollycoddling": "As a result of a total breakdown in law enforcement and the district attorney's 'game plan' an estimated 6,000 drunk drivers will be poured back onto Erie County streets—the majority of them unpunished and with little incentive for rehabilitation" (quoted in Galanter 1976, p. 11). At another level, there is the frequent criticism by police officials, prosecuting attorneys, or citizens that court leniency in punishing is responsible for the continuation of the drinking-driver problem. In 1976, the Los Angeles city attorney put the theory in a nonjudicial form by publicly advocating a higher fine and a two-day jail term for all first offenders: "The threat of jail is the best deterrent I know of [to drunk driving]!" (quoted in *Los Angeles Times*, July 3, 1976, p. 21).

Such demands for tough policies in sentencing usually end with a whimper rather than a bangful of jail sentences and heavy fines. The threat of higher punishment is met by defense attorneys' threats of more jury trials. Is the drinking-driver offender treated as a criminal? as an ordinary traffic violator?

Despite the array of potentially crimelike sentences made available by legislation, in the practical, routine negotiations of courtrooms the drinking-driving arrestee comes off not much worse than the routine traffic offender. The typical, common, and usual disposition is a fine of at least $100 and rarely more than $250.[20] Jail sentences are uncommon even with repeaters, and even when given are most often suspended. While license revocation or suspension is mandatory, it is seldom used against first offenders. Such low levels of enforcement indicate a status of traffic offense rather than crime elsewhere as well as San Diego (Ross 1976; Ross and Blumenthal 1975; Zylman 1970; Robertson, Rich, Ross 1973; Galanter 1976; Gusfield 1972; Shover et al. 1977).

This limited enforcement of the judicial and legislative classification of drinking-drivers as morally corrupt underlines the fact that a different perspective on drinking-driving exists situationally, in the particulars of the routine transaction of daily events, rather than in the public pronouncements of official governing agents. The failure to revoke or suspend driving licenses is one illustration of the ambiguities of public and of routine law. Where the automobile is essential to daily work, as in Southern California, judges appeared reluctant to be so punitive to the defendant and to his family. Further, they were aware of studies concluding that license revocation, in California and elsewhere, is as much honored in the breech as in the conformity (Coppin and Van Oldenbeek 1965).[21]

Whatever its status in the legislative corridors and councils, in the appellate courts, or in the newspapers, in day-to-day enforcement and adjudication DUIA is treated *as if*, like other traffic offenses, it is the normal behavior of motorists. Perhaps a Buffalo district attorney expressed this when he said: "DWI defendants aren't criminals—they're vice-presidents of banks, stock brokers, truck drivers" (Galanter 1976, p. 69).

The Legal Style as Public Culture

In a sense the differing levels of the legal process described in this chapter are inherent in much of human life and probably accentuated by the large-scale, diverse, and interdependent character of modern societies. The law that law students study, that law reviews note, and that legislators and common law judges assert is a more abstract statement of principles than the prescriptions and practices which govern the actions of courts, police, and attorneys (Rubinstein 1973; Blumberg 1967b). This is an instance of a more general disparity between the idealized nature of cultural symbolizations and the situational nature of actions. Human behavior occurs in specific contexts which present pragmatic problems in which immediate interests and goods and evils are symbolized and stated in instant and concrete cases. In the form of general principles, the set of statements provided by culture are often belied by behavior. The tension between the priest and the prophet is a persistent theme in human life. Dostoevsky portrayed it with clarity in the story of the Grand Inquisitor in *The Brothers Karamazov*. Christ returned to earth is again condemned, this time by his own Church. The stable and predictable society symbolized by the priests is threatened by the uncompromising program of the prophet whose appeal to Culture, as a set of general, abstract, and ideal norms, is more than the world of sinners and practical people can accept.

Judged by the abstract standards of official and publically enunciated norms, social institutions are almost always corrupt—negotiated schemes between people of specific interests and powers. A great many sociological studies have been illustrative of this, finding the kernel of practicality under the shell of ideal principle.[22] They have engaged in a process of irony which debunks official statements and programs, as I have done in this chapter and throughout this work. But that debunking is not my major aim. I want to examine the abstract and general character of law as itself an attribute with a level and a "seriousness" of its own; an aspect sui generis and constituting a dimension apart from the way in which it affects the law in routine legal procedures of enforcement.

There is a customary disjuncture between legal scholars and sociologists which makes them frequently talk past each other. When legal scholars talk about "the judicial process" what they refer to is the style and logic of appellate court decisions rather than what the sociologist refers to—the acts of police, attorneys, and courts (Levi 1949; Cardozo 1921; Ross 1976; D. Black 1976). This disjuncture is itself an instance of levels of culture. At one level the law itself creates a public culture through the definition and elaboration of principles of law. That public culture is not an accurate map to the geography of courts and police, but an abstraction. It is its abstract quality and its public character that commands my attention here.

In reflecting on primitive and modern law Paul Bohannon has written: "Law is one of the devices by means of which men can reconcile their actual activities and behavior with the ideal principles that they have come to accept in a way that is not too painful or revolting to their sensibilities, and in a way that allows ordered . . . social life to continue" (Bohannon 1973, p. 308). This is an excellent description of the routine process of law described in this chapter, but it is not appropriate to the judicial process as a public ceremony in which legislation and common law is defined and refined into a set of working principles, to what is meant when the layman asks, What is the Law? The ideal principles to

which Bohannon alludes are themselves the product of the judicial process as it becomes embodied in the Anglo-American legal institution.

The form of a legal statement is symbolic of the public character of its
message; it presents its commands in a style which underlines the official,
societal character of the principles. Laws are *not* specific reactions of
particular people to particular conditions and persons. The style in which
legislation is announced and judicial results promulgated is public in the
sense that it is visible and open, that of a body speaking for the society.
In the process, that society as an objective "fact" is both assumed and
created. In stating a general set of principles as publically held norms,
laws grant an orderliness to the diversity of behaviors that enable us to
"see" a society (Gusfield 1979a).

The style of DUIA legislation is illustrative of the universality, consistency, and rationality which also characterize the judicial decision. The
statute has the trapping of universality and certainty. It gives no indication of the particularism and negotiation in which police, attorneys, and
courts act. The definitive (note the word) version of the drinking-driving
statute is stated in the vehicle code and thus also made a recorded and
permanent statement. There is no comment on it, no history of its passage, no indication of the vote entailed in its passage or of who initiated
it. The date of its passage is irrelevant as long as it is current. Such
material is available but is neither included nor relevant. It is the action of
the state and as such possesses a quality abstracted from its origins or its
applications. It has finality and definiteness. "It *is* unlawful..." "*Any*
person convicted...*shall* be punished..." (italics mine). It is the language of assumed obedience, of definite authority.

The style of common law similarly presents a public culture in the form
of abstract rules or principles, even though they emerge in the context of
specific cases. As Walton Hamilton once wrote: "There is in fact something universal about the judicial process...because courts keep records
which are read and criticized. If businessmen, university faculties,
baseball players or debutantes were forced to set down the good reasons
for the decisions which make up their streams of conduct, the result
would be a crude miniature of the judicial process. In law the rationalization of judgment has become a convention" (quoted in Wetter 1960,
p. 54).

For the lawyer attempting to determine legal direction governing the
case of his client the past decision of an appellate court (for or against the
plaintiff) or the order directing how a lower court should proceed is not
the significant "fact" of the opinion (Friedman 1975, chap. 2). It is the
statement of a rule or principle by which the court explains the reasoning

which ostensibly led to the decision that is the principle directing future cases. Indeed much of the discussion of cases by lawyers is about the *ratio decidendi* (the decisive reasons) of particular cases (Levi 1949; Goodheart 1972; Stone 1972).

The legal decision is couched in the style of impersonal rule. Despite the differences between individual cases which engross law students in their endeavor to reconcile seemingly conflicting judicial opinions, the emphasis of the legal opinion is the rule and not the individual case. John Noonan has complained about this aspect of legal reasoning. The person hides behind the masks of legal generalities, as the judge cloaks "itself" in the robes of "the Court." The opinions are about rules, not about persons. "A good law student can answer a professor's dream of an examination question. The answer will be about P and D" (Noonan 1976, p. 7).

From the robed appearances of the judges to the statement of cases as *People* v. . . . the ritual of the legal process is an implicit drama of an imputed authority and a statement of law in the form of rules invested with generality and certainty. Science creates a factual order of imputed certainty. Law posits a public standard of behavior and presents it as an accepted canon of society. The names of the judges who write and concur in an opinion are to be found in the appellate reports but only the first initial of the first name. Even that may not be given for the parties. The disembodied abstractions help create the sense of legal rules as, in Holmes's famous line, "a brooding omnipresence in the sky."[23] The style and form of the presentation of the legislative act and the legal appellate decision, the "stuff" of what law students study, maintain an illusory sense of a public order that is certain, consistent, and powerful, of a "society" for which Law speaks.

That form contributes to a particular view of the drinking-driver and the act of driving after drinking. The law, in its formal attributes, underlines the factual dangerousness *to others* of the drinking-driver and his greater moral dereliction in comparison with other traffic violators. Drinking-driving occupies a special place in the panoply of traffic violations. It is not in the same moral situation as speeding, making an improper turn, or driving without lights. The punishments for it, and its evidentiary importance for establishing criminality, are greater than is the case with other driving irregularities.

Drinking-driving emerges as a publically condemnable action, its threat to public order of graver import than its relationship to private persons. The argument of Chatham's lawyers has had a better reception in tort law, where disputes between private persons are at issue, than in criminal actions, where the aggrieved party is the state, "the People." Although the law is not entirely clear and consistent and is often affected by legislative acts on the matter, intoxication is not per se evidence of negligence in tort cases. The plaintiff must show that the intoxication was a cause, or a contributing cause, of the accident and the injuries sustained (Dooley and Mosher 1978). This is clearly not the case with drinking-driving as a criminal action. It is a misdemeanor whatever the state of the defendant's driving at the time and a felony if an accident with injuries occurs. It is reprehensible per se. Good public order is predicated on the sobriety of the driver. Common law and legislation present drinking-driving as the paradigm, the myth and model of what is fearful and condemnable.

Law, like other forms of public action, becomes a part of public, societal culture. It is a presentation of a patterned, stereotyped, and abstract set of criteria presented as the perspective of "society" functioning in a collective capacity. That collectivity is itself a fiction, created and reinforced in the public act of its presentation. It thus enters into the experience of the individual as what George Herbert Mead calls "the generalized other" and what I call "the sense of the collective."

In a well-known study analyzing sources of demands for order and repugnance for disorder in human societies, Mary Douglas writes:

> Culture, in the sense of the public, standardized values of a community, mediates the experience of individuals. It provides in advance some basic categories, a positive pattern in which ideas and values are tidily ordered . . . it has authority, since each is induced to assent because of the assent of others. But its public character makes its categories more rigid. A private person may revise his pattern of assumptions or not. It is a private matter. But cultural categories are public matters. They cannot so easily be subject to revision [M. Douglas 1966, p. 39]

I find it useful to see the various parts of the legal process less as artillery weapons aimed at a target than as self-contained games, only tangentially part of a linear strategy instrumental to traffic safety. The police and the courts are attuned to the drinking-driver as criminal offender, not to the traffic analyst's knowledge and concerns. They operate in a world of practical realities, of defense attorney maneuvers, crowded court calendars, competing crimes, a dubious public opinion, and an openly hostile, often unrepentant defendant. That the offense is more "serious" than the average traffic offense is not a judgment acted on by many of the participants on both sides of the law. All of this operates in a milieu of middle class defendants and a public for whom the courts are already suspected of being in league with enemies of virtue.

The law game of drinking and driving is thus a microcosm of a political process that survives at multiple levels of reality and practice. Pushed by legislators and by a visible public of newspapers, letter writers, safety agencies, and organized interests toward an activist stance, the legislation and the legal decisions reflect the politics of organized groups and public officials; they state a culture that operates in the public arena. The police and the courts are sobered by an opposite, ambivalent perception of drinking-driving as a minor sin, no more mortal than other traffic violations. The legal game becomes an arena of pulls and tugs in which the issue of drinking and driving is confronted in a way which legislatures and appellate courts can afford to avoid.

At the level of routine daily events, the legal process continues the political process with a cast of unorganized interests and values. Drinking-drivers do not constitute a group in American life. They do not lobby for a version of DUIA as traffic offense like any other. That point of view becomes expressed at other levels, however.

To see each level of the political and legal process as playing its own game is not to deny the linear, instrumental metaphor of the cannon firing at distant targets. But the considerations I wish now to explore suggest that the firing of the cannon is as much a matter of the love of noise as of a desire to reach a target.

6

The Legal Myth
of Social Order

The abstract character of legislation and common law discussed in the previous chapter
should have prepared the reader for analysis of
law as a self-contained cultural product, a form
of communication rather than an instrumental
mechanism for achieving compliance. It is now
my intention to read the law of drinking-driving
as a response to the question, What does it tell
us to *be?* I am not reading it as a response to the
question, What does it tell us to *do?* This is not
to deny that there is an instrumental, utilitarian
relationship to the materials under consideration. That relationship is problematic in its impact on behavior. My concern here is with
another aspect of legal acts, their symbolic
forms as communications—as narratives,
stories, tales, as public legend and myth. Seen as
culture, law takes its place alongside other
forms of art—literature, painting, sculpture,
science, religious ceremony. "The directly observed interactions between individuals, which
the functionalist empiricist perceives as *economic transactions,* are reinterpreted as *acts of
communication*" (Leach 1976, p. 5).

Analysts of legal acts, including legislation,
have generally shied away from such aspects of
law, although they have recognized their existence. In a leading study of the legal decision,
Wasserstrom remarks that an important assumption of his analysis is that the legal system
ought to perform a utilitarian function although

he recognizes that this assumption is "as much a matter of convenience as commitment" (Wasserstrom 1961, p. 10). The analysis presented here is far from utilitarian in the usual sense of that term.

During the 1920s and '30s a wave of "legal realism" among American legal scholars challenged the view of law as a consistent, logical scheme to be discovered in judicial opinions (Friedman and MacCauley 1977, pp. 4ff). The emphasis fell on the uses of law, its impact or lack of impact on behavior, and the practical operation of municipal courts, lawyers, and police. The study of judicial decisions became suffused with the analysis of appellate courts as vehicles for the determination of social policy. In emphasizing economic interests, group ideologies, and political power, such realism produced another kind of rational interpretation of the legal process. It either ignored legislative acts and legal decisions as insignificant or sought to explain them entirely within the boundaries of political and economic interests.

Exceptions to this have been those legal realists who, in attacking the view of a "scientific" legal system, attempted to analyze its symbolic and ceremonial aspects. Interestingly, two major works by legal scholars both stem from the 1930s period of legal realism. Thurman Arnold and Jerome Frank both published their major works then (Arnold 1935; Frank 1936, 1949). For Frank, legal procedures were permeated by the basic fiction of the certainty and logical rationality of law. This "childish" (Frank's term) demand for a father-authority produced an inflexibility which in turn required elaborate and often unwieldy procedures to make it more flexible and inculcate a belief in a more humane attitude. Thus Frank saw the jury system and the judge's instructions to the jury as rituals, based on false assumptions but functioning to preserve a sense of both certainty and humanness in trials (Frank 1936, pp. 170–85).

Thurman Arnold had somewhat more appreciation for the role of myth and symbol in human affairs, but his Veblenian irony was also consistent with an underlying legal realism. He saw the ceremonial and symbolic character of government as an impediment to that clear thought and direct action by which human problems could be solved. Despite their shock and revulsion at the rhetorical usage of law, Frank and Arnold were alive to the ritual and drama by which legal acts created a sense of seriousness, certainty, and rectitude. No one has put the perspective of this chapter better than Thurman Arnold in *The Symbols of Government*.

The first important thing to be noted about Law Enforcement is that while it always appears to be very closely related to the problem of public order and safety, actually it has very little to do with it. Its effect is rather on the public utterances of those interested in the criminal law and on the appearance of the judiciary to the public. In order to understand this we must recognize that there are two very distinct problems of criminal administration: first, the keeping of order in the community; and, second, the dramatization of the moral notions of the community.

The first is primarily a police and prosecutor's problem, little concerned with, and only incidentally affected by, any governmental philosophy. . . .

The second function of criminal law administration, to dramatize the moral notions of the public, is probably the most important function of the criminal courts, as distinguished from the prosecutor, because they work in the limelight of public observation [Arnold 1935, pp. 152–54][1]

The legal realism of Frank and Arnold meant that they "put down" the symbolic and ritualistic elements of legal decisions and procedures. That is not my intention. I am contending that the dramatic qualities of legal acts infuse a situation with a visible meaning an understanding of which can be attributed by the observers to the general public. Whatever the situated acts may be, the public, official, communal meaning is portrayed and fixed by public legal acts.

Alcohol, Control, and Release in American Life

The laws against driving under the influence of alcohol constitute a moral drama which states the public definition of moral conduct in American life. In differentiating the drinking-driver from the traffic offender these laws create an identity for the moral person and a counteridentity of deviance and guilt. The law in this area symbolizes a public commitment to the centrality of work, safety, and individual responsibility in American society. It supports and enhances a view of a "generalized other," of a "society" committed to the legitimacy of a style of living in which alcohol is a symbol of risk and danger and its control a mark of morality and social responsibility. The modern world has not been the first to discover the joys of inebriety. It is, however, unique in defining these also as woes that call for public actions.

One way of thinking about why alcohol is so much a threat as well as a benefit in contemporary life is to contrast the daily routine of modern life with that of the preindustrial world.[2] The rational organization of work accompanying the rise of industrial organization has often been interpreted in the light of Max Weber's compelling analysis in *The Protestant*

Ethic and the Spirit of Capitalism as involving the appearance of internalized compulsions toward a disciplined and organized life. Frugality, punctual appearance, scheduled activities are all part of an institutional structure in which loose, erratic, and spontaneous behavior threaten the coordination of parts and whole which interdependent organization necessitates. The emergence of rational organizations and the appearance of jobs as the location of work have meant a sharp separation between work and play in the daily agenda. The factory is the model and the metaphor for this process that pervaded nineteenth-century America irrespective of social and economic class. The rationalization of economic organization made it important to maintain a boundary between the attitudes and activities of work and those of play. Insofar as drinking and drunkenness were appropriate at all, it was only within the confines of a specific and bounded area of social life, part of one of several enclaves around which the individual organized his segregated life.[3]

Until about the 1840s in America it was still believed that drinking was a valuable adjunct to work, and drinking was tolerated, sometimes even encouraged, in many work situations (Levine 1978). One of the major causes of changes in American drinking habits was that this connection was broken so thoroughly that its opposite is now widespread. Industrial life changed the concept of work time itself from one of spurts and splutters, of long bursts and short rests, into one of regularized and repetitive process (Thompson 1967; Gutman 1977, pp. 3–79; Kaplow 1980). It made the experience of life less that of an even flow of continuity between diverse areas and more that of impermeable membranes.

> The change in methods of production at last created a class with a direct interest in curbing drunkenness. Traditionally, work-rhythms had fluctuated both within the day and within the week; idleness on "Saint Monday" . . . followed by frantic exertion and long hours at the end of the week. . . . Essential but exhausting tasks had hitherto been accomplished largely through wielding the incentives of hunger and festivity, and the inseparability of drinking from customary recreations made it difficult to obtain precise and regular workmanship. . . . The frequency of early nineteenth-century protest against working-class drunkenness is as much an indication that the ancient inseparability of work and recreation had become inconvenient as that drunkenness itself had become more prevalent. [Harrison 1971, p. 40]

It is not so much that industrial and capitalist life made work more disciplined but that it separated the areas of control and regulation from the areas of release and spontaneity. It now became important to maintain those boundaries; to be sober and abstinent in some situations and to prevent insobriety or drunkenness from infringing upon them. While Americans quarreled bitterly over the place of alcohol, by the early twentieth century there was great consensus in the belief that drinking was a threat in areas and at times in which worklike competence was demanded. Philip Rieff has suggested that cultures may usefully be conceived as both controlling and releasing (Rieff 1966). What the rationalistic impulse demanded was that these two not be blurred, at least that the hedonistic not be allowed into the precincts of the "serious" segments of living and livelihood.[4]

The concern for alcohol as a "problem" owes much to the changed context within which drinking occurred. During the nineteenth century, to be drunk took on a new set of meanings, became more threatening and more closely connected to moral character in a world in which the boundaries between work and play, sobriety and drunkenness were more carefully stressed. It is not that the boundaries once delineated were always or usually respected but that the consequences of crossing or seeming to cross them were now more dangerous than they had been. There is yet another historical dimension that is pertinent to the questions raised by alcohol use in contemporary life. What constitutes an acceptable level of disorder in a society? Violence, crime, civil disturbance, riot, drunkenness are hardly the invention of modern men, capitalism, the industrial revolution, or other deities and devils to whom we so often refer for quick explanations of social change. How men and women respond to such disorderly conduct may change, however. Recognition of this is crucial in this book.

In many accounts of the growth of antidrinking movements in Europe or the United States much is made of the effect of increased drinking in stimulating mob violence, riot, criminal actions, and generally rowdy behavior, especially among the lower classes. In explaining the origin of the police in England, Jonathan Rubinstein places great importance on the disorder consequent upon increases in drinking among the lower classes after the invention of gin in the seventeenth century. Prior to that only the rich could afford hard liquor: "Their near-monopoly on hard liquor may help to explain the attachment of the rich to brawling, fighting and killing, habits which most people today associate with the poor. Gin democratized drunkenness and brought new terrors to London and then to all cities" (Rubinstein 1973, p. 4).[5]

I do not mean to deny either fluctuations in the use of alcohol or the impact of rowdiness and crime on social responses. But they do not in themselves constitute explanations of such responses. This is a point which Allan Silver has made in understanding public reactions to the riots of blacks in the 1960s and in accounting for the rise of the police in Britain in the nineteenth century (Silver 1967, pp. 1–25; 1968, pp. 151–63). In England a tradition of collective violence had existed, as it had on the Continent. Crowd violence was frequent and understood as a mechanism of communication between the poor and ruled, on the one hand, and the rich and powerful rulers on the other. It was perceived as a corrective to specific acts of injustice but not as a threat to the political order.[6] No such tradition existed in the United States where the integration of populations into the electoral system made for a higher level of expected orderliness. In England the emergence of politically oriented crowds, especially in the Chartist movement, influenced the development of police and raised the acceptable level of public violence well above that of the past, though the crowds of the past look so fierce when seen in hindsight.

An idea of legitimate collective violence, shared by both the upper and the lower orders, never existed in the United States. Especially among the powerful, belief in the efficacy of the electoral system as a mechanism of protest has made riots and protests a matter to be explained. Where violence and crowd disorder are seen as a natural and expected response, "diagnostic sociology is not required because collective violence as a response to injustice is rooted in the innate order of things" (Silver 1968, p. 158; R. Turner 1969).

The point here is that it is not only the objective behavior which must be explained but the response to it as well. The aphorism "One man's moral turpitude is another man's innocent pleasure" is a succinct way of putting it. "Civil disorder" is not a given, waiting only to be observed. Neither is drunkenness. When we turn to drinking-driving we need to account not only for its occurrence but also for the expected level of safety and fear of danger. We need to analyze its place as a public issue, one which public (governmental, communal) authorities are charged with resolving. We need to understand its singular place in the panoply of traffic misconduct.

The Myth of the "Killer-Drunk"

If good traffic order is predicated on the sobriety of the driver, then good people are sober drivers. The drinking-driver is the social delinquent, but in a manner distinctly apart from the ordinary traffic offender. This is the explicit theme of the legislation, the case law, and the many volatile commentaries in public print. They sustain the description of the drinking-driver as someone who is morally flawed, heedless of others, and deserving of both moral condemnation and legal punishment. The drinking-driver has committed a "serious" offense. It is not murder or burglary or rape, but it is nevertheless not a casual and "normal" act of most motorists. In both a moral and a factual sense, the normative order has been broken.

What the legislators, the appellate judges, and the reporting agencies are doing can be described as creating the sense that a normative order exists which assigns deviant status to the drinking-driver. The language of moral revulsion expressed by Justice Wiest in *People* v. *Townsend*, with which I began the last chapter, is heard again and again. A governmental report has a more moderate tone: "The *antisocial* manifestations of immoderate alcohol use have long been regarded as legal problems to be dealt with through the criminal process" (U.S. Congress, Committee on Public Works, 1968, p. 100; italics mine).

As with many nontraffic crimes, there are recurrent campaigns to increase penalties for drinking-driving. These are efforts to make the image of the drinking-driver more pointedly deviant and thus place that act further outside the social order, as not typical of good citizens or approvable and acceptable. In such campaigns the image of the offender as the potential "killer-drunk" is given prominence. Advocates point to instances of innocent victims of drunken drivers and demand a tougher policy. "How many of us could be the grieving survivors, or indeed the victims of an irresponsible fool that is let loose on our streets and highways with a dangerous weapon" (*Los Angeles Times,* October 27, 1973, Letter to the Editor, pt. 2, p. 4). The advertisement shown in figure 2 calls for a "way to teach them a lesson."

What are being constructed in these ceremonial, generally ineffective attempts to diminish the events of drinking-driving are a consciousness of the drinking-driver as a rules breaker and an assurance of the law-abiding citizen and the casual traffic offender that he or she is not in the same social space as the drinker who gets behind the wheel. Whatever may be the eventual fate of the offenders, they *deserve* punishment. They are not you or I. The opposite cannot be publicly admissible and the law teaches us that this is so.

Much of the apparatus of law—legislative acts, appellate court cases, police enforcement—upholds a public version of acceptable behavior. It points to the sources of disorder, the threats to safety as symbolized in the drinking-driver. In these ceremonies the linkage between danger and rejection of boundaries is continually perceived as a part of the moral order; throughout the staged narrative of the crime of driving while under the influence of alcohol the central figure is clearly and at all times villainous and condemned.

What is his villainy? I want to point to three aspects of it as portrayed
in the legal ceremonies enshrined in the acts of legislatures and the decisions of appellate courts—the law of the books—and given visible presentation in the arrest and conviction of offenders.

The first is the *antisocial character of drinking-driving*. Here the concern of law is with alleviating accidents and deaths to the sober. The
myth of "killer-drunk" is exemplified in the case of *People* v. *Townsend*
where the passenger was killed and the driver walked (or staggered)
away. It is the story which justifies the attempted severity of drinking-
driving penalties without any show of improper or erratic driving. To
drive after drinking is, then, to show disregard for others—to place self-
indulgence above orderly conduct toward others. It takes risks not only
with self but with "society." Every drinking-driver is the "killer-drunk."

A second aspect of the drinking-driver's villainy is his *responsibility for
his actions*. For the Christian theologian there is no sin without free will.
The concept of fault in law, though not as ubiquitous, is nevertheless
similar in its function. The drinking-driver has committed an act that he
could and should have avoided. He chose to drink and he chose to drive.
A person in command and control of his behavior, he is liable for the
crime committed. Not the store that sold the alcohol, not the bar or the
hosts that served the drinks, not the automobile that can be driven under
the influence of alcohol or the manufacturer of it is at all guilty of a
crime.[7] The individualistic character of the driving experience is again
prominent. The "good" man is either sober, or plans ahead for his
drinking and provides means of transportation, or is sufficiently rational
to do so after drinking. The boundary between work and serious activity,
on the one hand, and play and irresponsible release on the other hand, is
the duty of Everyman to recognize and maintain.

The third aspect of the drinking-driver's villainy is his *status as
deviant—morally and factually*. His crime is not the minor one of traffic
offense. In the California vehicle code it is included among "public offenses," as is reckless driving and hit-and-run. It is separated from other
"infractions" or misdemeanors such as speeding, improper equipment, or
going through a stop sign (*West's Annotated California Codes* 1971, p.
127). Many actions also connected with accidents are not treated at law
with the same severity as is drinking. Speeding, inexperienced driving,
wrong turns, improper passing, old age are among variables associated
with high rates of accidents and deaths on the highway, like drinking-
driving aggravating the risks of accident (Zylman 1974a, b).

The use of alcohol accentuates the moral degradation and the antisocial character of the drinking-driver delict in public arenas. His behavior
is not that of the average motorist. The greater punishment is not a

reflection of the greater typicality of the offense. It may in part be redemptive—to cleanse and purify the offender. But it is mainly a statement of the greater magnitude of the offense to orderly conduct, to public behavior, a reflection of danger to an ordered world in which work and play are not mixed. In this confrontation between divergent modes of behavior and arenas of action can be found the ceremonial drama of driving while under the influence of alcohol.

The Theory of Accidents and the Drama of Drinking-Driving

The drama of drinking-driving is then a drama of moral character. There is a world of dangerous and complicated machinery, a world of risk and chance, of danger and safety. That world demands a rational attitude of constant discipline, self-control, and concern for the implications of your behavior for others. The operation of a motor vehicle is an apt arena for these moral characteristics to be displayed or ignored, for the opposite of order and safety to emerge. Attributing automobile accidents to drinking-driving creates a drama in which moral failing is responsible for human injury. The motorist who ignores the authority of the rational, serious person is the one who causes death and destruction; he has ignored the boundaries between work and play. The driver who commits error or takes a human, normal risk is not morally flawed or to be dishonored.

But the automobile is also an apt cultural arena for the conflicting images of the good man in the modern, complicated world of work and obligation, of consumership and enjoyment. Arrests, the ceremonies of detention, release to friends or family, courtroom appearances, the law itself are all capable of being described as degradation ceremonies, in which the drinking-driver is held up against the standard of sobriety and moral obligation and lowered in the eyes of self and the world. "Finally, the denounced person must be ritually separated from a place in the legitimate order, i.e., he must be placed 'outside.' He must be made 'strange.'" (Garfinkel 1956).

It is this which the law establishes—the casting out of the drinker who has been unable to hold his drinking in check or to plan his activities so as not to become a "menace."

But who is it who is being degraded? We have met this issue in another form earlier, in my analysis of the rhetoric of scientific presentation. There the difference between the drinking-driver seen as the average social drinker and the drinking-driver seen as alcoholic and/or of lower class and status was crucial to whether he was an insider or an outsider to the spectator (chap. 4). How "strange" is the drinking-driver?

A glance at the defenders of drinking-driving quickly makes the point that, in the context of routine daily life and routine daily law, the effort to portray the drinking-driver as deviant and outside the communal life fails. Those defenders of the moral character of the drinking-driver are not to be found on the official pages of newspapers or on the talk show panels. They are to be found in the offices of defense attorneys, but not in public arenas. Here the defense attorney has the jury of peers and often the judge as the model of what he can utilize to support his client. The juror, writes Roger Cramton, is likely to identify with the defendant: "We all live it up once in a while, only he was unfortunate enough to get caught" (Cramton 1969, pp. 102–3).

While the drinking-driver as defendant must cope with the general image of himself as the "bad guy," the antisocial delinquent, he is also the recipient of empathy from the social drinker (Erwin 1965, pp. 831ff; Erwin 1976; Hollopeter 1957, pp. 817–30). Hollopeter, in advice to defense attorneys, says that while there is concern about drinking-driving by many people and a general antipathy against the use of intoxicating beverages, a majority of people use alcohol. From his perspective, the issue of "wet" and "dry" was still evocative in 1957, and the defense lawyer should select a jury with tolerance for drinking, who can identify with the defendant: "If the jury, as finally selected, includes a goodly number who would say of the defendant, 'There go I but for the grace of God' you are well underway to the trial of the case before an open-minded jury" (Hollopeter 1957; Freeman 1970, p. 821).

It is this theme of the drinking-driver as deviant and the countertheme of him as average, frail, and sometimes delinquent that is at work in the two levels of the legal process. On the public level of appellate court, of legislatures, and of public officials the crime of drinking-driving is justifiably dealt with as action demanding more than the response to traffic violations, the "folk crime" of "ordinary" people. At the level of the daily acts of courts and police, what has been shown in the previous chapters is that driver's licenses are seldom suspended or revoked on a first offense, jail sentences are seldom invoked, charges are reduced to lesser offenses in many instances, and the characteristic "punishment" for drinking-driving, especially as a first offense, is a fine of between $150 and $300, depending on the court involved. A different portrayal of the drinking-driver emerges from the routine legal act than from the public ceremony of official behavior.

In his dramaturgical analysis of police, Peter Manning points to similar processes for handling the discrepancies between public and private meanings. Many of the sources of crime and disorder are beyond the control of police. As public agents, however, they must be identified as persons of authority and control. They must substitute appearances for realities: "They must display a unity of purpose and of action regardless of the varying statuses and roles of police personnel and of their own political, moral and personal attitudes...and they must through the management of appearances create the sense of commitment to and enforcement of rules and tenets on which there is only an 'as if' public agreement" (Manning 1977, p. 18).

The moral status of the drinking-driver is not completely unambiguous, however. Drinking is a source both of condemnation and of sympathy. There is now a debate in legal circles about chronic alcoholism as an excuse for otherwise criminal behavior, especially public drunkenness. There is a vast literature on this subject, and a movement is now in existence to bring alcoholism within the exculpatory legal boundaries now occupied by pleas of insanity (Epstein 1977; Kittrie 1973; McCoid 1956; Room 1979, chap. 8). From the standpoint of the law the drinking-driver is a villain—irresponsible, hedonistic, antisocial, undisciplined. From another standpoint he is a victim—unable to control himself, more likely to hurt himself than others. Drunkenness has provided privileges as well as sanctions both in law and in life.[8]

This view of drunkenness as mitigating the guilt of drinking-driving does *not* govern the image projected through the legislation, the common law, and the fact of law enforcement. It is not the role of the drinking-driver to be the victim in the dramatic presentation of his legal status. It is not his public status.

The Symbolism of Order and Disorder

We can depict the contrasts of order and disorder which the public drama of law stages as a drama of moral character. The list of contrasts is not exhaustive but it suggests the moral and factual order which is being validated by the law at the public level.

Order   v.   Disorder

Sober	v.	Drunken
Safety	v.	Danger
Social	v.	Antisocial
Altruistic	v.	Hedonistic
Controlled	v.	Uncontrolled

Planned	v.	Spontaneous
Obedient	v.	Disobedient
Wise	v.	Foolish
Serious	v.	Frivolous
Work	v.	Play

The law comes down hard on the attributes in the righthand column. If drinking and drunkenness are condoned, it is only if the drinker at the same time joins the lefthand side of the list, segregating drinking and drunkenness and otherwise observing the boundary between the two columns. The sharpness with which the law paints this boundary is manifest whenever the drinking-driver is apprehended, put in the back seat of a squad car in which the inside door handles have been removed, and perhaps hadcuffed. If he has not committed murder he has done something more "serious" than going through a stop light, making an improper left turn, or doing sixty-five in a fifty-five-mile-an-hour zone. He is arrested, not just cited.

That there are far more drivers riding the roads than are or can be apprehended is a point made again and again ad nauseum in these pages. If the ritual of legislation and legal decision is aimed at this audience, it also vindicates those who drink and never drive after drinking. The punishment of the offender is the ritual action which attests to the validity in fact and morality of the law. There is much doubt of the practical effect of increasing arrests on preventing auto accidents and deaths. The inauguration of special drinking-driving squads in the San Diego Police Department in 1965 was followed by a sharp increase in arrests, but it did not lead to a significant diminution in automobile deaths or in deaths involving drinking-drivers (Gusfield 1979b). While the British inauguration of the breathalyzer did lead to a reduction it proved not to be lasting (Ross 1970, 1973, 1977). Although the Scandinavian countries have long had a reputation for effective use of "tough" laws, closer scrutiny has not found that to be the case. My discussions with Scandinavian researchers in 1973 revealed that the testing of fatalities for blood levels, typical in the United States, was not done in Norway, Sweden or Finland. Thus there was no empirical support for the popular view of Scandinavian "success." In a more searching analysis of data and results, Ross concluded that the Scandinavian reputation was "mythical" and unfounded (Ross 1975).[9]

More striking support for doubting the deterrence function of increasing enforcement is found in the experience of the Alcohol Safety Action Projects of the NHTSA then (1970) Office of Alcohol Countermeasures. Their experience with programs subsidizing increased en-

forcement and auxiliary measures in twenty-nine cities was not unlike the
experience of San Diego's "deuce" squads. "No simple relationship of
enforcement and crashes has been established in the ASAP projects. In
several instances fourfold and fivefold increases in arrests have not been
able to have an impact on the crash level" (U.S. Department of Transportation 1974, p. 23; also see Zador 1976; Zylman 1975a, b).

The impact of the law as a moral dramatization of cultural and public
ideals lies in its compression and magnification of the contrasts between
order and disorder. The stages of law and law enforcement are testimony
to public commitments. They reinforce the meanings of action. Anthropologists have often interpreted initiation or transition rituals as
functional to role passage or to maintenance of the solidarity of the
society. They see them as providing resolutions to important anomalies
and contradictions in the culture, as easing over the passage from one
status to another (M. Douglas 1966; Young 1965; Van Gennep 1960;
V. Turner 1969). Young suggests that this function is performed through
the intensification which dramatizing makes possible. They are rites of
intensification, "dramatizing and thereby clarifying the meaning maintained by the group" (Young 1965, p. 157). While the ceremonies may
reinforce meaning in both contemporary modern and primitive societies,
the ceremonies described by anthropologists are more likely to be a guide
to private behavior in primitive than in modern societies. That is the
central point in this analysis. Nevertheless, the perception of the legal
ceremony as intensifying the public attitude, what G. H. Mead called
"the generalized other," is an insight that will prove of considerable value
in the remainder of this chapter.

Two commentators shed light on this order of ceremony. Emile Durkheim's analysis of legal norms led him to conclude that the disposition to
punish criminals was necessary to the social order as a means of maintaining a respect for law and morality. Crime shows that obedience to the
norm is not universal. The anomaly of crime threatens the unanimity
from which norms derive their authority, says Durkheim. Punishment is
essential if that authority is to be restored (Durkheim 1947, pp. 96ff;
Gusfield 1963a, pp. 111–13).

Kenneth Burke's attitude toward the function of punishment, which he
calls "scapegoating," is similar. Burke understands much of public ritual
as a purification of the sacrificer by his identification with the presumed
evil of the sacrificed. The punishers transfer to the scapegoat their own
impurities and are purified in the vicarious atonement of sacrifice. The
purification of the punishers is just as significant as the general deterrent
effects of punishment on potential lawbreakers (Andenaes 1966):

"Criminals either actual or imaginary may thus serve as scapegoats in a society that 'purifies itself' by 'moral indignation' in condemning them" (Burke 1945, p 406).

In both of these theories, as in my analysis so far, it is not the utilitarian effectiveness of the law that is served by its promulgation so much as it is the cultural meanings of behavior. In Manning's work (Manning 1974, 1977), the police represent the visible presence of those meanings, meanings that are always somewhat fictive and problematic, but which are nevertheless maintained. Even when he breaks the law, the criminal, the lawbreaker, may and usually does accept the meaning of his action as crime. This is the considerable difference between criminals and revolutionaries (Sykes and Matza 1957).

An observation drawn from fieldwork with a metropolitan police force may illustrate the principle. Driving on a city street about 12:30 A.M. with a drinking-driving squad officer, our right-of-way was cut off by a vehicle which shot into the intersection from a side street. The driver was a middle-aged black man, well-dressed in suit, vest, and sport shirt. He spoke well and with pleasant and accommodating manner. He admitted having had a few drinks, said he was a veteran of Viet Nam, was wounded and couldn't walk well, thus explaining his unwillingness to take the field sobriety test although he did so anyway. He was apparently under the influence (and later tested at a lowest score of .21 on the breathalyzer). He was not handcuffed and did not protest the arrest. At one point he said, "Okay, you got me." In the car he asked about the possible punishment. The white police officer said the judge would probably be lenient on a first offense. The offender said he didn't want lenience; if he's caught, he's caught. It emerged that he was a Navy career man, with eighteen years service. He was worried over the effect of this arrest on his possible advancement in the Navy. The officer asked if they need hear of it. After the breathalyzer test was completed the officer said to me that since the offender had been so cooperative he'd see what he could do for him and would not report his occupation as military, but as unemployed.

This is not an atypical instance of the value which police give to the acceptance of their authority (Skolnick 1966). Viewed structurally it is a case of making police work easier and less dangerous. Viewed culturally, as I am doing here, it instances sharing of the meaning of the drinking-driving norm between the two parties, police and offender, and the willingness of the "scapegoat" to cooperate in dramatizing law enforcement. I am not examining motives or feelings but actions and the meanings of those actions. (Other instances, and I have seen those, in which the offender verbally abuses the police for "picking on me," stand as contrasts to the easy acceptance of authority in this case.)

At the public level, the laws regarding drinking-driving seem to have great consensus behind them. "No one's against crackdowns on drinking-drivers. It's like being for apple pie and motherhood," a police captain told us. Even the legal disputes before the appellate courts deal almost entirely with issues of proper and improper evidence, hardly at all with the propriety of punishing drinking-driving more severely than other traffic offenses.

Law as Negotiated Social Order

The difficulties with functional theories such as Durkheim's emerge when we leave the pubic halls and walk downstairs and observe the municipal court, ride with the police, and listen to the stories of attorneys. In the public halls, the law has a consistency and finality about it. The two columns of the list of orderly versus disorderly attributes are clearly separate, and it is clear who are the lawgivers and who are the law receivers. Not so when we move away from the public arena into the routine events of daily operation. Here the consistency of enforcement is absent, the connection between act, apprehension, and punishment unstable, the treatment of the offender less condemnatory, and the entire process far less criminal in its meanings.

It is useful to think of law as encompassing both levels, not as a system of authority structuring a normative pattern of rules and punishments but as a negotiated social order in which compromise, flexibility, and resistance exist at all levels: "Religious and legal institutions, among others, only cease to be bundles of dead or cold rules when they are seen as phases in social processes, as dynamic patterns right from the start" (V. Turner 1974, p. 37).

Sociologists of law have long made the point that the study of law as embodied in legislative acts and common law decisions yields a highly inaccurate description of what takes place in the behavior of police, the actions of attorneys, or the day-to-day events of courtrooms and primary-level judges. The law becomes a point in the negotiation between the different parties in the legal process, to be ignored or reinterpreted according to the organizational needs and specific interests of those involved in its implementation.[10] The impact of the public presentation of law on the routine legal events and of both on behavior have remained the central problem of the sociology of law (Abel 1973).

This problem of the "gap" between levels of law has been described in the previous chapter in my account of the way in which drinking-driving behavior becomes arrest, charge, conviction, and recorded event. What I described there was an orderly process in which the outcomes were results of negotiations of meaning and event rather than a consistent, direct implementation of a clearly stated rule and a clearly perceived instance of its violation. This account of social order as constantly being negotiated is not unique to law or to this book. It forms a generalized perspective toward social behavior shared by many social scientists.

Sitting in arraignment court in San Diego, El Cajon, or other San Diego jurisdictions, I was struck by the common, casual dress of defendants. The court is an attempt to surround law with the ritual appurtenances of sacredness. The ceremony of standing as the judge enters, the robes, and titles of respect are all there. The shelves of lawbooks on the wall make the concept of stated rules manifest. The suits, ties, and muted shirt colors of the male lawyers and the bland dress of female attorneys and the court staff continue the mien of seriousness and specialness. The defendants are conspicuous by casual appearance. Ties or jackets are hardly ever seen. Sport shirts are common; blue jeans are not untypical and even tank-top shirts and T-shirts. Women wear casual pantsuits. There is little to distinguish defendants from men or women attending a party, a casual dinner, or going to work in Southern California. They do not seem to regard the court as a sacred place in their lives.[11]

Here as elsewhere, there are two aspects which need to be differentiated, the structural and the cultural. Structurally the negotiation is influenced by the relative power and organizational needs of the participants. For example, the decision to prosecute on a particular charge is much affected by the ability of the defendant to create organizational problems for the prosecution by taking the case to trial (Cloyd 1975). The "facts" of the case are important but not governing. The courts, the lawyers, the police all have their own degrees of power and interest which operate to shape the outcomes at the municipal level into a less severe treatment of the drinking-driver than would appear from law at the higher level. These considerations are at work in other types of cases as well, as other studies indicate (Blumberg 1967a,b; Levine and Becker 1973).

From a cultural perspective the enforcement level of the law of drinking-driving is a ritual of upgrading. The judge in one small city court said to me that he always gives first-time drinking-driving offenders a stern lecture but then is lenient in punishment. In the large municipal courts, even the lecture is lacking. The process is routinized, each defendant having approximately one and one-half minutes before the arraignment court in San Diego City. The "traffic offense" outcomes and the random, nonrepresentative character of police apprehension present the observer with something other than the "killer-drunk" condemnation of the mass media, the legislation, and the common law. Drinking-driving becomes less of a crime and more of a "folk crime." Many judges, police, and even prosecution give voice to this in statements akin to that quoted from a juror above to the effect that we all live it up once in a while and this poor soul happened to get caught.

The enforcement of drinking-driving, as I have studied it, ends in a ritual of redemption through redefinition. It is a redefinition which presents, in implicit fashion, the case for the opposite side of the coin of criminality—the naturalness and commonality of play, spontaneity, danger, foolishness, and the antisocial. It diminishes the deviance of the drinking-driver and restores him to community, slightly dented but still intact.

Law as Cultural Performance

What I am doing in this analysis is treating behavior, including the written behavior of laws, as "cultural performances," and examining them not for their structural consequences of outputs and conclusions but as embodiments of meaning and definition to me and, insofar as I can make inferences based on observation and interaction, to the participants.[12] Viewed as cultural performances, the two levels of law constitute two divergent meanings of drinking-driving and carry two diverging conceptions of social order. This duality is at the heart of my analysis and must be probed further. At its ceremonial level law treats drinking as a peculiarly significant form of behavior, morally more condemnable than "ordinary" lapses from proper driving conduct. At more routine levels, that character is diminished, if not fully absent.

The Two Levels of Social Order

In his essay "The Art of Donald McGill," George Orwell examines the genre of quasi-pornographic postcards in England—the kind that get humor out of women with big breasts, impotence in men, and the human impulses to disobey at least eleven of the Ten Commandments. Orwell remarks that such humor gives vent to the underside of human beings, all that is nasty, perverse, and unsocialized. Official establishments recognize only the heroic, the unselfish, and the noble and shut out the underside:

> The two principles, noble folly and base wisdom, exist side by side in nearly every human being. If you look into your own mind which are you, Don Quixote or Sancho Panza? Almost certainly you are

both. There is one part of you that wishes to be a hero or a saint, but another part of you . . . is your unofficial self, the voice of the belly protesting against the soul . . .
  . . . Society has always had to demand a little more from human beings than it will get in practice. It has to demand faultless discipline and self-sacrifice, it must expect its subjects to work hard, pay their taxes, and be faithful to their wives, it must assume that men think it glorious to die on the battle field and women want to wear themselves out with child-bearing. The whole of what is called official literature is founded on such assumptions. . . . It is only that the other element in man, the lazy, cowardly, debt-bilking adulterer who is inside all of us, can never be suppressed altogether and needs a hearing occasionally. [Orwell 1954, pp. 120–22]

Orwell's focus on the dualities in human beings has in one way or another been touched upon at different points in this book; in discussing the work-play distinction, the ambivalence of American attitudes toward drinking, and the severe and lenient modes of law enforcement. The issue of dualities in culture and social structure has assumed importance in recent years in the work of symbolic anthropologists, especially Victor Turner (V. Turner 1967, 1969, 1974). Turner describes a basic cultural duality between hierarchical and institutional norms, which he calls *structure,* and norms of personal and intimate response, which he calls *communitas.* Structure defines the social order in terms of differentiations. Those norms which stress the commonality and equality of human beings refer to *communitas* and sometimes *antistructure.* He interprets many primitive African rituals as mechanisms through which these disuniting impulses are united and social order is integrated. His work has been deeply influential upon me, both directly in suggesting methods for analyzing the cultural content of public performances, and indirectly in leading me to see some crucial differences between the primitive ritual and the modern.
  I will return to the characterization of the drinking-driver as the "killer-drunk." It is an image implying social hostility, gross self-indulgence, lack of foresight, and foolhardiness. What is true of the sober man or the drunken man who recognizes his drunkenness as socially and mechanically dangerous is that he accepts the "rules of the road." At the level of public action, the law attributes the drinking-driver with having a high degree of hostility to others, with threatening the lives of others through indulgence in his own pleasure. He lacks the self-controls and discipline which establish moral character. He is deficient in a manner more open to condemnation and punishment than are other traffic offenders.

Natural Order and Social Order

This distinction between forms of traffic offense implies a cosmology, a system of thought which provides an understanding of otherwise inexplicable events. Automobile accidents are among the major threatening occurrences which human beings face daily in modern life. The explanation involves the same issues of religious theodicy which have absorbed human beings since even before Job. For the individual there are always the questions, Why me? Why *my* loved ones? For the aggregate there is the question applied to a larger, less personal unit. One answer might be that it is God's will—not a very comforting or acceptable response in an age that applies more secular explanations to events. Chance, luck, random selection might be utilized as well, and sometimes is. That makes a world in which prediction, thought, and care are useless, a world in which the good and the bad suffer equally without the solace of Job's God, even as a null hypothesis.

At least two sources for "accident" appear in the law. The source of the routine traffic offense lies in carelessness, in "human" disregard for norms, in misinterpretations. If there is a moral defect it is minor. The second source, drinking-driving, has another status. It explains automobile accidents as the result of Evil, of a double defect of morals—drinking plus an antisocial character. The public character of the drinking-driving law underscores and maintains this perception of the individualistic nature of auto accidents and the defective moral character of the drinking-driver. In a world in which individual actions count, in which goodness and badness affect life, if we could ensure adequate character the world could be made a safe place. There is implied a strong belief in the understandability of the world and the place of moral law in it.

In attempting to eradicate dangerous driving the institution of law makes a statement about the natural and the social order. "Accidents" can be diminished by enforcing an adequate standard of social behavior on people. Death and injury are not a natural consequence of using the technical equipment which mankind has developed, not the price we pay for progress. The social order needs to be propitiated, not a natural order in which accidents are an inevitable accompaniment of "normal" behavior. Primitive people need to bring their behavior into attunement with nature to obtain its aid. Moderns need to bring the individual into alignment with the social order, to keep the boundaries between proper and improper behavior clear, if evil is to be avoided and safety obtained.[13]

The distinction in punishment and in condemnatory language between

the drinking-driver and the common traffic offender rests on the portrayal of the drinking-driver as morally deviant—not the ordinary man
and thus not morally adequate. Speeding, driving with poor equipment,
inexperience, old age, passing improperly—however sober people cause
auto accidents and deaths—are not seen as moral defects of great proportions. They are treated as that which the other motorist or the pedestrian may rightfully anticipate as the common order of nature. The distinction reminds me of a conversation I once had with an official of the
Prohibition Party. In discussing alcoholism as a symptom of underlying
psychological problems, I remarked that if alcoholism were eradicated it
would only be supplanted by some other symptom. To which he then
replied, "Some symptoms are better than other symptoms." It is this
emphasis on alcohol that the DUIA law supports; the belief in the special
immorality of drinking as distinguished from other conditions of the
driver or the automobile also associated with accident and death.

In a discussion of issues of drinking-driving law, David Scholl writes:
"The only effective means of significantly eliminating the presence of the
drinking driver is to impress upon the public that driving after one has
consumed more than a token amount of alcohol is *unthinkable*" (Scholl
1969, p. 261). It is just this process of making what is thinkable unthinkable that constitutes the cultural impacts of law. The cultural performance that constitutes the law of public halls affects the public meanings,
the meanings that others can be expected to share.

At another level of law, that of the routine events of police enforcement
and court actions, the other side of the coin can be seen. One judge
expressed this in saying that drinking-driving was a matter of police
attitudes. By this, as he explained, he meant that whether or not one were
arrested for DUIA was a question of where and when police were pa-
trolling and their disposition to stop the car and to run field tests and
apprehend. From this standpoint the drinking-driver who is arrested is
just one of many, many out on the road. He just happened to get
caught—the true "scapegoat." His traffic violation may be minor, and
sometimes unrelated to poor driving. His driving record is often no worse
than that of others, and he often resents the implication of defective
moral character and criminality.

Seen in this light, the DUIA is not much different from the ordinary
traffic violator. Neither factually nor morally is he so deviant, so indulgent, and so socially hostile as to merit the denunciatory tones with
which the law portrays him. And a busy, organizationally complex court
cannot give him "the full measure of the law." He is defined in terms of
situations, not in terms of an ideal set of meanings which abstract law has

constructed. In San Diego City, the higher the blood-count level, or the more frequent or recent the offense, the higher the sentence. But in all events, both floor and ceiling are low.

It is after all the exceptional case among the many instances of driving when drinking-driving results in accident or even in arrest. Most of the time the driver manages his or her situation without hazard. Research now in progress leads me to believe that for many drinkers there is a body of experience with the phenomenon of drinking and driving which makes the assertion that "I can handle it" warrantable to them. Drinkers often distinguish instances and situations when they feel incompetent to drive and frequently relinquish the wheel when others point it out to them. Arrested offenders can point to circumstances which distinguish the arrest situation from their "normal" experiences with drinking and driving. There is a distinct possibility that what occurs in the experience of drivers are instances of competent drinking-driving contrasted with instances of incompetent drinking-driving.[14]

Though the outcomes are results of negotiations, the DUIA cannot yet afford to be sanguine, though his portrait is more flattering and makes him look more like Everyman than like Mephistopheles. Though he need not spend a night in jail in San Diego, he may find it embarrassing to have a friend or relative called to take him home. He is arraigned and may be forced to attend classes. Negotiation implies a give-and-take between the levels of the law and not just indifference. However, the offender can still attest to not having been jailed, to never having been arrested for anything but a traffic offense.

The Myth of Social Order

Social scientists are accustomed to thinking about politics as an interplay of groups. Analysis of police enforcement and courtroom processes suggests that the more benign view of the drinking-driver does not get a hearing in the halls of government, but it does in the courts of routine law. The major public dissent to drinking-driver legislation and to its enforcement has been based on civil liberties views of the right to withhold self-incriminating evidence (Breithaupt v. Abrams, 352 U.S. 432 [1957]; Schmerber v. California, 384 U.S. 757 [1966]; Erwin 1976; Murray and Aitken 1972). The status of drinking-driving as an offense, as distinguished from the driving behavior which may or may not be connected with it, is not at issue.

But at the level of legislative politics and appellate law the values of the drinking-driver are not heard. He does not constitute an interest group, although the alcohol beverage groups are hardly without influence. An alternative attitude to risk and an appreciative rather than a grudging acceptance of drinking and play have no standing in the public order. His is the politics of the situation; his only hope lies in the ability to create organizational trouble, to appeal to individuals on the basis of his specific person, or to be belligerent and resentful.

I consider this a continuation of the political process because there is still an interplay of power and influence brought to bear on actions of government. It is a situated politics, however. It is not oriented toward a general rule but toward its operation. Like politics at higher levels, it grants expression to competing values and interests. Here the ethic of serious work and the ethic of frivolous play at last come into collision.[15]

The public dramas of drinking-driving legislation, appellate cases, and the mass media exhortations display a definite consensus about the moral status of the DUIA. He or she is not a "normal traffic offender." The public dramas are a tacit denial of the situation of conflict both within the driver and between the elements of work and play in a technologically individualistic society. They sustain our belief in a moral order in which solutions to problems can be attained and a natural order which is not impervious to the control of science and the state. They hide the fact that the belief is imposed by authority. They also hide the fact that obedience to authority is an illusion.

It is in this consistency and imputed consensus that the legal process defines and describes a "society"—an aggregate of people engaged in an ordered and predictable set of relationships. It is through its certainty and uniformity that the legal process enunciates, at the public level, an orderly world in which the transgression of moral precepts is followed by danger and disorder. It presents us with a fictive world that is clear, understandable, and guided by moral directives. In the myth of the "killer-drunk" it provides the metaphor through which the individual can assess his or her environment. Invoked regularly, the law of DUIA is a visible ritual in which the conception of an orderly nature and an orderly society is persistently reestablished as the public, agreed upon, and shared vision of what is real and factual.

The fictive nature of that world is not insignificant. More than fifty years ago, the American novelist and critic Floyd Dell presented a view of unrealistic novels as similarly necessary. Fairy tales, wrote Dell, do not tell children what the world is *really* like but educate by providing an emotionally understandable world which makes sense of our feelings about such things as friendship and ambition and heroism. "We cannot learn life by living it—we must have some kind of notion about it to enable us to digest our experiences as we get them." It is the same for adults. We read novels for the same serious purpose we once read fairy tales: "We want to know more about our relation to the world. But we emphatically do not want the raw material of life; we want life made emotionally intelligible—and that can only be effected by a process of simplification and arrangement" (Dell 1922).

The fictive character of the moral and cognitive reality which law upholds has greater significance for behavior because it provides a legitimacy for the story, the narrative, the tale of the drinking-driver, of the killer-drunk and the innocent victim. By being a public act, one that is visible, persistent, official, and presumed to be powerful, law confers validity on the fiction of an orderly social organization which can then be used in living daily life. Only with the construction of the myth of society can the deviance of the drinking-driver be believable.

The paradigmatic status of the myth is conferred by a society. By stating and restating an abstract model of the drinking-driver in both cognitive and moral terms, the total apparatus of law enunciation—the legislature, the judiciary, and the police—reinforces a belief in the particular myth. The myth becomes for its audience the *fact* of social order. By that I mean that the ritual of law conveys a sense that the myth of the drinking-driver as a moral object is shared by others. The statement of law, acting within the public arena, reinforces its own presuppositions about what it is that is shared or believed to be right as the conditions of a shared social order. In this sense law creates our image of the society.

Functional interpretations of social actions have implicitly assumed this. They have suggested that the legislative and the judicial processes operate in ways which mitigate and soften conflict, especially where it is unavoidable. Thus in discussing the symbolic import of the cases on the First Amendment, Rozann Rothman writes: "Sharply divergent expectations are modified and the ambiguities of belief and perception which are the source of the controversy over the amendment are muted. Legal precedent, terminology and ritual surround the controversy, soften the impact of passion and help to maintain a complex interrelationship of divergent beliefs and perceptions" (R. Rothman 1978, p. 78).

As an element in the production of culture, law has a stylized content. Its patterned forms, discussed in chap. 5, and its modes of enunciation and passage provide an abstract mold for impressing rules of public order. This is the ritualistic aspect of legal process. Legal rules are the publicly admissible ones. The thinkability of conflict about the legitimacy of drinking-driving or the life-styles and values which such a conflict might entail are shunted out of the public arenas. In one of my favorite comic

as celebrate it, it becomes true, the social order

strips, "Miss Peach," the young pupils are told by their teacher that next week there will be a speaker on juvenile delinquency. "Oh goody," says one of the kindergarten children, "will he be for it or against it?" To be "for" drinking-drivers has no standing in the public forums; the issue is not at conflict at that level.

Yet as has been shown, the conflict emerges at the level of specific situated actions where human interests, organizational contingencies, ambiguities of perception, and other standards of morality intervene between the idealization stated in the abstract mythology and ritual and the specificity and facticity of the here and now. Although this discrepancy appears as corrupt or illegitimate it is partially inherent in the nature of the universal and abstract character of public culture.

As myth and as ritual the law of drinking-driving dramatizes the existence of a society in which there is a moral order, that is, a set of standards which operate universally. There is a public standard that carries the ring of authority and legitimacy. In that moral order, the dangerousness of drinking and driving does not have the same meaning as the dangerousness of imperfections and risks of "normal" driving. Drinking-driving is a moral lapse, the action of flawed people who fail to observe and obey the boundaries that should distinguish legitimate cultural releases from illegitimate ones. Theirs is the sin of not being rational about irrational behavior.

Where my point of view most significantly diverges from the functional is also where I find the work of the cultural anthropologists least useful in describing and analyzing modern societies. For me the emphasis in modern societies is on the public sphere as different from the routine sphere of situated acts. The law of drinking-driving is a drama about an orderly moral and cognitive world. It creates that world and in that sense enters the process of social control. It establishes a society against which the drinking-driver appears factually and morally deviant. It therefore invests the world with meaning. The relation of that law to behavior is a problematic, empirical question. One level of activity and understanding does not exclude the other but the two are analytically separate and follow separate directives.

This analysis of law and public drama seems close to Victor Turner's conceptions of ritual as displaying the unification of theme and countertheme in cultures. In my usage it is not so—quite the opposite—and the distinction is essential. For Turner, as for many anthropologists, ritual actions ("cultural performances") are expressions of latent conflicts which, through the action of ritual, are resolved. Through rituals, writes Turner, "people are induced to want to do what they must do. In this sense ritual action is akin to a sublimation process . . . symbolic behavior actually "creates" society for pragmatic purposes—including in society both structure and communitas" (Turner 1974, p. 56).

Three significant distinctions make the functionalism of Turner's perspective less applicable in the avenues and halls of modern life. First, modern societies are highly differentiated into groups whose experiences, categories of judgment, and criteria of morality as well as economic and material interests lead toward conflict. Alternate themes and counterthemes exist, both between and within groups, but they are often held by separate and conflicting communities. In modern pluralistic "society," the absolutist order is fictive, problematic, and often illusory. It is what the law works at, not within.

Secondly, the similarity of participation and observation which anthropologists assume in ritual is lacking in modern life. Only Catholics participate in the Mass; only Jews celebrate the Day of Atonement. If I were to view the entire legal process as one seamless web, a single cultural performance, I would ignore the fact that law—the higher level of acts—is not the experience of a large segment of the population. They know about drinking-driving, for example, know that it is against the law in a way other than a casual traffic offense. But they are an aggregate of drinkers and nondrinkers, of drivers and nondrivers, most of whom will never be arrested for drinking-driving or be close to those who have been; some will never experience the act of driving while under the influence of alcohol, although this is less true of DUIA than of other crimes. Knowledge of the character of "the law" is vicarious for them and may even require special studies. The entire "society" does not participate in the same way or at the same level.

This problem of the two audiences is precisely what has been involved in so much of the study of legal impacts. In Auden's famous poem it is only the judges who say "Law is the Law." Sociologists, political scientists, lawyers, and police know differently. The judge may know differently too, but they are not always acting toward the same audience as are the legal practitioners and enforcers who are in touch with crime and delinquency every day. This is the third distinction.

Both law and science construct a world of universal, abstract rules and values. It is an orderly and predictable world, intelligible and legitimate, a world of authority. In creating meaning the dramas of public action shore up a fence against the awesome skepticism of unending alternatives, ambiguous facts, and the confusion of the concrete and the particular.

Conclusions

The Drama of ~~make believe~~
Public Action

The Cultural Drama of Drinking and Driving

Both the science and the law of drinking and driving create an orderly account of danger in the contemporary world. It is an account of the conflict between self-control and self-indulgence. There is a cognitive order in which drinking renders the individual motorist unable to control the machinery of driving adequately enough to avoid danger to self and to others. There is a moral order in which the use of alcohol is singled out as especially heinous—an act which the motorist could have and should have avoided. The drama of the drinking-driver is a mythical story of the "killer-drunk"—the evil of the person who ignores the boundaries of prudent living and planning and by this action kills innocent victims and even himself.

At one level, and in relation to alternative possible accounts, it is a drama of individualism. The responsibility is in the individual, not in the social institutions or in the natural world. As the modern novel has been the drama of the individual making his way in confrontation with the world, so has modern American law emphasized the individual at fault as the source of praise, blame, and responsibility. So too does the drama of drinking and driving focus the explanation of danger on the flawed person—on moral failing. The drinking-driver has failed to live up to a standard of competence morally required on the road. And he has done so by choice and by indulging in pleasure to the eradication of rationality, prudence, and planning.

It is essential to remember that the focus on individual action is not inherent in the object—the phenomenon of auto accidents. In chapter 2 I pointed to other ways in which the phenomenon could be conceptualized. The approach of the "unsafe car" ignores the drinking-driver and seeks solutions through automobile designs which might enable drinking and driving to be conducted more safely. It ignores the individual as a source of danger and places the ownership of the problem outside the individual and in social institutions to regulate design of the auto. The story of the "killer-drunk" is then a story that is deeply embedded in an individualistic world in which moral actions lead to safety and immoral actions threaten me and you and the actor himself.

At another level it is a story specifically about alcohol. As I also pointed out in an earlier chapter, alcohol has a particular significance in the story. There is no research into the question of how it is that people under the influence of alcohol ever manage to drive safely or how they might do so. The law does not include other conditions, such as inexperience, incompetence due to age, temporary physical handicap, sedatives, sleepiness, or other limiting phenomena, either singly or as a general condition rendering the motorist unfit to drive at that time.

The lack of public conflict over this focus suggests the particular meaning of alcohol as a public symbol. The "prudent man" recognizes the boundaries within which he must observe norms of control and norms of release. The normal person observes the boundaries. It is a sign of irresponsibility and moral failing to do otherwise, not to recognize the particular risk and responsibility in using a substance which places one outside the mood of rational planning and self-control. Hence self-indulgence should not be condoned or even supported. The counterdrama—of the social person for whom drinking is a response to the rules of the group—is one in which drinking-driving is part of the "normal" risks of driving, in which the normal person is not faced with demands for so pristine a standard of self-control. In this drama, drinking-driving is no more heinous than are other traffic offenses; they are all within the risks of a standard of competence based on the "natural man."

Lastly the drama of the drinking-driver is a drama of order. It presents a model of an orderly world. There are generalizations which carry a ring of certainty. There is an orderly world in which disorder—the failure of people to act in acordance with social standards—produces natural disorder. Both cognitively, as a matter of science, and morally, as a matter of law, this is a world in which our actions explain our results. There is predictability, consistency, certainty. Lear's message in the Shakespearean play is *not* a paradigm for understanding life:

Like flies to the wanton gods are we.
They kill us for their sport.

The Public Drama

The study of drinking and driving has served me as a means to bring a
general perspective into the analysis of public action. I want to explore
that perspective in greater depth in this chapter. The two words that
comprise the title of this section—*public* and *drama*—both possess ambiguities which are clues to the nature of public drama. The term *public*
has at least two common usages. One is embedded in the meaning of
"public interest." Here the word acts as a contrast to *special, particular,*
and *personal,* which express the sense of being unconnected to the collective concerns. Public actions are attributed to the interests and values
of the total group. They are enunciated by persons who claim to speak
"for," or in a capacity representative of, the collectivity. People who
occupy public positions as officials of an institution often distinguish
between such acts and those in which they act as themselves, "in a private
capacity."

In another usage what is public is distinguished from what is private by
its observability. Acts conducted in private are not visible to anyone; they
are privileged and backstage. Public acts are out front, conducted where
the actors have no control over who may witness them and no means for
screening the audience.[1]

Drama, in one usage of the term, refers to staged presentations, as in
the theater. In another sense it includes an element of excitement and
heightened experience, as in someone's being described as theatrical or
dramatic (R. Williams 1976, pp. 94–95; Young 1965, p. 151). Conceptualizing public actions as drama means that we think about them *as
if* they were performances artistically designed to create and maintain the
attention and interest of an audience.

Public dramas are acts undertaken in the name of and in the sight of
the collectivity, visible and observable. They occupy a particular arena of
life. To portray them as dramas is to utilize a metaphor drawn from the
theater and apply it to another arena. It is to see public acts as presentations directed toward an audience which is the target of the actors
attention.

There is an irony inherent in the metaphor of drama. Is not drama
"make-believe"? Coleridge spoke of "the willing suspension of disbelief." That suspension is necessary to make an audience of Manhattan
sophisticates believe the actor who pretends to be in eleventh-century
Denmark when they "know" that he is, *in fact,* in a building on West

Forty-sixth Street in 1970 (E. Burns 1972). Drama would imply that action is not, as it seems to be, oriented toward the instrumental ends claimed but is instead, or in addition, a communication between the actor and the audience—not action but communication.

An amusing and apocryphal tale may make the point more "dramatic" (i.e., interesting and attention getting). About fifteen years ago the Department of Music at the University of Illinois at Urbana was one of the major centers in America for contemporary and electronic music. To more traditional classical tastes its concerts were often abominations. At one concert the pianist proceeded physically to take the piano apart. The widow of a former music faculty member was in the audience. She and her husband had both represented the "old guard" of classical tastes. Enraged at the desecration she saw before her, she leaped onto the stage and started throwing chairs at the "pianist." Police were called and came onto the stage brandishing clubs. Throughout the entire "action" the audience sat not mute or horrified but gleefully applauding what seemed to be a "performance"—a "happening." They could not distinguish between action meant as communication and action meant as instrumental means to a tangible goal. They were unable to shift frameworks (Goffman 1974, chap. 5).

Human behavior can be seen as involving both aspects, often at the same time and often one more than the other. Even the most instrumental act tells us something about the actor; something personal is communicated to the observer. The cashier at the supermarket conveys a commitment or lack of commitment to the "seriousness" of the *role* (itself a term borrowed from drama) by the manner of standing, speaking, and looking, by dress and demeanor. Every act is a presentation and a performance as well as a task (Goffman 1956). The cashier can take money, charge groceries, and make change in an attitude of burlesque, sarcasm, warm friendliness, or "pure business." In each instance different versions of the cashier and the transaction are conveyed, a different meaning of action is dramatized.

To see public acts through the metaphor of drama is not to deny a possible instrumental, utilitarian component. It is to emphasize the existence of a nonutilitarian, symbolic element, so that the action must be understood, like a staged drama, as intrinsic to its own performance; it is to see it from the standpoint of its ceremonial and ritualistic usage. Abraham Moles, discussing information processing research, has made a useful distinction between two levels of dimensions of all communication—a *semantic* and an aesthetic one:

Although materially connected, these two kinds of information, these two kinds of messages, obey independent structural laws. Without affecting the esthetic information, a theatrical play may have an incoherent, illogical or even senseless plot, increasing its semantic originality, or on the contrary a logical, rigid, inevitable, foreseeable plot, decreasing the originality and making the play easier to follow. [Moles 1968, p. 133][2]

On one level, public actions are presentations of the persons on stage. Public officials and public figures convey attributes of themselves by their behavior. They appear as heroic, cowardly, foolish, villainous, or otherwise possessed of character (Klapp 1962, 1964). That is an interesting aspect of public presentations but no different, in its analytical significance, from the analysis of interpersonal interaction. My concern is with the character of the public drama, both as visible and as infused with a collective import. How a priest conducts the Mass is a matter of his self-presentation, but the Mass is itself a form of presentation with attributes apart from its specific performers. From the standpoint of authority, the play's the thing and not the actors.

The description and analysis of public knowledge presented in this study have given a picture of the staging of an orderly and consistent system of alcohol information. This system was shown as a method for establishing a logical, consistent world and not as a direct reflection of the state of information and fact. This constructed quality appears as a ceremony in which a drama of logical parts is given public validity and credence. In it the performers create a drama of alcohol problems as serious and worthy of attention. They direct the attitudes of an audience toward a version of cognitive reality and moral order. There is a gap between this public and orderly world and the routine events which make up the scientific scholar's world or the day-to-day life of the drinker. They impinge on each other, but they are not the same.

This process of constructing or creating a public order, a public arena of actions, is at the heart of the theory of public actions as performances. I will begin with an analysis of private interactions and then move into public ones. Joan Emerson has analyzed how it is that the male gynecologist and the female patient act to define their interaction as nonsexual. The situation must be defined as one of medical practice, not of sexual encounter or experimental science. The staff must appear competent in the performance but yet not obliterate the sense of the patient as a human being. Such devices as draping the body segment under examination, using technical language, and wearing uniforms convey the medical character of the action and define the patient as a technical object, not a sexual one. Yet less technical language is also used and comments made which convey personal concern and attentiveness. ("Isn't it a nice day today.") The order constructed must face the precariousness of handling *both* the theme of medical situation and the countertheme of personal concerns (Emerson 1970). The entire action is invested with a logic and with ceremonies which serve to symbolize the ordered situation. (That such interactions "get out of hand" from time to time is indicative of their precariousness.)

The public drama follows its own rules and creates its own order. In the gynecological examination the parties to the interaction are face to face. Their ritual acts convey both rules and the appropriate attitudes to be presented in the interaction by each, including when and how the counterthemes are to be introduced and conveyed. They are stylized encounters. Public behavior is more often mass behavior, characteristically transmitted through newspaper, television, and radio, and/or reported through secondary levels of talk between interactants. Horton and Wohl coined the term "para-social interaction" to describe relations between television performers and members of their audience, who have no reciprocal obligations or relationships to other members of the mass audience to guide and influence their "behavior" as watchers (Horton and Wohl 1956). Mass relations go well beyond those of performers in front of intended audiences.[3] Public actions are "observed" by many to whom they are reported and their dramatic features conveyed. When a public figure acts, he or she may not do so with any specific audience in sight or in mind. Whether motivated or not, the reporting of the acts constitutes an audience relationship anyway. Public protesters are frequently aware of this and create events which will be reported in the news.

Viewed from the perspective of Emerson's analysis of rule setting and situation defining elements in interaction, in what manner, if any, is social organization being generated in public acts and events? How does the public event create a drama which communicates any elements of order in a significant fashion to its audience? Part of the problem of utilizing analysis of interaction to examine public behavior is the very lack of interactional features as we know them from face-to-face behavior. As Horton and Wohl suggest, we could examine such relations between performers and audiences as a unique kind of interaction and search for the ways in which new forms of intimacy are generated. My approach is very different.

Many things go on simultaneously in human action. I take as an example speeches or press conferences by the president of the United States. In one dimension they are direct exhortations to the vast population to do

something, as when President Carter sought in a press conference statement in 1978 to generate support for his energy program then getting a
cool reception in the Senate. Included in this dimension was the conveying of information. All this is instrumental understanding—speech as a
means to an end, as related to some reference points outside of the
communication. In another dimension the president was conveying
something about himself, that he is a "serious," informed, articulate
person, concerned with public interests. Here the press conference has
a dramatic quality as an arena in which the president "acts out" his
persona.

There is still a third dimension to the public drama which is our major
concern. The press conference is itself a drama of participation and governmental accountability. The president and the reporters convey and
communicate a statement about the rules of public action that portrays
openness and response as characteristics of governmental order that are
cherished. Were the president to refuse to answer questions or to answer
only written questions, the conference would have a different meaning. In
this sense, the conference is a ritual of democratic government. The other
two "functions" might well be carried out in other ways, but not this one.

That presidents use press conferences to "manage news" and that
newspapers construct events in ways differing from the "realities" are of
course part of the issues which concern me here.[4] That the participative
character of the press conference may be belied by everyday events of
government is at the heart of the gap problem analyzed here.

Another thing happening in the press conference is that a certain
content is brought into the sphere of public arenas. The question of
energy is now made a matter of debate, something that can sensibly and
naturally be a problem area. Many arguments about whether or not
governmental officials should discuss questions such as abortion,
homosexuality, or criminality are questions of this nature. What will the
very discussion of a topic as a public matter do for its legitimacy as an
issue? Will it convert into a problematic issue a mode of behavior toward
which a "taken-for-granted" public attitude has existed? Will it make
something thinkable? Murray Edelman asserts that once a mode of behavior or intended action has become a matter of public controversy it is
a signal that participants and partisans are prepared to accept a solution
that will not be their optimum. It conveys a sense that "people" seek a
viable resolution of the issue or, in my terms, that what was formerly not
an issue has now become one. The ensuing debate, Edelman suggests, will
not change the values and commitments of the partisans, but they are
willing to accept a less than favorable resolution: "The occurrence of

serious public debate between proponents and opponents is therefore also a signal that the issue is not worth fighting and dying or killing for" (Edelman 1971, p. 45). The visit of Sadat to Jerusalem in 1977 had this symbolic meaning. That gave it great political import.

I want to move beyond this insight to characterize the way in which the public drama creates and constructs that public order which Edelman views as occurring when an issue becomes public. From that perspective the press conference and its content are clues to what is in the public realm and what is the organization of public life as distinct from routine, situated, and personal interaction. To express this thought I need to discuss the concept of "pluralistic ignorance."

A degree of pluralistic ignorance underlies social institutions, especially in complex societies with diverse and conflicting cultures and differentiated social levels. The characteristic of pluralistic ignorance is that each member of the group imputes meaning and criteria to the others which he himself does not share. Each, ignorant of the others, believes in a wider consensus than exists. Such ignorance is often the basis for imputing a greater orderliness to a society than exists at the level of situated actions. What we construe as the content of "how others think," of what George Herbert Mead called the "generalized other," reinforces our nebulous perception of an orderly system of social organization: "society."[5]

Public presentations assume significance, from this perspective, because they convey a description of what is the public order, even though it is not the governing order of interpersonal and routine actions: "In seeing public morality as unassailable [people] tend far more to act in accord with that morality, even if privately they do not agree with the rules, than would be the case if they believed other individuals also disagreed with the rules" (J. Douglas 1971, p. 308).

The realization of the signifying character of public dramas underlies their importance to my analysis of authority. They assume importance whether or not they govern routine and situated behavior. The effect of marijuana legislation and the staunch public antipathy to the use of hallucinogenic drugs is to stamp drug use as deviant behavior, to support the view that it is the action of marginal and abnormal persons, that "society" possesses a consensus about morality from which such behavior is disapproved. It reassures those for whom the social and cultural changes in youth and in life-style are symbolized in drug use that the public order is consistent with their values and that it is their values which are dominant in American life (Kaplan 1970; Gusfield 1963a, 1975).

Public acts follow their own rules of decorum and demeanor; rules which are not the guiding principles of more private areas of life. The same individual may condone and accept behavior in the "backstage" of his life which he finds shocking, distasteful and even criminal when performed on the "front stage" of public arenas. In recent years in the United States, the public admission that a political candidate has told a joke, even among intimate friends, in which some ethnic group is ridiculed, is a matter for outraged responses from many, both within and outside the group lampooned. To learn that a presidential candidate has told friends a "Polish joke" offends others as well as Poles. The same people who are so offended may nevertheless share such jokes among their friends and family.

The distinction is not a simple case of hypocrisy. What happens on the public stage is made the standard of legitimacy, of what are the canons of the society. To grant acceptance to such behavior when it emerges in the light of public reports is to create the societal rule; to generate the perception of living in a society in which such action is legitimate.

In this way the public and the private constitute semiautonomous realms, each responsive to different norms. We do not seem to want public life to mirror our private behavior. A different face greets us when we look at social order portrayed in public actions. Their ritual character provides us with the fiction of a morality more aspiration than achievement.

The Cultural Autonomy of Legal Acts

What does this analysis mean for the phenomenon of the legal gap and analysis of deterrence? It does not "explain" the effectiveness or ineffectiveness of law and legislation to influence behavior in one direction or another. It brings to our attention the conceptualization of the drinking-driver on the level of public and routine orders. This conceptualization determines the categories with which social order is seen, and thus the character of the conflicts and the suppositions about obedience and violation toward which law and legislation also contribute. The public drama of law provides the expectations and perceptions of what is normal and acclaimed and what is deviant and condemned. It tells us what is publicly admissible.

In his intensive analysis of criminal law in eighteenth-century England, Douglas Hay has developed a thesis similar to mine about laws that seemed ineffective (Hay 1975, pp. 17–63). The criminal law of eighteenth-century England stipulated severe penalties, including death, for many crimes against property, but such penalties were seldom exacted.[6] Neither were efforts to reform the public statements of the law successful. Such seemingly irrational behavior on the part of elites makes sense, according to Hay, if we see those elites as contributing to the legitimacy of their authority through demonstrating their adherence to justice rather than impersonal law, to mercy rather than interest. For Hay, the problem of the gap is seen as serving to bolster authority in the eighteenth century. Hay also views law as a public as well as a routine show of character, in his case "the character of the ruling class."[7]

Both Hay and I look at law as something in addition to a system of commands. In this we differ from what Feeley refers to as "a view that emphasizes the 'command' of the official and the subsequent reaction by the subject" (Feeley 1966, p. 226). This is in contrast to what he describes as a "conception of law . . . emphasizing a system of rules with a 'life of their own.'" But it is exactly this quality of separation of public from routine acts that I wish to stress.

The problem needs to be assayed as the relation between public acts as communicative events on the one hand and the perception and attitude of the audience on the other. Implicitly I have presented considerable data to show that the communicative act of drinking-driving law is not a reflection of community behavior or norms. Drinking-driving is far from deviant action in a statistical sense or even in the sense of lying outside routine police and judicial enforcement. Drinking-driving law may, however, reflect the experience of audiences for whom drinking-driving is atypical. The reflection, I hypothesize, is a double reflection, like seeing the back of your head in a mirror held in front of you to reflect the picture from a mirror behind you. What is seen is a version of "society" in which one's experience and values are resonant and homologous with the dominant and the normal experience of the population.

From this standpoint law provides a reassurance to some that the society is indeed *their* society, its meanings their meanings and its morality their morality. The issue is *not* entirely, or even primarily, the reality of situational actions—the extent to which the mirrored image is a fictional account of a real world or not. The public order has a life of its own. It states the authoritative meanings of the culture as an absolutist, homogeneous culture in a homogeneous society. As such it is capable of assuring those whose values it reflects that there is a society of consistent values in a culture of logical and morally satisfying meanings. It creates the illusion of cultural dominance.

It is in this fashion that versions of social structure become taken as reality. We become prevented from seeing our own experience through our own eyes but wear instead the glasses of cultural categories that gain life in public acts. Thus the proliferation of youth culture through the mass media becomes the backdrop of normalcy through which parents and adolescents judge their own typicality. The pluralistic ignorance brought to bear on public conceptions of "society" hides the diversity and conflict which lie just outside the range of public monitoring. The separation of the immediate world of direct experience and the world constructed and created in public ceremonies, rituals, and dramas is sustained.

Murray Edelman, whose work on symbolic politics has been of enormous influence, characterizes such assurance as a form of "political quiescence," serving to hide advantages and influence of interest groups over the administration of legislative measures.[8] It is a record of "hollow victories," of reforms that failed to reform and interest groups defeated at the level of public drama, only to rise like the phoenix in the administrative corridors of government.

Edelman's thesis is one I agree is correct, and he is sensitive to the affective meanings of public and visible politics. But events have multiple dimensions. Sometimes at one and the same time, sometimes with one dimension overshadowing another contradictory to it. My intent in this work is to discover, study, and analyze a lesser known dimension and attempt to see where it is most useful. While the version of society may be taken as the description of how things are as behavioral acts, much of the affect surrounding public life emerges in contexts where the utilitarian, technical assumptions of effectiveness are widely recognized as weak. A public aware of the limited effectiveness of Prohibition legislation, death penalty, antiabortion laws, marijuana prohibitions, or the limited impact of pornography on behavior is not less moved to support the passage of laws to eradicate behavior which appears to be ineradicable (Gusfield 1963a; Zurcher and Kirkpatrick 1976; Carson 1976; Hellman 1975; Chandler 1976). Such assurance is symbolic assurance both in the sense of not being instrumental and technical but also in the sense of being about the symbolic structure of the society—its consistency and moral value. It assures by demonstrating that there is authority and that it is on the side of the audience. It is a culture-creating and culture-validating mechanism.

These considerations help me to recognize ways in which specific issues take on other symbolic properties in another sense and partake of the literary nature of symbols as items of language or action. Symbols in literature possess conventional meanings that establish linkages to wider elements than given in the act or term itself. Thus the title of Ibsen's *A Doll's House* has other meanings besides that of a child's toy. The poet uses darkness and light to stand for optimism and pessimism. It is just such metaphorical usages that enable laws and legislation to be more than they seem. The battle over marijuana legislation, because of its emotional level, could be understood as a drama about the authority of adult culture and its power over youth. The ferocity of punishment in the marijuana laws must then be seen in the context of a historical period when adult public values were under attack in wide areas, including sex, work goals, public decorum, and dress. The drug issue was a microcosm of the general issue of youth versus adulthood, of older and younger generations. Whatever ocurred at the behavioral level, the marijuana laws had their own meaning as culture (Gusfield 1975).

This realization makes the struggle over the content and form of public dramas understandable whatever their instrumental importance (Warner 1959). If culture is being shaped and society being formed as a public entity, then whose culture and whose society it is to be becomes an important counter in political acts. Many public issues contain a moral dimension and a cultural consequence. The campaign to extend the retirement age from sixty-five to seventy is not only a movement with structural consequences in the form of longer earning years. It is also a movement to redefine the point of entry into old age as a part of American consciousness and thus a bid for greater respect and power by a portion of the population. In that sense it contains a moral meaning. So too has the drinking-driver issue emerged as an issue of morals and law, as a definer of superior and inferior styles of life.

Watergate: An Example of Public Drama

I will bring this chapter to a close with an example of public dramas as mechanisms for the creation of public order. My vehicle is the Watergate case but especially the interview series which Mr. Nixon gave on television in Spring 1977, almost three years after his resignation.

The assertion that the events of the Watergate "coverup" revealed a profound dereliction of duty on the part of Mr. Nixon as president and his staff to uphold the law was sometimes countered by the statement that such "derelictions" were common in American political life. Other presidents have done the same but were not exposed. From this perspective, the move to impeach Nixon was motivated by personal vendetta and political advantage. The public attention given to the Senate investigation of the Watergate events and the House committee on impeachment, the actions of the jury, the indictments and Judge Sirica's actions culminating in the evidence of the tapes and the resignation all created a dominant belief in the guilt of the president. As a public drama Watergate has many meanings, but one of those is its dramatizing of the rule of law—the doctrine that no person, even the president, ought to be beyond responsibility for illegal acts. At stake, then, is the legitimacy of the political order, and the focus of inquiry could not be more visible and dramatic—the office of the chief executive, the highest elected post in the country. The focus is not the legitimacy of this or that particular president but of the presidency as an institution.

In his initially aired interview with a television "personality," David Frost, Mr. Nixon discussed the events that led up to his resignation. For much of the two hours he maintained an air of innocence, sometimes claiming that his complicity in the Watergate "coverup" had been exaggerated, sometimes implying that he had tempered law and discretion no more than had previous presidents. Toward the end of the interview, he dropped the posture of wronged innocence for one of humility and even shame. Here are his relevant words: "I let down my friends. I let down the country. I let down our system of government and the dreams of all those young people that ought to get into government but think its all too corrupt and the rest . . . Yep I . . . I let the American people down and I have to carry that burden with me for the rest of my life" (*New York Times*, May 5, 1977, B 11:6).

The *New York Times* headlined the story on page one as, "I Let the American People Down." In covering himself with shame, Mr. Nixon helped restore the sense of a consistent public order. It matters not if we live in a cynical world, where we disbelieve the motives and statements of authorities. What is crucial for this interpretation of the Watergate events is that when evil was visible it was recognized as such. Only in showing his accord with the principle of a public order did Nixon contribute to its legitimacy. It does not matter what are the actor's motives, in political drama as on the theatrical stage. Even if there is no sincerity there, as in the playing of any role, a deference to the values of the audience validates them.[9] It is in the honor that Vice pays to Virtue by masking itself that Virtue mounts its pedestal.

The world to which so many of us respond is a world "out of reach, out of sight, out of mind," as Walter Lippmann characterized it (Combs and Mansfield 1976, p. 180). The work of public officials, of lawmakers and lawgivers, creates an orderly and morally directed society. It is fictive in many ways and a flawed guide to the daily life of its audiences. Yet its consequence for human life and human behavior is by no means slight. The magic of the great statesman has often come from his realization that such illusions are also realities.

8 The Perspective of
Sociological Irony

In 1974 I participated in an international conference on the prevention of drinking problems, held in Berkeley, California (Room and Sheffield 1975). During much of the research and writing that has ended in the completion of this book I have constantly reminded myself of a discussion at that conference. It raises a pertinent question on which to bring this study to closure.

Several of us at the conference had presented a view of alcohol fact, theory, and policy consistent with the general perspective of sociological constructivism and epistemological relativism that underlies this study (Gusfield 1975; Room and Sheffield 1974). In an exasperated tone, Griffith Edwards, the researcher and clinician at Maudsley Hospital in London, berated us. He accused us of having our fingers in our ears so that we needn't hear the suffering (Room and Sheffield 1975, pp. 141ff). It is a criticism not unlike that occasioned by my Goldsmiths College critics (cf. chap. 4, p. 106). In positioning ourselves "above the battle" were we denying the experiential reality of alcohol problems, of alcohol addiction or, in this case, of drinking-driving? in these last pages I want to bring into clear focus both the nature of the perspective taken here and what I see as its value. My intention is not to deny Griffith Edward's complaint but rather to justify my use of earmuffs.

This has been a book about how technical and moral realities are created and given form as socially shared facts and values. I have tried to show how particularistic data are interpreted and cast into definitive and generalized results of scientific knowledge. In this process scientific personnel, journalistic and policy groups, and occupations and movements committed to diminishing alcohol and/or automobile problems have constructed a cognitive reality about alcohol and auto accidents. In the style of presentation social knowledge is dramatized as certain, definitive, and accurate as a base for justifiable policies. The drinking-driver is further presented in a language and style which command or induce an attitude toward him and his actions. In this sense, a moral as well as a cognitive posture is being taken. Science possesses a rhetoric as well as a rationale.

not "wrong" but over-simplified

It is not that such knowledgeable conclusions and theories are "wrong," in the sense of being incorrect and invalid as general statements. It is that the style of scientific presentation and its transmission to interested publics create a reality of undoubted certitude. It is not that alcohol is unrelated to automobile accidents. It is that the system of asking questions excludes alternative ways of asking. Thus the auto itself—its design and mass consumption—is *not* viewed as a possible source of accidents that are capable of being controlled. Neither are such variables as age or nonintoxicated conditions of the motorist (sleepiness or emotional distress, for example). Nor is the interaction of variables displayed. Alcohol alone is singled out as *the* cause.

It is the emphasis on alcohol as the problem and the location of auto accidents in individual motorists that are part of the culture described here. Whether phenomena are viewed as problems or not prefigures the research and policy. It is what I mean by cultural assumptions. Every perspective is a way of *not* seeing as well as a way of seeing.

This may seem like a restatement of much of what recent writers following Gramsci have referred to as "cultural hegemony" (Joll 1977; Gramsci 1971; Bauman 1976). Here the emphasis is on the way in which ruling groups create legitimation and functional response to their power and interests not by direct assertion of power but by construction of a cognitive and moral reality, a set of motives and directions in the ruled which are consonant with the needs and interests of ruling groups.

I have chosen not to examine the hegemonic character of the drinking-driving culture in this volume. That is, I have avoided examining the relation of drinking-driving knowledge to the interests, values, and sentiments of particular groups, classes, or occupations in the United States. In part, that task has been done, but it necessitates a separate volume in which I examine technical knowledge as the rationale of professional groups and the use of the medical metaphor as the invented foundation of alcohol expertise (Gusfield, forthcoming). The relationship of the alcohol and automobile industries to the policy orientations of alcohol studies and safety knowledge is still another facet of the social structure of alcohol and automobile abuse.

The relation of culture and social structure can, and should, be examined in a more macrohistorical perspective. The individualism that is apparent in so much of the drinking-driving orientation to auto safety can itself be set in the context of American individualism, a historical study of considerable magnitude and well beyond this volume. So too, the changes in orientation toward auto safety represented in the consumer movement of the 1960s and in the welfare state orientation of the medical metaphor need to be analyzed.

But there is still another reason for my not discussing hegemony. The cultural categories depicted here are not significantly hegemonic in their impact on day-to-day behavior, either in controlling the act of drinking and driving or in establishing the working rules of legal enforcement. It is the symbolic and mythic character of that culture which I have emphasized in the last section of the book. Legislation and judicial decisionmaking are seen as public culture. They create a version of a consensual "society" which is ordered, consistent, and predictable. In doing so they support a moral order and a cognitive order, ritualistically repeated and supporting enforcement as public authority. The public culture of drinking-driving maintains the acceptance and indisputability of a culture of rational, responsible risktaking and the evil of self-expressive, hedonistic action. When ordinary traffic infractions are sharply distinguished from drinking-driving, the use of alcohol is given a special status; it becomes morally deviant, and auto accidents become results of moral turpitude.

The authority of public culture, like that of public knowledge, is often illusory. Its illusionary quality is evidenced in the casual and widespread existence of drinking-driving as a "normal" event in American life. It is further seen in the situated actions of police, lawyers, and courts where practical contingencies, specific justice, and the interests and power of parties influence outcomes and actions. The public culture is an abstraction. Its relation to specific, situated actions of participants in the "society" is problematic. It cannot be taken for granted.

What I have been about in this study is the development of an added dimension, a different perspective toward public acts of knowledge creation and legal policy. What is stressed in this study is their existence as dramatic events—as presentations of reality and of society. The scientific "state of the art" has been shown to be dependent on "taken-for-granted" assumptions about what constitutes significant data, to be couched in language which builds abstract and mythic generalization from specific and particularistic data. What results is a rhetoric of an orderly world, a dramatization of causal and political responsibility which creates a basis for policies and actions.

Similarly legal acts of legislating and making judicial decisions dramatically state a set of principles of human behavior which create a world in which moral responsibility is clear and in which the natural order of cause and effect in auto safety is influenced by the moral character of motorists. The hedonism of drinking is a symbol for the irrational pursuits of self-expressive and indulgent attitudes. These clash with the rational and instrumental attitudes necessitated by industrial life. The "good man" keeps these attitudes separate and avoids risk.

What I have done may indeed be seen, as my critics in Berkeley and in London suggested, as "reducing" knowledge and law to something less than has been their claim. My relativism carries with it a tone of skeptical disbelief in the "reality" of the problem. The authority of knowledge and of law is part of the world's illusion, a Pirandellian play before an audience that expects realism and is given fantasy. I am not sure that I can succeed in resisting the claim that my perspective is anarchistic and nihilistic. What I can do is clarify its value to the general perspective of sociology and defend its use.

The Ironic Stance

Having examined the documents of research and the decisions and statutes of lawmakers, how shall I characterize my own work? In chapter 4 I analyzed the rhetorical elements in a research document which is part of the "state of the art" in drinking-driving research. I was concerned, among other aspects of its style of presentation, with the point of view of the writer toward his object—the drinking-driver. The distance which he observed toward his object is in many ways similar to the distance which I have been observing toward the scientific study and the legal actions in drinking-driving knowledge and legal policy. I find it useful to discuss the two approaches toward science and law as matters involving the use of figures of speech, of tropes.

Literary and linguistic analysis frequently uses four species of major tropes: metonymy, synecdoche, metaphor, and irony (White 1973a, pp. 31–38; Burke 1945, pp. 503–17). The distinction between metonymy (in which a part stands for the whole, e.g., "He is all heart") and metaphor (in which similarities are discovered between differences, e.g., "She is tough as nails") has been used by linguists and cultural anthropologists following Roman Jakobson and Claude Levi-Strauss to characterize the technical, scientific language of realism and the metaphorical, artistic language of myth and poetry (Jakobson 1966; Levi-Strauss 1966, pp. 191–216).

The knowledge about drinking-driving discussed in part 1 of this study is presented by its creators and its broadcasters as metonymic—as a realistic description of nature arising from a representative sample of contiguous relationships of cause and effect. Contiguous relationship is metonymic. The legal acts of lawmaking bodies described in part 2 also are presented as realistic—as becoming causes for the action of subjects for whom the law is a rule of behavior. That is what the concept of law as deterrent implies.

In describing each of these areas of institutional life as couched in metaphorical language, I have acted to discount an implicit claim to realism which both science and law affect in their modes of presentation. In that process of discounting or disclaiming I have operated with the language of irony, the trope which Richard Brown characterizes as "a seeing something from the viewpoint of its antithesis" (R. Brown 1977, p. 172). Thus I have analyzed science as if it were art, and law as if it were myth, and both as if reality were theater. In doing this I have been negating the series of claims of scientists and lawgivers to be taken as authoritative and legitimate representors of a positive reality. The irony comes in showing that the content and consequence of authoritative actions are not what is maintained but are instead or in addition something opposite. We affect irony in our language when we describe a cowardly action as that of a "real tiger"—the tone of voice carrying the ironical meaning. Here irony becomes satire, becomes humorous in displaying that things are not what they seem but are their opposite.

It is in this unmasking that the sociological ironist incurs resistance and anger. My Goldsmiths College critics were right. One cannot engage in irony without assuming a distance and detachment from those being described. The ironist sets himself above his subjects by claiming a higher level of insight and awareness; by saying that he sees that the assumptions taken for granted by the scientists or lawgivers are not, as claimed, in the nature of reality but are instead matters of choice, functions of the linguistic, epistemological, and ideological paradigms with which they have approached material. It leaves the subjects in a new status contrary to that presented. They are self-interested and found to be hiding behind a mask of objectivity or unaware of their limitations. They are shown as magicians whose magical "tricks" are patently apparent. This attitude puts the ironist on a higher level than those he studies. As Hayden White expresses it, irony tends "to inspire a Mandarin-like disdain for those seeking to grasp the nature of social reality in either science or art" (H. White 1973a, p. 38).

The ironic character of any presentation will depend not only on its content but on the degree of awareness of the audience. A study of Hitler's Germany which contrasted claims to German cultural superiority with the atrocities of concentration camps would not be ironic today but might have been in 1940. Edward Gibbon, that master of historical irony, inverted the beliefs of his audience about the intolerance of Rome toward Christianity by depicting Christianity and Judaism as distinguished from Roman society by their monotheistic intolerance of other religions. Thus Gibbon's famous sentence that to the Roman populace all religions were equally true, to the philosophers all were equally false, and to the magistrates all were equally useful.

The impact of irony is then to hold up that which is taken for granted, familiar, and commonplace as something strange and problematic. If phenomena are made into topics of analysis the audience may be moved into a new perspective toward them. The cultural frameworks otherwise unrecognized now become matters of awareness. In this is one of the major methods of sociology: to approach human behavior as if it were unfamiliar, as if the observer were a stranger and everything observed had to be explained and nothing could be taken for granted.

Sociological irony contains similarities to art. Like the artist, the sociologist creates the possibility of alternative worlds. In demonstrating the institutional and/or cultural frames within which actions are given meaning, he imagines that things could be otherwise. That possibility for developing new and alternative lines of action is the significant feature of sociological thought and study. As Richard Brown puts it: "to the extent that social science is itself composed of 'of course statements', that is, only when sociology fails to be dramatic, only when it does not reveal unexpected relationships that have an ironic necessity, does it become banal." (R. Brown 1977, p. 182).

The negativism of irony is then essential to sociological method. The debunking, unmasking criticism of the sociologist is crucial to the unleashing of imagination. Like Shiva, the great God of the Shaivite Hindus, we are both Destroyers and Creators.

Sociological Irony: Utopian and Olympian

Kenneth Burke, who has been so influential in the framing of this book, deserves and merits one of the final words. In *A Grammar of Motives* he writes: "Irony arises when one tries, by the interaction of terms upon one another, to produce a *development* which uses all the terms. Hence, from the standpoint of this total form (this 'perspective of perspectives'), none of the participating 'sub-perspectives' can be treated as precisely right or precisely wrong" (Burke 1945, p. 512). In this is contained the lead to my response to Griffith Edwards's sorrow, dismay, and anger at the detachment of sociologists from the concrete problems of alcoholics and problem drinkers.

What I have been about in this book is the interpretation of actions, events, and words from perspectives other than those presented by the actors. I see this as in a continuous line with the dominant sociological tradition since Marx, Durkheim, and Weber. The sociologist is interested in what is characteristic of cultures, societies, and groups, not of individuals. His subject matter is the socially shared rules, understandings, and meanings by which social life is pursued. The clinician, the practitioner, the official cannot afford to stand outside the frameworks within which action occurs, to examine their institutions and beliefs as only one among a number of possible worlds. Mathematicians are reputed to say, "Reality is only a special case." Also for the sociologist, the existing world is an object of scrutiny, not acceptance; one among possibilities. By the same token, the sociologist's perspective is seen also as one among a number, another mode of interpreting the world. It does something different from though not necessarily a substitute for other interpretations. Sociological irony creates a new view of the drinking-driving phenomenon, looks at it from another angle. Paul Ricoeur has likened the study of human behavior to the study of texts. Just as the discourse, seen as text, is not dependent on the intentionality of the author, so too human action is open to interpretations. "The world is the ensemble of references opened up by the texts" (Ricoeur 1979, p. 79).

Sociological method thus becomes a way of seeing, a perspective. I am not denying the existence of a world of fact, independent of the minds that understand it. What is suggested is that "fact" is enormously ambiguous and so heavily intertwined with "understanding," with the cultural apparatuses of conceptualization, that it can only be assumed to be problematic in any particular instance. The metaphorical image for what I am trying to express is the plight of the six blind men in the Indian legend of the elephant. Each places his hand on a different part of the elephant's anatomy, and each describes a different beast. The sociologist strives to do all six and a seventh.

Here I arrive at the political implications of my argument. To find alternative ways of seeing phenomena is to imagine that things can be otherwise. To display the sources of belief in historical paradigms, institutional influences, power, and sentiment is to *reduce* a phenomenon to something else, as the ironist does. This cannot but be a diminution of the legitimacy which authority gains from a belief in its facticity. When the sociologist is so operating, he presents a world that is political rather than a world of technical necessity. If choice is possible, if new and alternative modes of acting are possible and imaginable, then the existent situation hides the conflicts and alternatives which can be imagined. This disposition to go beyond the individual to scrutinize the frameworks of behavior is the continuing thread of sociology across the years.

But there are at least two sharply divergent ways of examining social life through the prism of alternative perspectives. I call one utopian. Here the uncovering of the ephemeral character of the dominant perspective provides the occasion for the creation of a newer and better one. Irony as dialectic leads to a new synthesis but one that resolves the contradictions of the old thesis and suggests a new one. Thus the paradigm of sociological irony results in an intensification of political action; it produces a critical attitude toward dominant authority but a supportive one toward change. Just as the Prohibitionist official I quoted above (p. 165) said that "some symptoms are better than other symptoms" so the utopian ironist presumes some reality, some perspective that is better than other perspectives.

[handwritten margin note: utopians uncover all untruths so can create a better one]

In contrast, the Olympian sociologist is more detached, more skeptical of *all* perspectives. He views each occasion for the use of sociological irony as a critical act fostering the development of many perspectives, no one of which is inherently better than the others, each open to the partiality of language, interests, and sentiments. To quote Hayden White again: "Existentially projected into a full-blown world view, Irony would appear to be transideological . . . [it] tends to dissolve all belief in the possibility of positive political actions. In its apprehension of the essential folly or absurdity of the human condition, it tends to engender belief in the 'madness' of civilization itself" (H. White 1973a, p. 38).

[handwritten margin note: many perspectives, all equal]

This perspective in turn presents the scholar as one of Karl Mannheim's "free-floating intellectuals," outside and uncommitted though his or her work inspires critical understanding and thus possesses political importance. Which stance the individual sociologist takes—the Olympian or the utopian—seems to me less a matter of method than of temperament and political attitude. That I find the Olympian more congenial and aesthetically pleasing does not diminish its source in an act of choice, and that too makes it a political act.

Science and Politics

Irony is also a facet of self-awareness, of the realization that our premises, our assumptions, are not so far from their opposite as they seem. Much of the cognitive basis for the law of drinking-driving and the moral condemnation of alcohol is presented in public as technical reasoning, the product of politically and morally neutral attitudes. I see in the case of drinking-driving an important illustration of how the language of the technical and instrumental attitude of science serves to hide from recognition and awareness that moral and political choices are being made. That assertion has been a constant theme in this book.

Alvin Gouldner has expressed a basic thought of this book as follows:

A fundamental vulnerability of the technocratic consciousness is that it is characterized by a prosaic matter-of-factness; it has painted God grey. . . . This lack of public bellicosity makes the technocratic consciousness seem apolitical, possessed of a disinterestedness placing it "above the struggle"; or, from another perspective, over to the *side* of the struggle [Gouldner 1976, p. 262]

This seemingly unattached and outsider sense of the technician is deeply bound up, I believe, with implications of the technical role of science for social and legal authority.

It is sometimes said that although Hobbes defended the power of the monarchy in his *Leviathan,* the work was hardly appreciated by the exiled king. What troubled monarchists was that Hobbes rested his argument on the self-interests of subjects rather than the divine, God-given right of the monarch to rule. The analogy between the Hobbesian problem of legitimating authority and the implications of technical expertise for contemporary rulers lies in a similar irony of minimizing authority while defending it.

Science is the idiom of our age. It is the language in which command is cast as the compulsion of external nature. Authoritative law that rests its claim to legitimacy and acceptance on the technical reasoning of the realm of science denies any moral status. It denies that a moral decision has been taken, that a political choice among alternatives has been made. The ownership and responsibility for social problems and their solution are given as a matter of fact and not of values.

how we've been controlled, how we can control

It is in this sense that my book is about social control, or at least control over the public sphere of action and reaction. The very noncontroversial character of drinking-driving has made it an apt place in which to examine the moral and political bases of what has seemed to be a technical problem of social orderliness. I have tried to reveal the ways in which the drinking-driving phenomenon is not solely a scientific or technical matter, but that it is pervaded by a public culture in which moral attitudes toward alcohol use are essential to understanding the bases for the cognitive reality and the legal position of drinking-driving. The place of drinking-driving in the symbolic system by which public culture dramatizes societal values is more than a reflection of technical understandings and conclusions. It reflects a political and ethical choice.

That the ironic stance leads to such reflexive awareness of the grounds of authority may be disturbing. In a society where hierarchy and elite rule can claim legitimacy as authoritative arbiters of public morals, the acts of political choice in public matters can be made with ease. The "monarch" need not defend his actions by denying their moral base. Contemporary societies, the United States for one, lack the solid structure of a commanding elite whose moral legitimacy is evident to themselves and to their subjects. Nineteenth-century public culture was clear about the moral supremacy of sobriety. There was little need for technical grounds to moral dominance.

Here the sociological ironist takes over again. To deny that political choice has taken place, that a moral commitment about alcohol is being made, is both convenient and useful to officials and publics who eschew authority. To deny authority serves to affirm authority. Such dialectic is deep in the nature of social processes.

The reflexive irony of the sociologist is here a means to penetrate the veil of the apolitical (R. Brown 1980). It makes us aware of the sheer difficulty of avoiding choice between alternatives, of having to engage in the world of politics and moralities, to have to take a stand without the benefits of a clear and commanding social vision.

There is irony here too. Sociology has been a continuation of the Enlightenment's faith in science and progress, promising to bring technical method to bear on public problems, rescuing politics from the whirlpools of ideological division and self-interested power seekers. To demonstrate the role of the sociologist as the artistic developer of an ironic sense of alternatives is to minimize that claim to a technical authority. Like the scientist and the technician, the ironist too stands outside the struggles even though he understands the imperative to choose.

Notes

Chapter One

1. Also see the same approach in Spector and Kitsuse 1977, chap. 5; and Blumer 1971.
2. See the analysis of the automobile safety movement in chapter 2 below.
3. In my San Diego study we found that on such arrest forms, seventy percent of the respondents said they were coming from home and eighty percent said they were going home.
4. The issue of structure and process is a central one in the social sciences. For one noteworthy attempt to discuss it see Maines 1977.
5. This is in keeping with recent conceptions of social problems as "claims-making activities" rather than responses to social conditions (cf. Spector and Kitsuse 1977, chap. 5). Amitai Etzioni refers to power in the area of social problems as "the ability to make one's definition of what is problematic and what is to be done about it 'stick'" (Etzioni 1976, p. 146). While the concept of "ownership" has much in common with that of Howard Becker's "moral entrepreneurs," the former concept stresses the effectiveness of groups in gaining control and the role they play in defining the problem itself (cf. Becker 1963, pp. 147–63; also see Room 1978).
6. This draws on a variety of secondary data presented by Ralph Nader in Senate hearings and in his book, *Unsafe at Any Speed* (Nader 1973, pp. 280–90).
7. See the analyses of the Prohibition period in Sinclair 1963; Gusfield 1963a, 1968b; Clark 1977).
8. This is the model of politics implicit in

theories of group interests as determinative in American politics (cf. Truman 1951; Easton 1963).

9. Although in this book I do examine aspects of social structure, these will be more thoroughly treated in a future volume, tentatively titled *Technics and Therapy: Studies in Alcohol Policy.*

10. A similar theme, emphasizing the distinction between public and private culture, is to be found in Manning's analysis of police work (Manning 1977).

11. For general introductions to dramaturgical analysis see the anthologies *Drama in Life* (Combs and Mansfield 1976) and *Life as Theater* (Brisset and Edgley 1975). An excellent illustration of dramaturgical analysis applied to the problem of public and private meanings is Peter Manning's *Police Work* (1977).

12. There are many works of Kenneth Burke in which his method is utilized but no single theoretical book. I think the best introduction to dramatism, as he calls it, is his *Grammar of Motives* (1945). There is a vast literature on metaphor, some of which is discussed in chapter 4, below.

13. Elizabeth Burns has probed the specific similarities between human behavior and theatrical behavior in her book *Theatricality* (1972).

Chapter Two

1. For purposes of this section, I am ignoring the issues of strict liability in tort cases. In these the defendant is liable even though exercising care and avoiding negligence, as in cases of liability for injury resulting from dynamiting. The issue is highly significant for the automobile and is discussed later in this chapter and, in its legal aspects, in chapter 5.

2. Haddon also points out that the unknowing ingestion of polio or pneumonia virus is not considered "accidental," but the ingestion of a poison by a child is so considered, while the knowing ingestion of a poison is "suicide." These uses give us some insight into the non-

logical characteristics of the term (Haddon et al. 1964, pp. 28–29).

3. The issue of strict liability is discussed in chapter 5, pp. 116–19.

4. Of course, much of the production of "fact" in the form of records is by persons closer to the events described. Police, auto accident victims, medical personnel are responsible for primary data. That activity is part of the larger story. In this chapter I am concerned with the aggregators, who also influence the categories and with the data collected by primary gatherers.

5. In the 1965 hearings before Senator Ribicoff's subcommittee on executive reorganization, General Motors officials pointed with pride to a grant of one million dollars to the Massachusetts Institute of Technology for auto safety research. Under angry questioning by Senator Robert Kennedy they admitted profits of 1.7 billion dollars in the same year (Nader 1972, p. 287). Nader reports a Ford executive who estimated the cost of designing a new rear end at more than twenty-five million dollars. That, wrote Nader, was more than the total spent on auto safety research by the entire automobile industry in the period 1950–65 (Nader 1972, pp. 281–82, 138–40).

6. In 1926, Calvin Coolidge, in a public speech calling attention to the large number of deaths from auto accidents (24,000) supported efforts to develop uniform state and local laws but added: "The control of the highways is, of course, a matter for state and not national government" (*New York Times*, Jan. 21, 1926). This is still fairly accurate. Neither a national vehicle code nor a national speed law nor a national auto license has ever existed in the United States. The first effort at a uniform speed law occurred in 1974 as a federal requirement for state highway appropriations. Since 1968, however, there has been a set of national automobile standards through the National Highway Traffic Safety Administration.

7. In studying drinking-driver reports in San Diego County, I found the responses to ques-

tions about source and destination of journey to be unusable. Seventy percent of the reports listed "Home" as source of journey and eighty percent listed "Home" as destination. Unless the use and importance of the data are evident to its gatherers, their collection cannot be expected to be useful.

8. All items pertinent to auto safety were identified through the *New York Times Index* and all such items were read for every fifth year between and including 1922 and 1972. (I am grateful to Jerold Cloyd for assistance in this project.)

9. The utility of the emphasis on speeding and on driver education as countermeasures is considerably in doubt. The early correlations between low accident rates and teenage driver education now appear to reflect the students who chose such courses (Robertson and Zador 1978). The issue of speed is more complex but appears to entail the relation between the character of the road, the speed of other autos, and that of the specific motorist (O'Connell and Myers 1966; Haddon et al. 1964).

10. The position of the automobile industry was articulated most early in the hearings on the National Highway Safety Act of 1966. Auto company officials argued that "safety does not sell cars." A more detailed response made the case for consumer choice, maintaining that a safer auto would be a costlier one and that, when given the choice between safety and expense, consumers had always opted for cheaper but riskier driving.

11. The story of the auto safety movement is significant in the development of consumer protection and the environmental orientation in American politics. Other aspects of the movement are treated in Halpern 1972. While many people were associated with the movement, William Haddon, Jr., Daniel Patrick Moynihan, and Ralph Nader can be singled out at that time as the major then nonpolitical figures leading it, while Senators Ribicoff, Magnuson, and Robert Kennedy played key parts in the drama of its passage.

Chapter Three

1. See the work of Bruno Latour (Latour and Woolgar 1979; Latour 1979). See also the studies of Harry Collins (1976) and Michael Lynch (1978). Less empirical but useful works in the same direction are Ravetz 1973; Ziman 1968; Bloor 1976.

2. This characteristic use of analogy and metaphor in scientific presentation is discussed in works of Max Black (see Black 1962) and of Mary Hesse (see Hesse 1965, 1966) and described in the next chapter and its footnotes. Also see the discussion of Vaihinger by Lon Fuller (1967, chap. 3).

3. Later in the text of the 1974 report, material is presented on American drinking practices, including problem drinking. The text describes several surveys by Harris and associates commissioned for NIAAA and states that these, carried out in 1972–74, are the source for materials presented. A chart (p. 27) lists percent of problem drinkers by age in U.S.A., 1973. No other information is given about the survey or the overall figure of ten million (NIAAA 1974, pp. 7–8, 18). In the 1978 report (NIAAA 1978), the number of problem drinkers is given in three different statements, each based on the same study, commissioned for the NIAAA and presented in June 1977 (Johnson et al., 1977). First the report states, "There are an estimated 9.3 to 10 million problem drinkers (including alcoholics) in the adult population" (p. v). This is in the section titled "Highlight." Following this, in the introduction, the Report states, "We currently estimate that there are 10 million problem drinkers (including alcoholic people) in the United States" (p. xvii). The third statement, in chapter 1, is identical to the first except that the mood shifts from the indicative ("There are . . ."), to the subjunctive ("It is estimated that there are 9.3 to 10 million problem drinkers [including alcoholics] in the adult population" [p. 9]).

4. The earlier estimate of 4–5 million alcoholics had come from the work of Mark Keller and associates at the Rutgers Center of Alcohol Studies. It was based on the formula

developed by E. M. Jellinek which utilized rates of cirrhosis of the liver and a complex ratio between alcoholics with liver complications and those with no liver complications. The formula has been hotly debated and remains, at best, a systematic guess (Keller 1962; Seeley 1960; Popham 1956).

5. Conversations with personnel who supervised the surveys indicate that the figure was obtained from the Social Research Group by the then director of the National Bureau on Alcoholism, the percursor of NIAAA, under pressure from Congressional committee chairmen who wanted a prevalence rate. This occurred in 1969. According to my informant, the director was told that if he wanted a figure for the persons under treatment for alcoholism, it was several hundred thousand. The surveys had not measured "alcoholism" but "alcohol problems," a very different concept (see below). If that figure was to be used, the director was told, then projecting the nine percent who had a high score for problems in that survey on the total U.S. population of drinking age yielded a figure of ten million. That sounded too "pat" and was decreased to nine.

6. In a recent publication Room points out that he and his staff reporting on alcohol and casualties specifically avoided any modal figure for homicides "due to" alcohol. Government reports using this review referred, however, to figures "up to ——" using the high end of the reported range (Room 1978, p. 196).

7. I am indebted to Tracy Cameron for her superb description and analysis of the literature on drinking-driving. The reader is directed to that for an exhaustive treatment of drinking-driving studies (Cameron 1977, chap. 3). Richard Zylman's work in this field has been the most informed and critical of all the many reviews and analyses (see esp. Zylman 1974b).

8. In her exhaustive review of the drinking-driving literature, Tracy Cameron compiled a bibliography of 353 items. (The figure is not rounded to 350 in order to show that I actually

counted them.) These may be said to constitute the "state of the art" in knowledge about drinking-driving. They consist of articles in books and in journals, books, government reports—published, unpublished, and partially published (available from governmental agencies, sometimes with difficulty).

In a number of cases separate items report the same research. Often there is a report to the sponsor, an article in an academic journal, and a paper presented at a conference and later published in a proceedings volume. Of the 353 separate items in Cameron's bibliography I have read 113. I have tried to include those which loom most prominently in the literature and in Cameron's analysis.

9. More exactly, most states, like California, use .10 as prima facie evidence of DUIA and .05 as prima facie evidence of *not* DUIA. In between is a "shadow zone" where behavioral evidence is necessary to prove DUIA. Many European countries use .08 and some, in Eastern Europe, use .03 as the minimum for DUIA. A few American states even use .15.

10. The 1968 Alcohol and Highway Safety Report refers to "800,000 crashes every year" resulting from the use of alcohol (U.S. Congress 1968, p. 1).

11. There were also six foreign studies. In these, two report the base of percentage and the total number of accidents as the same, and one reports a testing base about 95 percent of all accidents. Thus these ignore the testing problem. A fourth study is based on only 29 cases (Cameron 1977, p. 130–33).

12. The full report states that all fatalities occurring within 24 hours of crash were used and that this included "nearly all fatalities" in the county during the period studied.

13. The concept of responsibility is itself, as the discussion in chapter 2 has shown, open to much criticism as a selection from alternative modes of perceiving causal elements. The concept, as used in accident reporting, is related to insurance purposes and legal decisions. Even

there, the need to find responsibility is greatly under attack in the issue of "no-fault" insurance (Calabresi 1970).

14. That Art is not Life is an old adage. Criticisms of the dramaturgical mode of analysis have pointed out the differences between the stage and naturally occurring events (Messinger et al. 1962). For a general discussion of the conventions utilized in stage performances, see Burns 1974, esp. chapters 4–7; Goffman 1974, chap. 4.

15. "Dramatism, as so conceived, asks not how the sacrificial motives revealed in the situations of magic and religion can be eliminated in a scientific culture, but what new forms they take" (Burke, in Combs and Mansfield 1976, p. 15).

Chapter Four

1. In criticizing a previously published version of this chapter Bruno Latour made a valuable point about the use of methods as a validating device. In personal communication to me, he suggested that the less than "hard" sciences are often more defensive about their work than are the biologists he studied. Consequently the attentiveness to method in the Waller study is not typical of science. However, in the flow of policy events, this research is part of an imputed science which does serve as grounds for justifying policies.

2. Paul Ricoeur also points out in an issue of *Critical Inquiry* how metaphorical thought organizes feelings as well as cognition (Ricoeur 1978). In the same issue also see articles by Cohen and by Booth.

3. The studies reporting occupational and/or racial characteristics of arrested or nonarrested drinking drivers have not been uniform in their findings. Though Cameron's general statement is that blue collor workers appear to be drinking-drivers more frequently than white collar workers, there are also several contrary studies. For analyses see Cameron (1977) and the items cited there as well as Zylman 1972b.

For qualified and opposing results see Cosper and Mozersky 1968; Hyman 1968a; Marshall and Purdy 1972.

4. Room has written that the Department of Transportation and the casualty insurance companies, based on the existent research, set out to change the image of the drinking-driver from that of social drinker to that of problem drinker/alcoholic "with the explicit purpose of increasing the perceived deviance of the drunk driver" (Room 1979, p. 189).

Chapter Five

1. For uses of the concept to analyze sociological thought see R. Brown 1977, pp. 125–78.

2. See the materials on the law of deodands and jeofails, under which animals and inanimate objects, such as furniture, were "put to death" after trials for commission of crimes (Pollock and Maitland 1923, II, pp. 473–74). For analyses of changing objects of deviance and of victimization, see Rock 1973, chap. 1 and pp. 147–49.

3. Friedman maintains that the introduction of fault and negligence as necessary to fix responsibility in torts was largely a concession to expanding business enterprise, especially railroads, in the American nineteenth century. It enabled growing businesses to avoid a wide circle of possible risks and limited their liability to imprudent and negligent acts (Friedman 1973, pp. 261–64; also see J. W. Hurst 1956).

4. For discussions of the *mens rea* doctrine see G. Williams 1961; J. Hall 1952; Wasserstrom 1961; H. L. A. Hart 1968, chap. 6.

5. This distinction is used at law in the body of cases and comments concerning search and seizure of automobiles, passengers, and drivers. The distinction is used to determine when and how police may "frisk" persons or search cars. For a discussion and bibliography see Alwin 1976. Alwin's discussion must be qualified by the recent U.S. Supreme Court decision in the Mimms case (Pennsylvania v. Mimms 430 U.S. 106 [1977]).

6. Estimates of the number of autos in use in

the United States before 1920 should be taken with a grain of salt (or a pint of oil). Licensing was irregular and not well enforced everywhere before then. Nevertheless there was a steady and considerable growth. Approximately 144 million passenger cars and taxis were registered in the fifty American states in 1977 (U.S. Department of Commerce 1978, p. 650).

7. An excellent discussion of the criminological status of traffic law can be found in Willett 1964, chapter 1; Ross 1960; Cressey 1975.

8. Willett conducted a study of serious motoring offenses in England with the hypothesis that white collar workers were more likely to commit these than were blue collar workers. His findings were the opposite: blue collar workers were more often arrested and convicted of such offenses. However he had no data on other "crimes" to compare for stratificational differences (Willett 1964, pp. 194ff).

9. For an analysis of state statutes as of 1967 and a suggested uniform statute see "Note" 1970.

10. "It is self-evident that inward intoxication cannot be the proximate cause of one's injury unless the inward condition is translated into outward conduct . . . mere intoxication in the absence of any evidence of conduct is [not] sufficient to take to the jury an issue of negligence proximately contributing to an accident" (Benoit v. Wilson, 150 Texas 273, 239 S.W. 2d 792 [1951], quoted by McCoid in Freeman 1970, p. 340).

11. In the most recent Supreme Court case (Mackey v. Montrym), the same premise is used of the greater "seriousness" of drinking-driving compared with other traffic offenses. In his majority opinion Chief Justice Burger refers to studies establishing the high frequency of alcohol involvement in auto accidents as part of his argument for the compelling interest of the state in suspending hearings on license revocation as a prior requirement to such revocation after a licensee refuses the breathalyzer test. The court was split, however, with four members

dissenting on grounds that the Massachusetts Department of Motor Vehicles' procedure of not requiring prior hearing was not essential to the protection of safety (Supreme Court of the United States, No. 77–69, June 25, 1979; see esp. pp. 15–17 of Burger's opinion and p. 7 of Stewart's dissent).

12. There are other, and often well-understood, functions of traffic enforcement. In providing a base for "probable cause" to stop cars it enables police to maintain a general surveillance of the community. In some jurisdictions it also provides a source of municipal revenue. Cf. Cressey 1975.

13. This is almost a standard conclusion in texts and treatises on crime in America. Some typical works are Gibbs 1975; Hartjen 1974; Reid 1976; and Wilson 1975.

14. In referring to this as a "normative" perspective I am using a term commonly employed in the social sciences to designate a system described as rule-following and studied as a set of rules or norms. This should be differentiated from views of law or legality as involving norms and distinguishing the legal institution from other institutions. Such nonpositivist views of law can be found in Fuller 1969 and among sociologists in Selznick 1961 and Gusfield 1977.

15. "Law can be seen as a thing like any other in the empirical world. It is crucial to be clear that from a sociological standpoint, law consists in observable acts, not in the rules as the concept of rule or norm is employed in the literature of jurisprudence and in everyday legal language" (D. Black 1972, p. 1091). The entire paper is an excellent statement of the sociologist's view of law. Also see D. Black, 1976.

16. In this chapter I refer to experiences and materials drawn from my study of the courts and law enforcement agencies in San Diego county (Gusfield 1972).

17. I have referred earlier (p. 62) to roadside studies concluding that for every one arrest

there are two thousand other drivers DUIA and undetected or unarrested. The 1973 national sample roadside study reported 12–13½% of all drivers on the road between 10:00 P.M. and 3:00 A.M. on Friday and Saturday night were DUIA. Another similar study reports 200 DUIA for every one arrested (Beitel 1975). An ethnographic bar study of mine leads me to a similar conclusion: drinking-driving is commonly accepted and occurring American behavior (Gusfield, Kotarba, and Rasmussen 1979). Survey studies of unreported crime have led investigators to maintain that about four out of five crimes are unreported. It seems the ratio is far greater for DUIA. Whatever the reception of the studies, the police officer's observation that, "there are a helluva lot of them out there" seems a good working hypothesis.

18. In California, as in most American states, a blood-alcohol level of .10 and above is prima facie evidence of DUIA and a count of .05 or below is prima facie evidence of sobriety. The "twilight zone" between the two is one governed by other data of police observation. As I explain below, however, in working procedures the B.A.L. is the most significant datum in determining the final charge.

19. In riding with the special "drinking-driving" squads in San Diego my assistants and I observed arrests in one out of three "stops." We also found an informal quota of one to two arrests per night. At the national level, nonspecialized police make two DUIA arrests per year (Borkenstein 1975, p. 664). One officer on the special squad told us that the ordinary police dislike the reports involved in DUIA arrests and that he often gets accident cases turned over to him to make the DUIA arrest. This discretionary situation is also observed by Ross who suggests that when the breathalyzer came into use in Britain, while DUIA arrests increased, traffic offense charges decreased (Ross 1973, pp. 46–50).

20. This is based on data from the early 1970s in San Diego County and among the cities participating in the Alcohol Safety Action Project

program of the Department of Transportation (Gusfield 1972; U.S. Department of Transportation 1974, chap. 3). This does not take account of costs of legal fees. By 1979 according to conversations with San Diego judges, fines of $300 were common. Inflation knows no barriers!

21. "Jail sentence" also is a term of public clarity but situational ambiguity. The "suspended" character of many jail sentences has already been commented upon. In the San Diego study we did not find that such sentences were routinely "picked up" on a rearrest for another DUIA charge. Even when carried out the sentence might be served by donation of work, as when a carpenter spent weekends repairing children's toys at a youth center. The rule relating to mandatory jail sentence where there was a prior DUIA offense was also rendered ambiguous since a plea-bargained DUIA charge which became a "reckless" was no longer a "prior offense." Sometimes, in the bargaining negotiation the prosecuting attorney agreed not to recognize the existence of DUIA "on the record."

22. A good illustration of this, applied to the courts, is Abraham Blumberg's "The Practise of Law as Confidence Game." The title alone, in connecting law and a criminal act, suggests the way in which the author will "put down" the presumption that courts adhere to a set of ideal principles. The bulk of the paper proceeds to demonstrate that the relations between the actions of judges and lawyers belie the adversarial model and follow a logic based on the custodial needs of the social organization of courts (Blumberg 1967a).

23. Noonan 1976 points out that in stating the facts of the famous torts case of *Palsgraf* v. *Long Island Railway,* only the grammatical necessity for a personal pronoun made the reader aware that Palsgraf was a female (chap. 4). Yet, as our observation of San Diego enforcement showed, this is often a significant element in enforcement of DUIA and in trials.

Chapter Six

1. I read *The Symbols of Government* in a late stage of preparation for writing this chapter. I had first read Arnold's *The Folklore of Capitalism* in the 1940s when it was an important book for undergraduates. Rereading Arnold now is an ego-deflating reminder of Louis Wirth's aphorism to his students that "originality is the result of a faulty memory."

2. I am not offering here "an explanation" for antialcohol movements in America. That is a more complex subject which I have partially treated in *Symbolic Crusade* (Gusfield 1963a). For a recent superb analysis see H. Levine 1979.

3. In this view of boundary maintenance as significant to understanding drinking issues in American life, especially the strictures against public drunkenness, see Room 1978; Gusfield 1978. In my conception of boundaries, as in much else in this study, I am indebted to Robin Room, without whose published and unpublished writings and illuminating conversations this study would be infinitely poorer.

4. It is possible to see the issue of temperance as being about play, in which one group demands that it be clearly related to the next day's work and the other demands that it be sharply distinguished. A nineteenth-century Protestant preacher made a distinction between recreation, which he labeled purposeful and utilitarian, and amusement, which is pleasure for its own sake. Recreation, he argued, strengthens us for the work of the world, while amusement provides "stimulant and excitement" but not refreshment (quoted and cited in Gusfield 1963a, pp. 30–31). Many "hard" drinkers make a distinction between competent and incompetent drinkers. The incompetent are unable to keep their drinking from spilling over into other compartments of their lives (LeMasters 1975; Kotarba 1977). See fuller discussion of this distinction in *The World of the Drinking-Driver* (Gusfield, Kotarba, and Rasmussen 1979).

5. For a general account of the spread of distillation and liquor in Europe during the sixteenth to nineteenth century see Braudel 1973.

Also see T. G. Coffey, "Beer Street, Gin Lane" (1966), for an account of British reaction through price and licensing policy that encouraged beer drinking and discouraged gin use.

6. This is a major point in other studies of "preindustrial" crowd violence (Hobsbawm 1959; Rudé 1959, 1964).

7. This, of course, is less so in tort law, where dram shop acts and common law may make tavern owners, and even hosts, responsible in whole or in part for damages (Dooley 1977). Although there are movements in criminal law toward recognition of the chronic alcoholic, these are not yet, except for some cases of public drinking, exculpatory defenses (Kittrie 1971; Room 1979, chap. 8).

8. The case of *Callaway* v. *Hart* is illustrative. Hart was a passenger on the Central of Georgia Railway. While intoxicated he opened a door between cars and stepped from the train while it was in motion, sustaining injuries. The Alabama Supreme Court held that the railway could be liable for damages since, knowing he was drunk, they owed him a higher degree of care (Callaway v. Hart, 146 F 2d 103 [1945]). The question of the responsibility for the drunk has been a consistent and vexing one for law, analogous though not similar to issues of insanity and drug addiction as exculpatory defenses (Dooley 1977; Hall 1944; Kittrie 1973; Greenwalt 1969; Powell v. Texas, 392 US 514 [1968]).

9. A necessary caveat must be introduced. In the United States there are no states without a DUIA law. Whether or not the absence of a DUIA law would lead to a rise in deaths is therefore a moot question. Comparative statistics are deeply confounded by the tendency, discussed earlier (chap. 2), of countries which do not emphasize DUIA also to gather little data on deaths involving alcohol.

10. The literature on these questions is vast. The anthology by Friedman and MacCauley (1977) is an excellent compendium of typical materials. For general overviews and bibliogra-

phy see the papers on law in *The Encyclopedia of the Social Sciences,* 1968.

11. It may be objected that what I have seen are the less affluent of the defendants while the more affluent are represented by their lawyers. This may be true, but the large number of those arraigned and the generally wide range of incomes among the drinking-drivers does not suggest a homogeneously poverty-stricken group. Weddings, funerals, other sacred occasions, though often marked by more casual attire than is typical of other parts of the country, are nevertheless, even in California, marked by particular attention to dress as a way of demonstrating the ritual character of the occasion.

12. The concept of "cultural performance" is derived from the work of Milton Singer on Hinduism in modern India. He uses it to describe the unit of his observation, including both religious rituals and festivities as well as the usual plays, concerts, and lectures (Singer 1972).

13. In an analysis of stateless and state societies and the regulation of sexual behavior—adultery, violation of celibacy, and incest—Yehudi Cohen makes a significant distinction. Stateless societies portray antisocial behavior as interfering with the natural order of the universe. State societies utilize law to portray the authority of the state over the order to which the individual is responsible, whatever the degree of compliance (Y. Cohen 1969).

14. The research referred to was conducted under National Science Foundation Grant No. SOC77-18068, for which I am the principal investigator. It is based on barroom ethnography and on interviews with convicted DUIA offenders. It was reported in *The World of the Drinking-Driver* (Gusfield, Kotarba, and Rasmussen 1979).

15. An analogy by which I have been much influenced is the experience of Indian society in the decade following independence. Having been shut out of the power to influence public policy during British rule, Indians learned to

gain their objectives by influencing administration through personal attachments and bribery. Following Independence they continued to avoid attempts to support their interests through political pressure, preferring influence on situational acts (Weiner 1962).

Chapter Seven

1. This distinction, and some aspects of this section, have been presented in my paper "The (F)Utility of Knowledge? The Relation of Social Science to Public Policy toward Drugs" (Gusfield 1975).

2. Similar distinctions emphasizing the non-utilitarian can be found in Edelman 1972; in my 1963 usage of instrumental and symbolic action (Gusfield 1963a); and in Kenneth Burke's semantic and poetic meaning (Burke 1957, discussed in chap. 4 above).

3. The concept of mass relationships as distinguished from traditional social organization has been an effort to capture the unique qualities of the mass as a social aggregate. Among notable attempts, in addition to Horton and Wohl, see Blumer 1939, pp. 241–45; Kornhauser 1959, pt. 1; Bramson 1961; Arendt 1951, chap. 10.

4. See the analysis of "pseudoevents" in Boorstin 1964.

5. Questionnaire data of sociologists and survey researchers are suspect of telling us what respondents think others think rather than their "own" beliefs. The classic study of occupational prestige conducted by the NORC has been interpreted and studied not as the respondents' individual judgments of occupations but as their judgments of what others think— their view of "society," not of self (Gusfield and Schwartz 1963).

6. This was equally the case in thirteenth-century England (Pugh 1973).

7. Hay's analysis has reference to a society in which relations between rules and subjects were more localistic, face to face, and direct than is the case in contemporary societies.

8. This theme is dominant in much of Edel-

man's writing (Edelman 1964, chap. 2; 1972; 1977). It is also the dominant conclusion of Goodlad's analysis of popular dramatic entertainment (Goodlad 1970).

9. I am quite aware of the performance character of the Nixon interviews. They were presented in an order other than that in which they were made. They were edited to provide a sense of narrative—of beginning, middle, and end. The "shots" were made from a selection of several at each moment. Such "staging" is precisely what is characteristic of much of public events.

References

Abel, Richard

1973   "Law Books and Books about Law." *Stanford Law Review* 26. Repr. in L. Friedman and S. Macauley, eds., *Law and the Behavioral Sciences,* pp. 21–26. Indianapolis: Bobbs-Merrill.

Addiction Research Foundation

1975   "Alcohol—Do You Know Enough About It?" Pamphlet.

AFL-CIO Community Service Activities and National Council on Alcoholism

N.d.   "What Every Worker Should Know about Alcoholism." Brochure. N.p.

Alwin, Ronald

1976   "Searches during Routine Traffic Stops after *Robinson* and *Gustafson:* A Re-Examination of the Illinois Distinction between 'Ordinary Traffic Violators' and 'Criminals.'" *Loyola University Law Journal* 7:853–99.

Andenaes, Johannes

1966   "The General Preventive Effects of Punishment." *University of Pennsylvania Law Review* 114:949.

Arendt, Hannah

1951   *The Origins of Totalitarianism.* New York: Harcourt, Brace.

Aristotle

1941   *Basic Works,* Trans. Richard P. McKeon. New York: Random House.

Arnold, Thurman

1935   *The Symbols of Government.* New Haven: Yale University Press.

Aubert, Vilhelm, and Messinger, Sheldon

1958   "The Criminal and the Sick." *Inquiry* 1:137–60.

Auden, W. H.

1942   "Law, Say the Gardeners, Is the Sun." In Louis Untermeyer, ed., *Modern British Poetry,* pp. 481–82. New York: Harcourt Brace.

Auerbach, Erich

1953   *Mimesis: the Representation of Reality in Western Literature.* Princeton, N.J.: Princeton University Press.

Austin, J. L.

1962   *How to Do Things with Words.* Cambridge, Mass.: Harvard University Press.

1971   "Performative Constative." Repr. in J. Searle, ed., *The Philosophy of Language.* London: Oxford University Press. (Orig. pub. 1963.)

Baker, Robert F.

1971   *The Highway Risk Problem.* New York: Wiley-Interscience.

Baker, Susan, and Spitz, Werner

1970   "Age Effects and Autopsy Evidence of Disease in Fatally Injured Drivers." *Journal of the American Medical Association* 214, no. 6: 1079–88.

Baker, Susan; Robertson, Leon; and Spitz, Werner

1971   "Tattoos, Alcohol and Violent Death." *Journal of Forensic Sciences* 4:219–25.

Barthes, Roland

1967 *Elements of Semiology.* Boston: Beacon Press.
1973 *Mythologies.* London: Paladin.

Bauman, Zygmunt

1976 *Socialism: The Active Utopia.* New York: Holmes and Meier.

Becker, Howard D.

1963 *Outsiders.* Glencoe, Ill.: The Free Press.
1967 "Whose Side Are We On?" *Social Problems* 14 (Winter): 239–47.

Beitel, G. A.; Glanz, W. D.; and Sharp, M. C.

1975 "Probability of Arrest while Driving under the Influence of Alcohol." *Journal of Studies on Alcohol* 36:870–76.

Bell, Daniel

1972 "On Meritocracy and Equality." *The Public Interest* 29 (Fall).

Ben-David, Joseph

1971 *The Scientist's Role in Society.* Englewood Cliffs, N.J.: Prentice-Hall.

Black, Donald

1971 "The Social Organization of Arrest." *Stanford Law Review* 23 (June): 1087–1111.
1972 "The Boundaries of Legal Sociology." *Yale Law Journal* 81 (May): 1086–1100.
1976 *The Behavior of Law.* New York: Academic Press.

Black, Max

1962 *Models and Metaphors.* Ithaca: Cornell University Press.

Bloor, David

1976 *Knowledge and Social Imagery.* London: Routledge and Kegan Paul.

Blum, W., and Kalven, H.

1967   "The Empty Cabinet of Dr. Calabresi: Auto Accidents and General Deterrence." *University of Chicago Law Review* 34:239.

Blumberg, Abraham S.

1967a   "The Practice of Law as Confidence Game." *Law and Society Review* 1:15–39.
1967b   *Criminal Justice.* Chicago: Quadrangle Books.

Blumer, Herbert

1939   "Social Movements." In Robert Park, ed., *An Outline of the Principles of Sociology.* New York: Barnes and Noble.
1969   "The Methodological Position of Symbolic Interactionism." In *Symbolic Interaction.* Englewood Cliffs, N.J.: Prentice-Hall.
1971   "Social Problems as Collective Behavior." *Social Problems* 18 (Winter): 298–306.

Bocock, Robert

1974   *Ritual in Industrial Society.* London: George Allen and Unwin.

Bohannon, Paul

1973   "The Differing Realms of the Law." In Donald Black and Maureen Mileski, eds., *The Social Organization of Law.* New York: Seminar Press.

Boorstin, Daniel

1964   *The Image: A Guide to Pseudo Events in America.* New York: Harper Colophon.

Booth, Wayne

1961   *The Rhetoric of Fiction.* Chicago: University of Chicago Press.
1969   "Distance and Viewpoint." In R. M. Davis, ed., *The Novel: Modern Essays in Criticism.* Englewood Cliffs, N.J.: Prentice-Hall.
1978   "Metaphor as Rhetoric: The Problem of Evaluation." *Critical Inquiry* 5 (Autumn): 49–72.

Borkenstein, R. F.

1975   "Problems of Enforcement: Adjudication and Sanctioning." In S. Israelstam and S. Lambert, eds., *Alcohol, Drugs and Traffic Safety,* pp. 655–62. Toronto: Addiction Research Foundation.

Borkenstein, R. F.; Crowther, R. F.; Shumate, R. P.; Ziel, W. B; and Zylman, R.

1964   *The Role of the Drinking Driver in Traffic Accidents.* Bloomington, Ind.: Department of Police Administration, Indiana University.

Boston University School of Law–Medicine Institute

1969   "Investigation of Thirty-one Fatal Automobile Accidents: Final Report." U.S. Department of Transportation: Bureau of Highway Safety.

Bramson, Leon

1961   *The Political Context of Sociology.* Princeton, N.J.: Princeton University Press.

Braudel, Fernand

1973   *Capitalism and Material Life 1400–1800.* New York: Harper Torchbooks.

Brissett, Dennis, and Edgley, Charles, eds.

1975   *Life as Theater.* Chicago: Aldine.

Brown, Richard

1977   *A Poetic for Sociology.* Cambridge: Cambridge University Press.
1980   "Dialectical Irony: Literary Form and Sociological Irony." In Edmond Wright, ed., *Irony.* London: Harvester.

Brown, Stuart

1968   *Drivers Who Die: A Safety Study.* Houston, Tex.: Baylor University College of Medicine.

Bruyn, Severyn

1966   *The Human Perspective.* Englewood Cliffs, N.J.: Prentice-Hall.

Bryant, Donald

1965   "Rhetoric: Its Function and Scope." In J. Schwartz and J. Rycenga, eds., *The Province of Rhetoric.* New York: The Ronald Press.

Burke, Kenneth

1945   *A Grammar of Motives.* New York: Prentice-Hall.
1950   *A Rhetoric of Motives.* New York: Prentice-Hall.
1954   *Permanence and Change. Indianapolis:* Bobbs-Merrill.
1957   *The Philosophy of Literary Forms.* New York: Vintage Books.
1968   "Dramatism." In *International Encyclopedia of the Social Sciences.*

Burns, Elizabeth

1972   *Theatricality.* New York: Harper Torchbooks.

Cahalan, Don

1970   *Problem Drinkers: A National Survey.* San Francisco: Jossey-Bass.

Cahalan, Don; Cisin, Ira; and Crossley, Helen

1969   *American Drinking Practices.* New Brunswick, N.J.: Rutgers Center of Alcohol Studies.

Cahalan, Don, and Room, Robin

1974   *Problem Drinking among American Men.* New Brunswick, N.J.: Rutgers Center of Alcohol Studies.

Calabresi, Guido

1970   *The Costs of Accidents.* New Haven: Yale University Press.

California Department of Justice

1976   *Crime and Delinquency in California.* Sacramento: Bureau of Criminal Statistics, State of California.

Cameron, Tracy

1977   "Alcohol and Traffic." In Marc Arrens, Tracy Cameron, Ron Roizen, Robin Room, Dan Schneberk, and Deborah Wingard, eds., *Alcohol, Casualties and Crime.* Report C-18. Berkeley: Social Research Group.

Cardozo, Benjamin

1921   *The Nature of the Judicial Process.* New Haven: Yale University Press.

Carlson, W. L.

1973   "Age, Exposure and Alcohol Involvement in Night Crashes." *Journal of Safety Research* 5:247–59.

Carson, W. G.

1975   "Symbolic and Instrumental Dimensions of Early Factory Legislation." In Roger Hood, ed., *Crime, Criminology and Public Policy: Essays in Honor of Sir Leon Radzinowicz.* New York: The Free Press.

Chandler, David

1976   *Capital Punishment in Canada.* New York: Macmillan.

Cicourel, Aaron

1964   *Method and Measurement in Sociology.* New York: The Free Press.

1968   *The Social Organization of Juvenile Justice.* New York: Wiley.

Clark, Norman

1976   *Deliver Us from Evil.* New York: Norton.

Cloyd, Jerold

1972   "News Coverage of Auto Safety Issues, 1922–1972: An Analysis of the *New York Times*." Unpublished report.

1975   "The Ideals of Justice and the Practical Organizational Contingencies Affecting Criminal Cases Involving Intoxicants." Ph.D. dissertation. Department of Sociology, University of California, San Diego.

Coffey, T. G.

1966   "Beer Street, Gin Lane..." *Quarterly Journal of Studies on Alcohol* 27:669–92.

Cohen, Abner

1976   *Two-Dimensional Man.* Berkeley: University of California Press.

Cohen, Ted

1978   "Metaphor and the Cultivation of Intimacy." *Critical Inquiry* 5 (Autumn): 3–12.

Cohen, Yehudi

1969   "Ends and Means in Political Control: Punishment of Adultery, etc." *American Anthropologist* 71:658–81.

Collins, Harry, and Cox, Graham

1976   "Recovering Relativity: Did Prophecy Fail?" *Social Studies of Science* 6 (September): 423–44.

Combs, James, and Mansfield, Michael, eds.

1976   *Drama in Life.* New York: Hastings House.

Coppin, R., and G. Van Oldenbeek

1965   "Driving under Suspension and Revocation." Sacramento: Department of Motor Vehicles.

Cosper, Ronald, and Mozersky, Kenneth

1968   "Social Correlates of Drinking and Driving."

Quarterly Journal of Studies on Alcohol.
Supplement no. 4 (May), pp. 58–117.

Cramton, Roger

1969   "Driver Behavior and Legal Sanctions," *Michigan Law Review* 67:421.

Cressey, Donald

1953   *Other People's Money.* Glencoe, Ill.: The Free Press.

1975   "Law, Order and the Motorist." In Roger Hood, ed., *Crime, Criminality and Public Policy.* New York: The Free Press.

Crocker, J. Christopher

1977   "The Social Functions of Rhetorical Forms." In J. D. Sapir and J. C. Crocker, eds., *The Social Use of Metaphor.* Philadelphia: University of Pennsylvania Press.

Davis, J. H.

1974   "Carbon Monoxide, Alcohol and Drugs in Fatal Automobile Accidents: Dade County, Florida, 1956–1968." *Clinical Toxology* 7:597–613.

Dell, Floyd

1922   "The Difference between Life and Fiction." *New Republic* (April 12), pp. 7–8.

Dooley, David, and Mosher, James

1978   "Alcohol and Legal Negligence." Unpublished report. Alcohol, Casualties and Crime Project. Working paper no. F-62. Berkeley: Social Research Group, School of Public Health.

Douglas, Jack D.

1971   *American Social Order: Social Rules in a Pluralistic Society.* New York: The Free Press.

Douglas, Mary

1966   *Purity and Danger.* London: Routledge, Kegan Paul.
1973   *Natural Symbols.* London: Pelican Books.

Douglas, R.

1974   "The Operational Meaning of Reported Alcohol Involvement in Official State Accident Data." *HIT Lab Reports,* vol. 5, pp. 1–15. Ann Arbor: Highway Safety Research Institute.

Duncan, Hugh D.

1962   *Communication and Social Order.* London: Oxford University Press.
1969   *Symbols and Social Theory.* London: Oxford University Press.

Durkheim, Emile

1947   *The Rules of the Sociological Method.* Glencoe, Ill.: The Free Press. (Orig. pub. 1895.)
1951   *Suicide.* New York: The Free Press.

Eastman, Crystal

1910   *Work, Accidents, and the Law.* New York: Arno.

Easton, David

1963   *The Political System.* New York: Knopf.

Edelman, Murray

1964   *The Symbolic Uses of Politics.* Urbana, Ill.: University of Illinois Press.
1971   *Politics as Symbolic Action.* Chicago: Markham.
1977   *Political Language.* New York: Academic Press.

Eliade, Mircea

1963   *Myth and Reality.* New York: Harper Torchbooks.

Emerson, Joan

1970   "Behavior in Private Places: Sustaining Definition of Reality in Gynecological Examinations." *Recent Sociology 2: Patterns of Communicative Behavior*. London: Macmillan.

Epstein, Thomas

1977   "A Socio-Legal Examiniation of Intoxification in the Criminal Law." Working paper no. F-53. Berkeley: Social Research Group.

Erwin, Richard E.

1965   "Defense of Persons Accused of Driving while under the influence of Alcohol." *Practical Lawyer* 11:73.

1976   "Another Slant—There Is No Danger of a Fair Trial in a Drunk-Driving Case." *California State Bar Journal*. 51:214.

Etzioni, Amitai

1976   *Social Problems*. Englewood Cliffs, N.J.: Prentice-Hall.

Feeley, Malcolm

1966   "Coercion and Compliance: A New Look at an Old Problem." In Samuel Krislov et al., eds., *Compliance and the Law*. Beverley Hills, Ca.: Sage Publications.

Feyerabend, Paul

1975   *Against Method*. London: Verso.

Filkins, L. D., and Carlson, W. L.

1975   "Analysis and Reporting of Blood Alcohol Concentrations of Michigan Traffic Fatalities." *HIT Lab Reports*, vol. 3, no. 7. Ann Arbor: Highway Safety Research Institute.

Filkins, L. D.; Clark, C. D.; Rosenblatt, C. A.; Carlson, W. L.; Kerlan, N. W.; and Manson, H.

1970   "Alcohol Abuse and Traffic Safety: A Study of Fatalities, Offenders, Alcoholic and Court-Related Treatment Approaches." University of Michigan: Highway Safety Research Institute.

Firth, Raymond

1973   *Symbols: Public and Private.* Ithaca: Cornell University Press.

Foucault, Michel

1965   *Madness and Civilization.* New York: Random House.

Frank, Jerome

1936   *Law and the Modern Mind.* New York: Tudor.
1949   *Courts on Trial.* Princeton: Princeton University Press.

Freeman, Brian, ed.

1970   *Drunk-Driving Cases: Prosecution and Defense.* New York: Practicing Law Institute.

Freidman, Norman

1969   "Point of View: The Development of a Critical Concept." In R. M. Davis, ed., *The Novel: Modern Essays in Criticism.* Englewood Cliffs, N.J.: Prentice-Hall.

Freud, Sigmund

1938   *The Psychopathology of Everyday Life.* In *The Basic Writings of Sigmund Freud.* New York: Modern Library, Random House.

Friedman, Lawrence

1973   *A History of American Law.* New York: Simon and Schuster.
1975   *The Legal System: A Social Science Perspective.* New York: Russell Sage Foundation.

Friedman, Lawrence, and Macauley, Stewart
1977 *Law and the Behavioral Sciences.* Indianapolis: Bobbs-Merrill.

Friemuth, H. C.; Watts, S. R.; and Fisher, R. S.
1958 "Alcohol and Highway Fatalities." *Journal of Forensic Science* 3.

Frye, Northrop
1957 *Anatomy of Criticism.* Princeton, N.J.: Princeton University Press.

Fuller, Lon L.
1967 *Legal Fictions.* Stanford, Ca.: Stanford University Press.
1969 *The Morality of the Law.* New Haven and London: Yale University Press.

Galanter, Marc
1976 "Drunk Driving Law Enforcement." Unpublished manuscript.

Gardiner, John
1969 *Traffic and the Police.* Cambridge, Mass.: Harvard University Press.

Garfinkel, Harold
1956 "Conditions of Successful Degradation Ceremonies." *American Journal of Sociology* 61 (March): 420–24.
1967 *Studies in Ethnomethodology.* Englewood Cliffs, N.J.: Prentice-Hall.

Gay, Peter
1966 *The Enlightenment.* New York: Vintage Books.

Geertz, Clifford
1973a *The Interpretation of Cultures.* New York: Basic Books.
1973b "Thick Description: Toward an Interpretative Theory of Culture." In *The Interpretation of Cultures.* New York: Basic Books.

Gerber, S. R.

1963   "Vehicular Fatalities in Cuyahoga County, Ohio, 1941–60." *Proceedings of the Third International Conference on Alcohol and Road Traffic, 1962*, pp. 38–44. London: British Medical Association.

Gerber, S. R.; Jolist, P. V.; and Feegel, J. R.

1966   "Single Motor Vehicle Accidents in Cuyahoga County, Ohio, 1958–1963." *Journal of Forensic Sciences* 11:144–51.

Gibbs, Jack P.

1975   *Crime, Punishment and Deterrence.* New York: Elsevier.

Goffman, Erving

1956   *The Presentation of the Self in Everyday Life.* Edinburgh: Social Sciences Research Center, University of Edinburgh.
1974   *Frame Analysis.* New York: Basic Books.

Goodheart, A. L.

1972   "The Ratio Decidendi of a Case." *Yale Law Journal* 40. Repr. in Lloyd, Lord of Hamstead, ed., *Introduction to Jurisprudence*, pp. 766–71. New York: Praeger.

Goodlad, J. S. R.

1971   *A Sociology of Popular Drama.* London: Heinemann.

Gordon, John E.

1949   "The Epidemiology of Accidents." *American Journal of Public Health* 39:504–15.

Gouldner, Alvin

1968   "The Sociologist as Partisan: Sociology and the Welfare State." *American Sociologist* 3 (May): 103–16.
1976   *The Dialectic of Ideology and Technology.* New York: Seabury.

Gramsci, Antonio

1971   *Selections from the Prison Notebooks of An-tonio Gramsci,* ed. Q. Hoare and G. N. Smith. New York: International Publishers.

Greater Tampa ASAP

N.d.   "You'll Be the Death of Me Yet . . . If You're a Drunken Driver." Pamphlet.

Greenawalt, Kent

1969   "'Uncontrollable' Actions and the Eighth Amendment: Implications of Powell v. Texas." *Columbia Law Review* 69:927.

Gregory, Charles O.

1951   "Trespass to Negligence to Absolute Liability." *Virginia Law Review* 37:359.

Gusfield, Joseph

1963a   *Symbolic Crusade: Status Politics and the American Temperance Movement.* Urbana, Ill.: University of Illinois Press.

1963b   "The 'Double Plot' in Institutions." *Patna University Journal* 18, no. 1.

1968a   "On Legislating Morals: The Symbolic Process of Designating Deviance." *California Law Review* 58 (January): 54–73.

1968b   "Prohibition: The Impact of Political Utopianism." In John Braeman, Robert Bremmer, and David Brody, eds., *Change and Continuity in Twentieth-Century America: The 1920s.* Columbus: Ohio State University Press.

1972   *A Study of Drinking Drivers in San Diego County.* San Diego: Urban Observatory.

1973   *Utopian Myths and Movements in Modern Societies.* Morristown, N.J.: University Programs Modular Studies, General Learning Press.

1975   "The (F)Utility of Knowledge? The Relation of Social Science to Public Policy toward Drugs." *Annals of the American Academy of Political and Social Sciences* 417:1–15.

1976   "The Prevention of Drinking Problems."
        In William Filstead, Jean Rossi, and Mark
        Keller, eds., *Alcohol and Alcohol Problems.*
        Cambridge, Mass.: Ballinger.
1977   "Power, Justice and Sociological Cynicism."
        Stanford Law Review 29 (January): 371–81.
1978   "Passage to Play: A Ritual Theory of Social
        Drinking." Paper presented to the Food and
        Nutrition Section of the Eighth International
        Congress of Anthropological and Ethnologi-
        cal Sciences, New Delhi, India, Dec. 6, 1978.
        To appear in a forthcoming publication of
        section proceedings.
1979a   "The Sociological Reality of America: An Essay
        on Mass Culture." In H. Gans, N. Glazer, J.
        Gusfield, and C. Jencks, eds., *On the Making
        of Americans: Essays in Honor of David
        Riesman.* Philadelphia: University of Penn-
        sylvania Press.
1979b   *The Illusion of Authority: Rhetoric, Ritual and
        Metaphor in Public Action.* Report to the
        National Science Foundation.
1979c   "The Modernity of Social Movements: Public
        Roles and Private Parts." In Amos Hawley,
        ed., *Societal Growth.* New York: The Free
        Press.
Forthcoming   *Technics and Therapy: Studies in Alcohol
        Policy.*

Gusfield, Joseph; Kotarba, Joseph; and Rasmussen, Paul

1979   *The World of the Drinking-Driver.* Report to
        the National Science Foundation.

Gusfield, Joseph, and Schwartz, Michael

1963   "The Meanings of Occupational Prestige: A
        Reconsideration of the NORC Scale."
        American Sociological Review 28 (April):
        265–71.

Gutman, Herbert

1977   *Work, Culture and Society in Industrializing
        America.* New York: Vintage Books.

Habermas, Jurgen

1970   "Technology and Science as 'Ideology.'" In *Toward a Rational Society*. Boston: Beacon Press.
1975   *Legitimation Crisis*. Boston: Beacon Press.

Haddon, William, Jr.

1970   "The Problem Drinker and Driving: Questions of Strategy in Countermeasure Choice and Development." In L. Filkins and N. Geller, eds., *Community Response to Alcoholism and Highway Crashes*. Ann Arbor, Mich.: Highway Safety Research Institute.
1972   "A Logical Framework for Categorizing Highway Safety Phenomena and Activity." *Journal of Trauma* 12:193–207.

Haddon, W., and Bradess, V. A.

1959   "Alcohol and the Single Vehicle Fatal Accident Experience in Westchester County." *Journal of the American Medical Association* 169:1587–93.

Haddon, William, Jr.; Suchman, Edward, and Klein, David

1964   *Accident Research*. New York: Harper and Row.

Halebsky, Sandor

1976   *Mass Society and Political Conflict*. Cambridge and New York: Cambridge University Press.

Hall, Jerome

1944   "Intoxication and Responsibility." *Harvard Law Review* 57:1045.
1952   *Theft, Law and Society*. 2d ed. Indianapolis: Bobbs-Merrill.

Halpern, Paul Joseph

1972   "Consumer Politics and Corporate Behavior: The Case of Automobile Safety." Ph.D. dissertation. Department of Government, Harvard University.

Harrington, D. M.

1972   "The Young Driver Follow-Up Study: Human Factors in the First Four Years of Driving." *Accident Analysis and Prevention* 4:191–240.

Harrison, Brian

1971   *Drink among the Victorians.* Pittsburgh: University of Pittsburgh Press.

Hart, H. L. A.

1961   *The Concept of Law.* Cambridge: The Clarendon Press.

1968   *Punishment and Responsibility.* Oxford: The Clarendon Press.

Hart, H. L. A. and Honoré, A. M.

1959   *Causation in the Law.* London: Oxford University Press.

Hartjen, Clayton A.

1974   *Crime and Criminalization.* New York: Praeger.

Havelock, Ronald

1971   *A National Problem-Solving System: Highway Safety Researchers and Decision-Makers.* Ann Arbor, Mich.: Institute for Social Research, University of Michigan.

Hawkes, Terence

1977   *Structuralism and Semiotics.* Berkeley and Los Angeles: University of California Press.

Hay, Douglas

1975   "Property, Authority and the Criminal Law." In D. Hay, P. Linebaugh, J. G. Rule, E. P. Thompson, and C. Winslow, eds., *Albion's Fatal Tree: Crime and Society in Eighteenth-Century England.* New York: Pantheon Books.

Heise, H. A.

1934   "Alcohol and Auto Accidents." *Journal of the American Medical Association* 103:739–41.

Hellman, Arthur D.

1975   *Laws against Marijuana: The Price We Pay.* Urbana, Ill.: University of Illinois Press.

Hesse, Mary B.

1965   "The Explanatory Function of Metaphor." In Y. Bar-Hillel, ed., *Proceedings of the 1964 International Congress for Logic, Methodology and Philosophy of Science.* Amsterdam: North Holland.

1966   *Models and Analogies in Science.* Notre Dame, Ind.: University of Notre Dame Press.

Hirschi, Travis, and Selvin, Hannan

1967   *Delinquency Research.* New York: The Free Press.

Hobsbawm, E. J.

1959   *Primitive Rebels.* New York: Praeger.

Hoffman, Lilly

1973   "Alcohol and Traffic Safety: Screening Out the Drunken Driver." In A. Etzioni and R. Remp, eds., *Technological Shortcuts to Social Change.* New York: Russell Sage Foundation.

Hofstadter, Albert

1955   "The Scientific and Literary Uses of Language." In Lyman Bryson, Louis Finkelstein, Hudson Hoagland, and R. M. MacIver, eds., *Symbols and Society.* New York: Conference on Science and Religion in Their Relation to the Democratic Way of Life, Inc.

Holcomb, R. L.

1938   "Alcohol in Relation to Traffic Accidents."

Journal of the American Medical Association
111:1076–85.

Hollopeter, Charles

1957   "The Trial of a 'Drunk Driving' Case." *Practical Lawyer,* vol. 3 (December).

Hood, Roger

1972   *Sentencing the Motoring Offender.* London: Heinemann.

Horton, Donald, and Wohl, R. Richard

1956   "Mass Communication and Para-Social Interaction." *Psychiatry* 19:215–29.

Hurst, James Willard

1956   *Law and the Conditions of Freedom in the Nineteenth-Century United States.* Madison, Wisc.: University of Wisconsin Press.

Hurst, Paul M.

1973   "Epidemiological Aspects of Alcohol in Driver Crashes and Citations." *Journal of Safety Research* 5 (September): 130–48.

Hyman, Merton M.

1968a   "The Social Characteristics of Persons Arrested for Driving While Intoxicated." *Quarterly Journal of Studies on Alcohol,* Supplement no. 4, pp. 138–77.
1968b   "Accident Vulnerability and Blood Alcohol Counts of Drivers by Demographic Characteristics." *Quarterly Journal of Studies on Alcohol,* Supplement no. 4, pp. 34–57.

Insurance Institute for Highway Safety

1976   *Status Report.* May 3; August 30. Washington, D.C.

International Conference on Alcohol and Road Traffic

1950   *Proceedings.* Stockholm: Karolinska Institute.

Isherwood, Christopher

1954   *The Berlin Stories.* New York: J. Laughlin.

Israelstam, S., and Lambert, S., eds.

1975   *Alcohol, Drugs and Traffic Safety.* Proceedings of the Sixth International Conference on Alcohol, Drugs, and Traffic Safety. Toronto: The Addiction Research Foundation.

Jakobson, Roman

1966   "On Metonymy and Metaphor in Aphasia." Repr. in J. V. Cunningham, ed., *The Problem of Style,* pp. 260–65. New York: Fawcett. (Orig. pub. 1956.)

Johnson, Bruce

1973   "Discretionary Justice and Racial Domination: A Study of Arrest without Prosecution in Urban America Today." Ph.D. dissertation. Department of Sociology, University of California, Berkeley.

Johnson, Paula; Armor, David; Polich, Susan; and Stambul, Harriett

1977   "U. S. Adult Drinking Practices: Time Trends, Social Correlates and Sex Roles." Draft report no. ADM 281-76. Washington, D.C.: National Institute on Alcohol Abuse and Alcoholism.

Joll, James

1977   *Antonio Gramsci.* London: Penguin Books.

Judicial Council of California

1978   Annual Report of the Administrative Office of the California Courts.

Kaplan, John

1970   *Marijuana—The New Prohibition.* New York and Cleveland: World.

Kaplow, Jeffrey

1980   "Saint Monday and the Artisanal Tradition in Nineteenth-Century France." Lecture sponsored by the Department of History, University of California, San Diego, March 14, 1980.

Keller, Mark

1962   "The Definition of Alcoholism and the Estimation of Its Prevalence." In David Pittman and Charles Snyder, eds., *Society, Culture and Drinking Patterns*. New York: John Wiley.

Kern, J. C.; Schmelter, W. R.; and Paul, S. R.

1977   "Drinking Drivers Who Complete and Drop out of an Alcohol Education Program." *Journal of Studies on Alcohol* 38 (January): 89–95.

Kitsuse, John, and Cicourel, Aaron

1963   "A Note on the Official Uses of Statistics." *Social Problems* 11 (Fall): 131–39.

Kitsuse, John, and Spector, Malcolm

1973   "Toward a Sociology of Social Problems." *Social Problems* 20 (Spring): 407–41.

Kittrie, Nicholas

1971   *The Right to Be Different*. Baltimore: Johns Hopkins University Press.

Klapp, Orrin

1962   *Heroes, Villains, and Fools*. Englewood Cliffs, N.J.: Prentice-Hall.

1964   *Symbolic Leaders*. Chicago: Aldine.

Klein, David, and Waller, Julian

1970   *Causation, Culpability and Deterrence in Highway Crashes*. Washington, D.C.: U.S. Government Printing Office.

Knowles, John, ed.

1977   *Doing Better and Feeling Worse.* New York: W. W. Norton.

Kornhauser, William

1959   *The Politics of Mass Society.* Glencoe, Ill.: The Free Press.

Kotarba, Joseph

1977   "The Serious Side of Tavern Sociability." Paper presented to the annual meeting of the Society for the Study of Social Problems, Chicago, August, 1977.

Kuhn, Thomas

1962   *The Structure of Scientific Revolutions.* Chicago: University of Chicago Press.

LaFave, Wayne R.

1965   *Arrest: The Decision to Take a Suspect into Custody.* Boston: Little, Brown.

Latour, Bruno

1979   "What Does It Mean to Study Science?" Unpublished manuscript.

Latour, Bruno, and Woolgar, Stephen

1979   *Laboratory Life: The Social Construction of Scientific Fact.* Los Angeles: Sage.

Leach, Edmund

1954   *The Political Systems of Highland Burma.* Boston: Beacon.
1976   *Culture and Communication.* Cambridge: Cambridge University Press.

LeMasters, E. E.

1975   *Blue Collar Aristocrats.* Madison, Wisc.: University of Wisconsin Press.

Levi, Edward H.

1949   *An Introduction to Legal Reasoning.* Chicago: University of Chicago Press.

Levine, Harry Gene

1978   "The Discovery of Addiction." *Journal of Studies on Alcohol* 39 (January): 143–74.

1979   *Demon of the Middle Class: Self-Control, Liquor, and the Ideology of Temperance in Nineteenth Century America.* Ph.D. dissertation. Department of Sociology, University of California, Berkeley.

Levine, James B., and Becker, Theodore

1973   "Toward and beyond a Theory of Supreme Court Impact." In Theodore Becker and Malcolm Feeley, eds., *The Impact of Supreme Court Decisions.* New York: Oxford University Press.

Levi-Strauss, Claude

1966   *The Savage Mind.* Chicago: University of Chicago Press.

Lippmann, Walter

1922   *Public Opinion.* New York: Penguin Books.

Lubbock, Percy

1957   *The Craft of Fiction.* New York: Viking Press.

Lynch, Michael

1978   "Art and Artifact in Laboratory Life." Ph.D. dissertation. School of Social Sciences, University of California, Irvine.

McBay, A. J.; Hudson, R. P.; Hamrich, H.; and Beaubier, J.

1974   "Alcohol Impairment in Highway Fatalities in North Carolina, 1972." *Journal of Safety Research* 6:177–81.

McCarroll, J. R., and Haddon, W.

1961   "A Controlled Study of Fatal Automobile Accidents in New York City." *Journal of Chronic Diseases* 15:811–26.

McCoid, Allan H.

1956   "Intoxication and its Effect upon Civil Responsibility." *Iowa Law Review* 42:38.

McRuer, J. C.

1963   "Liability without Fault in the Law of Torts." In R. St.-J. MacDonald, ed., *Changing Legal Objectives.* Toronto: University of Toronto Press.

Maines, David

1977   "Social Organization and Social Structure in Symbolic Interactionist Thought." In Alex Inkeles, James Coleman, and Neil Smelser, eds., *Annual Review of Sociology.* Vol. 3. Palo Alto, Ca.: Annual Reviews, Inc.

Manning, Peter K.

1974   "Dramatic Aspects of Policing: Selected Propositions." *Sociology and Social Research* 59 (October).

1977   *Police Work: The Social Organization of Policing.* Cambridge, Mass.: MIT Press.

Marcuse, Herbert

1964   *One-Dimensional Man.* Boston: Beacon Press.

1968   "Industrialization and Capitalism in the Work of Max Weber." In *Negations.* Boston: Beacon Press.

Marrus, Michael

1974   *The Emergence of Leisure.* New York: Harper Torchbooks.

Marshall, Harvey, and Purdy, Ross

1972   "Hidden Deviance and the Labelling Approach:

The Case for Drinking and Driving." *Social Problems* 19 (Spring): 541–53.

Matza, David

1966   "The Disreputable Poor." In N. Smelser and S. M. Lipset, eds., *Social Structure and Mobility in Economic Development*. Chicago: Aldine.

Mead, George Herbert

1934   *Mind, Self and Society*. Chicago: University of Chicago Press.

Merton, Robert

1949   "Social Structure and Anomie." Repr. in *Social Theory and Social Structure*. New York: The Free Press. (Orig. pub. 1938.)

1972   "Insiders and Outsiders: A Chapter in the Sociology of Knowledge." *American Journal of Sociology* 78 (July): 9–47.

Messinger, Sheldon, with Sampson, Harold, and Towne, Robert

1962   "Life as Theater." *Sociometry* 35:98–110.

Mileski, Maureen

1971   "Courtroom Encounters: An Observation." *Law and Society Review* 5 (May): 473–538.

Moles, Abraham

1968   *Information Theory and Esthetic Perception*. Urbana, Ill.: University of Illinois Press.

Monthly Vital Statistics Report

1979   Final Mortality Statistics, July, 1977. Hyattsville, Md.: National Center for Health Statistics.

Morrison, Robert

1970   "Agnew, Alcohol, Automobiles, and Assessment." Editorial. *Science* 69 (August 28): 3948.

Murray, Antony, and Aitkin, Robert E.

1972   "The Constitutionality of California's Under the Influence of Alcohol Presumption." *Southern California Law Review* 45:955.

Nadel, Mark

1971   *The Politics of Consumer Protection.* Indianapolis: Bobbs-Merrill.

Nader, Ralph

1972   *Unsafe at Any Speed.* New York: Bantam Books. (Orig. pub. 1965.)

National Council on Alcoholism

1976   "The Alcoholic Is a Sick Person Who Can Be Helped." Pamphlet.

National Institute on Alcohol Abuse and Alcoholism

1971   *First Special Report to Congress on Alcohol and Health–New Knowledge.* Washington, D.C.: U.S. Government Printing Office.

1974   *Second Special Report to Congress on Alcohol and Health–New Knowledge.* Washington, D.C.:U.S. Government Printing Office.

1976   "Here's Looking at You: The Drinking American." DHEW pub. no. (ADM)76-348.

1978   *Third Special Report to Congress on Alcohol and Health—New Knowledge.* Washington, D.C.: U.S. Government Printing Office.

National Safety Council

1977,   *Accident Facts.* Chicago: National Safety
1978   Council.

Newsweek

1974   "Alcoholism." April 22, pp. 39–45.

Nida, Robert

1971   "California Motor Vehicle Legislation." In *West's Annotated California Codes*, pp. lxiii–cxxix. St. Paul, Minn.: West Publishing Co.

Noonan, John Patrick

1976   *Persons and Masks in the Law*. New York: Farrar, Strauss, and Giroux.

"Note, A State Statute to Prevent the Operation of Motor Vehicles by Persons under the Influence of Alcohol."

1970   *Harvard Journal of Legislation* 4:280. In Brian Freeman, ed., *Drunk Driving Cases: Prosecution and Defense*. New York: Practicing Law Institute.

O'Connell, Jeff

1971   *The Injury Industry and the Remedy of No-Fault Insurance*. Urbana, Ill.: University of Illinois Press.

O'Connell, Jeff, and Myers, Arthur

1966   *Safety Last*. New York: Random House.

Orwell, George

1954   "The Art of Donald McGill." *A Collection of Essays*. Garden City, N.Y.: Doubleday Anchor Books.

Parsons, Talcott

1951   *The Social System*. Glencoe, Ill.: The Free Press.

Peacock, James

1969   "Society as Narrative." In Robert F. Spencer, ed., *Forms of Symbolic Action*. Seattle: University of Washington Press.

Pelz, Donald, and Schuman, Stanley

1974   "Drinking, Hostility and Alienation." In "Driving of Young Men." *Proceedings of the Third Annual Alcoholism Conference of the National Institute on Alcohol Abuse and Alcoholism*. Rockville, Md.; National Institute on Alcohol Abuse and Alcoholism.

Pelz, Donald, and Williams, Patricia A.

1975   "Impulse Expression through Cars in Young

Drivers." University of Michigan: Highway
Safety Research Institute.

Pepper, Stephen

1966   *World Hypotheses*. Berkeley and Los Angeles:
University of California Press.

Perelman, Chaim

1963   *The Idea of Justice and the Problem of Argument*. New York: The Humanities Press.

Perelman, Chaim, and Olbrechts-Tytecka, L.

1969   *The New Rhetoric*. Notre Dame: University of
Notre Dame Press. (Orig. pub. 1958.)

Perrine, M. W.

1970   "The Spectrum of the Drinking Driver." In Patricia Waller, ed., *North Carolina Symposium
on Highway Safety* 3 (Fall): 28–74.

Perrine, M. W., ed.

1973   *Alcohol, Drugs and Driving*. Technical Report
DOTHS 265-2-489. U.S. Department of
Transportation: National Highway Traffic
Safety Administration.

Perrine, M. W.; Waller, J. A.; and Harris, L. S.

1971   *Alcohol and Highway Safety: Behavioral and
Medical Aspects*. Technical Report DOTHS
800-599. U.S. Department of Transportation: National Highway Traffic Safety Administration.

Phillips, David

1977   "Motor Vehicle Fatalities Increase Just after
Publicized Suicide Stories." *Science* 196:
1464–65.

Platt, Anthony

1969   *The Child Savers*. Chicago: University of
Chicago Press.

Plowden, William

1971   *The Motor Car and Politics in Britain.* Harmondsworth: Penguin Books.

Polanyi, Michael

1962   *Personal Knowledge.* Chicago: University of Chicago Press.

Pollock, Sir Frederick, and Maitland, F. W.

1923   *The History of English Law before the Time of Edward I.* Vol. 2. Cambridge: Cambridge University Press.

Popham, Robert E.

1956   "The Jellinek Alcoholism Estimation Formula and Its Application to Canadian Data." *Quarterly Journal of Studies on Alcohol* 17.

Popper, Karl

1976   "The Logic of the Social Sciences." In T. Adorno, ed., *The Positivist Dispute in German Sociology.* New York: Harper and Row.

Pugh, Ralph

1973   "Some Reflections of a Medieval Criminologist." *Proceedings of the British Academy* 59:1–24.

Quinney, Richard

1971   "The Social Reality of Crime." In Jack Douglas, ed., *Crime and Justice in American Society.* Indianapolis: Bobbs-Merrill.

Rae, John B.

1971   *The American Automobile: A Brief History.* Chicago: University of Chicago Press.

Raleigh Hills Hospital

N.d.   Brochure. N.p.

Ravetz, Jerome R.

1973   *Scientific Knowledge and Its Public Problems.* London: Penguin Books.

Reid, Sue Titus

1975   *Crime and Criminology.* Hinsdale, Ill.: The Dryden Press.

Reiss, Albert J., Jr.

1971   *The Police and the Public.* New Haven: Yale University Press.

Ricoeur, Paul

1978   "The Metaphorical Process as Cognition, Imagination and Feeling," *Critical Inquiry 5* (Autumn): 143–59.

1979   "The Model of the Text: Meaningful Action Considered as a Text." In P. Rabinow and W. M. Sullivan, eds., *Interpretive Social Science.* Berkeley: University of California Press.

Rieff, Philip

1966   *The Triumph of the Therapeutic.* New York: Harper Torchbooks.

Robertson, Leon, and Baker, Susan

1974   "Prior Violation Records of 1,447 Drivers Involved in Fatal Crashes." *Accident Analysis and Prevention* 7:121–28.

Robertson, Leon; Rich, R. F.; and Ross, H. L.

1973   "Jail Sentences for Driving while Intoxicated in Chicago: A Judicial Action That Failed." *Law and Society Review* 8:497.

Robertson, Leon, and Zador, Paul

1978   *Driver Education and Fatal Crash Involvement of Teen-Aged Drivers.* Washington, D.C.: Insurance Institute for Highway Safety.

Rock, Paul

1973   *Deviant Behavior*. London: Hutchinson.

Room, Robin

1978   "Governing Images of Alcohol and Drug Problems." Ph.D. dissertation. Department of Sociology, University of California, Berkeley.

Room, Robin, and Sheffield, Susan

1974   *The Prevention of Alcohol Problems: Report of a Conference*. Sacramento: Office of Alcoholism, State of California.

Rosen, George

1968   *Madness in Society*. New York: Harper and Row.

Rosett, Arthur, and Cressey, Donald

1976   *Justice by Consent*. Philadelphia: Lippincott.

Ross, H. Laurence

1960   "Traffic Law Violation: A Folk Crime." *Social Problems* 8:231–41.
1970   *Settled out of Court*. Chicago: Aldine.
1973   "Law, Science, and Accidents: The British Road Safety Act of 1967." *Journal of Legal Studies* 2 (January): 1–78.
1975   "The Scandinavian Myth: The Effectiveness of Drinking-and-Driving Legislation in Sweden and Norway." *Journal of Legal Studies* 6 (June): 285–310.
1976   "The Neutralization of Severe Penalties: Some Traffic Law Studies." *Law and Society* 10 (Spring): 403–13.
1977   "Deterrence Regained: The Cheshire Constabulary's 'Breathalyzer Blitz.'" *Journal of Legal Studies* 6 (January): 241–49.

Ross, H. Laurence, and Blumenthal, Murray

1975   "Some Problems of Experimentation in a Legal

Setting." *American Sociologist* 10 (August): 150–55.

Rothman, David

1971   *The Discovery of the Asylum.* Boston: Little, Brown.

Rothman, Rozann

1978   "The First Amendment: Symbolic Import—Ambiguous Prescription." In R. Simon, ed., *Research in Law and Sociology.* Vol. 1. Greenwich, Conn.: JAI Press.

Rubinstein, Jonathan

1973   *City Police.* New York: Ballantine Books.

Rudé, George

1959   *The Crowd in the French Revolution.* London: Oxford University Press.
1964   *The Crowd in History.* New York: John Wiley.

Sahlins, Marshall

1976   *Culture and Practical Reason.* Chicago: University of Chicago Press.

Sapir, J. David

1977   "The Anatomy of Metaphor." In J. David Sapir and J. Christopher Crocker, eds., *The Social Uses of Metaphor.* Philadelphia: University of Pennsylvania Press.

Schmidt, W., and Smart, R. G.

1959   "Alcoholism, Drinking and Traffic Accidents." *Quarterly Journal of Studies on Alcohol* 20:631–44.

Schmidt, W.; Smart, R. G.; and Popham, R. E.

1962   "The Role of Alcoholism in Motor Vehicle Accidents." *Traffic Safety Research Review* 6:21–27.

Schneider, Joseph

1978   "Deviant Drinking as Disease: Alcoholism as a Social Accomplishment." *Social Problems* 25 (April): 361–72.

Scholl, David

1969   "The Drinking Driver: An Approach to Solving a Problem of Underestimated Severity." *Villanova Law Review* 14:97. Repr. in B. Freeman, ed., *Drunk Driving Cases: Prosecution and Defense,* pp. 246–61. New York: Practicing Law Institute.

Schur, Edwin

1965   *Crimes without Victims.* Englewood Cliffs, N.J.: Prentice-Hall.

Schutz, Alfred

1967   *The Phenomenology of the Social World.* Evanston, Ill.: Northwestern University Press.
1970   *On Phenomenology and Social Relations,* ed. Helmut Wagner. Chicago: University of Chicago Press.

Scoles, P., and Fine, E. W.

1977   "Short Term Effects of an Educational Program for Drinking Drivers." *Journal of Studies on Alcohol* 38 (March): 633–37.

Seeley, John

1960   "The Definition of Alcoholism." *Quarterly Journal of Studies on Alcohol* 21:125–34.

Selzer, M. L.

1961   "Personality versus Intoxication as Critical Factor in Accidents Caused by Alcoholic Drivers." *Journal of Nervous and Mental Disorders* 132:298–303.
1969   "Alcoholics at Fault in Fatal Accidents and Hospitalized Alcoholics: A Comparison."

Journal of Studies on Alcohol 30 (December): 883–87.

Selzer, M. L., and Weiss, S.

1966   "Alcoholism and Traffic Fatalities: A Study in Futility." *American Journal of Psychiatry* 122:762–67.

Selznick, Philip

1961   "Sociology and Natural Law." *Natural Law Forum* 6:84–108.

Shover, Neal; Bankston, William; and Gurley, J. William

1977   "Responses of the Criminal Justice System to Legislation Providing More Severe Threatened Sanctions." *Criminology* 14 (February): 483–99.

Silver, Alan

1967   "The Demand for Civil Order." In David Bordua, ed., *The Police.* New York: John Wiley.

1968   "Official Interpretations of Racial Riots." In Robert H. Connery, ed., *Urban Riots.* New York: Vintage Books.

Sinclair, Andrew

1963   *Era of Excess.* New York: Harper and Row.

Singer, Milton

1972   *When a Great Tradition Modernizes.* New York: Praeger.

Skolnick, Jerome

1966   *Justice Without Trial.* New York: John Wiley.

Spector, Malcolm, and Kitsuse, John

1977   *Constructing Social Problems.* Menlo Park, Ca.: Cummings.

Starr, Chauncey

1969   "Social Benefit versus Technological Risk: What Is Our Society Willing to Pay for Safety." *Science* 165 (September 19): 1232–38.

Sterling-Smith, R. S.

1975   "Alcohol, Marijuana and Other Drug Patterns among Operators Involved in Fatal Motor Vehicle Accidents." In S. Israelstam and S. Lambert, eds., *Alcohol, Drugs and Traffic Safety*, pp. 93–106. Toronto: Addiction Research Foundation of Canada.

Stewart, J. R., and Campbell, B. J.

1972   "The Statistical Association between Past and Future Accidents and Violations." Chapel Hill, N.C.: University of North Carolina, Highway Safety Research Institute.

Stoll, Clarice

1975   "Images of Man and Social Control." Repr. in Ronald Akers and Richard Hawkins, eds., *Law and Control in Society*. Englewood Cliffs, N.J.: Prentice-Hall. (Orig. pub. 1968.)

Stone, Julius

1972   "The Ratio of the Ratio Decidendi." In Lloyd, Lord of Hampstead, ed., *Introduction to Jurisprudence*, pp. 772–82. New York: Praeger.

Sudnow, David

1965   "Normal Crimes: Sociological Features of the Penal Code in a Public Defender Office." *Social Problems* 12:25–76.

Sykes, Gresham M., and Matza, David

1957   "Techniques of Neutralization: A Theory of Delinquency." *American Sociological Review* 22 (December): 664–70.

Tabachnik, Norman, ed.

1973   *Accident or Suicide?* Springfield, Ill.: C. C. Thomas.

Thompson, E. P.

1967   "Time, Work-Discipline and Industrial Capitalism." *Past and Present* 38 (December): 56–97.

Traffic Safety Magazine

N.d.   "The Facts about Drinking and Accidents."

Truman, David

1951   *The Governmental Process.* New York: Knopf.

Turbayne, Colin

1962   *The Myth of Metaphor.* New Haven: Yale University Press.

Turner, Ralph H.

1969   "The Public Perception of Protest." *American Sociological Review* 34 (December): 815–31.

Turner, Victor

1969   *The Ritual Process.* Chicago: Aldine.
1974   *Dramas, Fields, and Metaphors.* Ithaca and London: Cornell University Press.
1977   "Variations on a Theme of Liminality." In Sally Moore and Barbara Meyerhoff, eds., *Secular Ritual.* Assen/Amsterdam: Van Gorcum.

United Nations

1974   *Statistics of Road Traffic Accidents in Europe, 1972.* New York: United Nations.

U.S. Congress

1966   *Congressional Record.* 89th Congress. Vol. 112. Pt. 2. 2d Series. Washington, D.C.: U.S. Government Printing Office.

U.S. Congress, Committee on Public Works

1968   *Alcohol and Highway Safety.* Washington, D.C.: U.S. Government Printing Office.

U.S. Department of Commerce

1978   *Statistical Abstract.* Washington, D.C.: U.S. Government Printing Office.

U.S. Department of Transportation, National Highway Traffic Safety Administration, Office of Driver and Pedestrian Programs

1968   *Alcohol Safety Action Projects, Evaluation of Operations–1967.* Washington, D.C.: U.S. Government Printing Office.

1974   *Alcohol Safety Action Projects, Evaluation of Operations–1974.* Vol. 2. Detailed Analyses. Chapter 2. Evaluation of the Enforcement Countermeasure Activities. DOT HS801-77. Washington, D.C.: U.S. Government Printing Office.

1975   *Alcohol Safety Action Projects, Evaluation of Operations–1974.* Washington, D.C.: U.S. Government Printing Office.

N.d.   "The Drinking Driver and the Police." Brochure. N.p.

U.S. House of Representatives, Committee on Interstate and Foreign Commerce, Subcommittee on Public Health and Welfare

1970   *Hearings on Comprehensive Alcohol Abuse and Alcoholism Legislation.* 91st Congress, September 15–17. Washington, D.C.: U.S. Government Printing Office.

U.S. National Center of Health Statistics

1979   *Monthly Vital Statistics Report.* Washington, D.C.: Department of Health, Education, and Welfare.

U.S. Senate, Committee on Commerce

1966   *Hearings.* 89th Congress, March 16–April 6.

Vaihinger, Hans

1924   *The Philosophy of "As If."* London: Routledge and Kegan Paul.

Van Gennep, Arnold

1960   *The Rites of Passage.* Chicago: University of Chicago Press. (Orig. pub. 1909.)

Voas, R. B.

1975   "Roadside Surveys, Demographics and BACs of Drivers." In S. Israelstam and S. Lambert, eds., *Alcohol, Drugs and Traffic,* pp. 13–20. Toronto: Addiction Research Foundation.

Waller, Julian A.

1966   "Alcoholism and Traffic Deaths." *New England Journal of Medicine* 275:532–36.

1967   "Identification of Problem Drinking among Drunken Drivers." *Journal of the American Medical Association* 200:124–30.

1968   "Patterns of Traffic Accidents and Violations Related to Drinking and to Some Medical Conditions." *Quarterly Journal of Studies on Alcohol.* Suppl. no. 4, pp. 118–37.

1971   "Factors Associated with Police Evaluation of Drinking in Fatal Highway Crashes." *Journal of Safety Research* 3:35–41.

Waller, Julian, and Turkel, H. W.

1966   "Alcoholism and Traffic Deaths." *New England Journal of Medicine* 275 (July–September): 532–36.

Warner, W. L.

1959   *The Living and the Dead.* New Haven: Yale University Press.

Wasserstrom, Richard

1961   *The Judicial Decision: Toward A Theory of Legal Justification.* Stanford, Ca.: Stanford University Press.

Wedow, Suzanne

1979   "New Conception of Ritual in the Study of Contemporary Society." Unpublished manuscript.

Weiner, Myron

1962   *The Politics of Scarcity.* Bombay: Asia Publishing House.

West's Annotated California Codes

1971   St. Paul, Minn.: West Publishing Co.

Wetter, J. Gillis

1960   *Styles of Appellate Judicial Opinions.* Leyden: A. W. Sythoff.

Wheelwright, Phillip

1954   *The Burning Fountain.* Bloomington, Ind.: Indiana University Press.
1962   *Metaphor and Reality.* Bloomington, Ind.: Indiana University Press.

White, Hayden

1973a   *Metahistory.* Baltimore: Johns Hopkins University Press.
1973b   "Foucault Decoded." *History and Theory* 12:23–54.
1976   "The Fictions of Factual Representation." In Angus Fletcher, ed., *The Literature of Fact.* New York: Columbia University Press.

Willett, T. C.

1964   *Criminal on the Road.* London: Tavistock.

Williams, Glanville L.

1961   "Intention in the Criminal Law." In Herbert Morris, ed., *Freedom and Responsibility.* Stanford, Ca.: Stanford University Press.

Williams, Raymond

1976   *Keywords.* New York: Oxford University Press.

Wilson, James Q.

1975   *Thinking about Crime.* New York: Basic Books.
1976   *Varieties of Police Behavior.* New York: Atheneum.

Winterowd, W. Ross

1968   *Rhetoric: A Synthesis.* New York: Holt, Rinehart and Winston.

Wolfe, A. C.

1975   "Characteristics of Late-Night, Weekend Drivers: Results of the U.S. National Roadside Breath-Testing Survey and Several Local Surveys." In S. Israelstam and S. Lambert, eds., *Alcohol, Drugs and Traffic Safety,* pp. 41–50. Toronto: Addiction Research Foundation of Ontario.

Young, Frank

1965   *Initiation Ceremonies.* Indianapolis: Bobbs-Merrill.

Zador, Paul

1976   "Statistical Evaluation of the Effectiveness of 'ASAP.'" *Accident Analysis and Prevention* 8:51–66.

Ziman, J.

1968   *Public Knowledge.* Cambridge: Cambridge University Press.

Zimring, Franklin E., and Hawkins, Gordon

1973   *Deterrence.* Chicago: University of Chicago Press.

Zurcher, Louis A., and Kirkpatrick, R. George

1976   *Citizens for Decency.* Austin: University of Texas Press.

Zylman, Richard

1968   "Accidents, Alcohol and Single-Cause Explanations." *Quarterly Journal of Studies on Alcohol*. Supplement no. 4 (May), pp. 212–33.

1970   "Are Drinking-Driving Laws Enforced?" *Police Chief* 37:48–52.

1972a   "Age is More Important than Alcohol in the Collision-Involvement of Young and Old Drivers." *Journal of Traffic Safety Education* 20:7–8.

1972b   "Race and Social Status Discrimination and Police Action in Alcohol-Affected Collisions." *Journal of Safety Research* 4:75–84.

1973   "Youth, Alcohol and Collision Involvement." *Journal of Safety Research* 5:58–72.

1974a   "Semantic Gymnastics in Alcohol: Highway Crash Research and Public Information." *Journal of Alcohol and Drug Education* 19 (Winter): 7–23.

1974b   "A Critical Evaluation of the Literature on 'Alcohol Involvement' in Highway Deaths." *Accident Analysis and Prevention* 6: 163–204.

1975a   "Mass Arrests for Impaired Driving May Not Prevent Traffic Deaths." In S. Israelstam and S. Lambert, eds., *Alcohol, Drugs and Traffic Safety*. Toronto: Addiction Research Foundation of Ontario.

1975b   "DWI Enforcement Programs: Why Are They Not More Effective." *Accident Analysis and Prevention* 7:179–90.

Index

Blumenthal, Murray, 140, 246
Blumer, Herbert, 71, 218
Bohannon, Paul, 141–42, 218
Booth, Wayne, 87, 91, 93, 218
Borkenstein, R. F., 62, 64, 73, 74, 89, 219
Bradess, V. A., 61, 71, 231
breathalyzer, 63, 64
Breithaupt v. *Abrams,* 166
Brown, Richard, 84, 190, 191, 195, 219
Brown, Stuart, 68, 219
Bruyn, Severyn, 97, 220
Bryant, Donald, 27, 220
Bureau of Roads, 38
Burke, Kenneth, 21, 53–54, 77, 81, 86, 95, 100, 102, 107, 117, 158–59, 189, 192, 220
Burns, Elizabeth, 176, 220

Cahalan, Donald, 58–60, 98, 220
Calabresi, Guido, 117, 220
California State Highway Division, xi
Cameron, Tracy, 63, 65, 69, 70, 72, 73, 86, 221
Cardozo, Benjamin, 141,221
Carlson, W. L., 70, 73, 127, 221, 225, 226
Carson, W. G., 183, 221
causation, 13–16, 33
Chandler, David, 183, 221
Chatham, Robert, 128, 129, 143
Cicourel, Aaron, 135,

221, 236
Cisin, Ira, 58, 220
Clark, Ramsey, 131
class, social, 103, 124, 130
Cloyd, Jerold, 45, 138, 161, 222
Cohen, Abner, 17, 222
Cohen, Morris, 2, 50
Combs, James, 185, 222
Committee of Fifty, 11
consciousness, 30, 34
consumer movement, 48, 49
convincing, 74–76
Coppin, R., 140, 222
Cosper, Ronald, 62, 103, 222
Cramton, Roger, 155, 223
Cressey, Donald, 10, 121, 124, 138, 223, 246
crime, 9, 10; and punishment, 131–32, 139–40, 158; traffic violations as, 122–29; without victim, 123, 129, 134
Crocker, J. Christopher, 107, 223
Crossley, Helen, 58, 220

Davis, J. H., 70, 223
De Haven, Hugh, 46
Dell, Floyd, 167–68, 223
Department of Transportation, 30–31, 34
deterrence, 20, 45, 130–31, 133, 157–58, 161–62, 165, 181, 190
Devlin, Lord, 122, 124, 131
disorder, 150–51, 152, 156–62, 174
Dooley, David, 144, 223

Douglas, Jack D., 22–23, 180, 223
Douglas, Mary, 144, 158, 224
dramaturgy, 21, 77, 155–56
drinking, 11, 55, 58–59, 148–51, 155–62, 163, 186; and arrests, 87, 94; types of, 98–103. *See also* drinking-driving; driving under the influence of alcohol; drunkenness
drinking-driving, xi, xii, 1–4, 7–8, 17, 18, 20–22, 30, 44, 47, 50, 53, 54, 77, 123, 131, 135, 156, 159, 166–67, 173–74, 181, 188; as antisocial behavior, 152–56, 164; arrests in, 67, 87, 94, 100, 134–36, 138–39, 165, 166; as a cause of accidents, 45, 164; as a criminal offense, 114, 126–29, 132–33, 144, 166; described, xii, 6, 19, 21, 61–62, 65–66, 76–80, 94, 95, 98–99, 111–12, 151–52, 154–56, 187–88, 190, 195; as deviant behavior, 98–99, 115, 129, 151–52, 153, 155, 165, 168, 182; institutional responses to, 2, 6, 7, 11, 16, 19, 21, 115, 151; and the law, xii, 2, 6, 7, 18, 21, 61, 113–45, 146, 155, 157, 159–60, 166–70, 173, 182, 188, 194; as a medical problem, 6, 7, 82, 86, 88, 100–101, 115, 154; misconceptions